This Aging Society

William C. Cockerham
University of Illinois

This Aging Society

Prentice Hall
Englewood Cliffs, New Jersey 07632

Library of Congress Cataloging-in-Publication Data

Cockerham, William C.
    This aging society / William C. Cockerham.
        p.   cm.
    Includes bibliographical references and index.
    ISBN 0-13-919119-4
    1. Aging--Social aspects. 2. Aging--Social aspects--United
States. 3. Aged--Social conditions. 4. Aged--United States--Social
conditions.   I. Title.
HQ1061.C56 1991
305.26--dc20
                                                90-19776
                                                   CIP

Acquisitions editor: Nancy Roberts
Editorial/production supervision: Mary McDonald
Interior design: Karen Buck
Cover design: Patricia Kelly
Prepress buyer: Debra Kesar
Manufacturing buyer: Mary Ann Gloriande

© 1991 by Prentice-Hall, Inc.
A Division of Simon & Schuster
Englewood Cliffs, New Jersey 07632

Printed in the United States of America
10 9 8 7 6 5 4 3 2 1

ISBN   0-13-919119-4

Prentice-Hall International (UK) Limited, *London*
Prentice-Hall of Australia Pty. Limited, *Sydney*
Prentice-Hall Canada Inc., *Toronto*
Prentice-Hall Hispanoamericana, S.A., *Mexico*
Prentice-Hall of India Private Limited, *New Delhi*
Prentice-Hall of Japan, Inc., *Tokyo*
Simon & Schuster Asia Pte. Ltd., *Singapore*
Editora Prentice-Hall do Brasil, Ltda., *Rio de Janeiro*

To Eva Louise Mail Hunnicutt

Contents

Preface   xi

1. Social Perspectives on Aging   1

Growth in Aged Populations   1
Social Gerontology   3
What Causes Aging?   4
Aging and the Life Cycle   10
Summary   13

2. The Demography of Aging   15

Demographic Patterns in the United States   16
Demographic Patterns Worldwide   31
Summary   46

3. Social Theories of Aging   48

Disengagement Theory   49
Activity Theory   53
Continuity Theory   56
Age Stratification Theory   57

Modernization Theory   60
Symbolic Interaction Theory   63
Conflict Theory   66
Summary   68

4. Health of the Aged   70

Perceived Health Status   71
Physical Health   75
Mental Health   93
Health Policy and the Aged   101
Summary   104

5. The Aged Self   106

The Self   106
Awareness of Aging   111
Society's View of the Aged   116
The Aged Self   123
Summary   128

6. Ageism, Gender, and Racial Minority Status   130

Ageism   131
Gender   135
Minority Groups   138
Summary   148

7. Work and Retirement   150

Work   150
Retirement   158
Summary   167

8. The Aged as a Social Force   169

The Aged: A Minority Group?   169
The Aged as an Interest Group   171
The Aged and the Welfare State   175
Summary   183

9. Aging and Social Policy in Selected Countries   185

United States   186
Canada   189
Great Britain   191
Germany   194
France   198

Japan   200
China   205
Summary   208

10. Death and Dying   210

Death and the Individual   211
Death and Society   220
Changing Attitudes Toward Death   229
Summary   232

Postscript: The Future of Aging   233

References   237

Author Index   251

Subject Index   255

Preface

The aging of human society worldwide is rapidly becoming one of the most distinct features of modernity. The fact that older people will exist on this planet in greater numbers than ever before means not only significant changes in the age composition of society, but a corresponding change in the norms, values, and attitudes concerning the elderly and the social policies affecting them. In the 21st century, approximately one in five persons will be age 65 or over, a demographic reality that has enormous implications. Today's elderly have attained higher levels of education and economic position, and are larger in number, than in the past, and the aged are becoming a major social and political force.

Consequently, it is the intent of this book to assess both the causes and direction of social change in the modern world brought on by the aging of society. The focus is on the social aspects of the aging process, from the standpoint of both the individual and the wider society. In the social sciences, interest in and analysis of our aging society are likely to increase to the point that social gerontology will become one of the most important fields of study and research on human social behavior. This book is an effort to provide an overall view of the literature that currently represents this growing specialty. The views expressed are those of the author. However, the author wishes to thank Leonard D. Cain of Portland State University and Dale A. Lund of the University of Utah for reviewing the manuscript and providing important suggestions.

William C. Cockerham
Champaign, Illinois

Social Perspectives on Aging

The purpose of this book is to examine the social aspects of the aging experience. Growing old is not simply a biological process; it is also a social and psychological phenomenon that involves important changes in the aging person's perceptions, social roles, self-concept, behavior, and approach toward daily living. Aging also has important effects on society, because the trend worldwide is toward increasingly larger numbers and proportions of aged persons; in fact, the twentieth century can be described as a period of rapid growth for aged populations. In the twenty-first century, this process will become even more accelerated. Improved nutrition, sanitation, housing, and health care have combined to help promote longer lives for most people. Increasing longevity has, in turn, fostered a growing interest in both the biological and behavioral aspects of the aging process and the role of the aged person in society.

GROWTH IN AGED POPULATIONS

Overall life expectancy in the United States in 1987 was 75.0 years. This figure represents an increase in longevity of nearly 50 percent since 1900, when life expectancy was 47.3 years. The rise in life expectancy has brought a corresponding increase in the growth of the elderly population. In 1940, the elderly (those persons 65 years of age and over) constituted 9 million people, or about 7 percent of the total American population. By 1987, their number had increased to 29.8 million, or about 12.3 percent of the population.

Not only are more people living to reach older ages, but since 1958 the birthrate in the United States has been declining. The lower death rate coupled with the lower birthrate has resulted in a much higher proportion of older Americans in relation to the total population. Table 1–1 illustrates this trend by showing that in 1900 only 4 percent of the total United States population was age 65 or over. By 1987, as noted, older Americans constituted 12.3 percent of the total population, and by 2050 it is projected that 21.8 percent of all Americans will be in this age bracket. This means that persons over age 65 will make up more than *one-fifth* of the population in the twenty-first century. The point is obvious: Americans are living longer, and the percentage of elderly in the population is significantly increasing.

This trend will undoubtedly bring about a marked change in American society. The aged population will be healthier, better educated, and more affluent than any comparable cohorts of elderly persons in the past. They are likely to have not only a higher standard of living, but also increased political power because of their large numbers and experience with the political process. This means they will have the clout to bring about legislation for public services to meet their needs. Even though elderly Americans will be healthier than ever before, more pressure is likely to be put on health care delivery systems and public health insurance to keep them fit. Pressure will also be put upon the Social Security system to maintain or increase payments for old-age benefits. With the relatively fewer children resulting from the Baby Boom generation in the United States that was born between 1946 and 1964 and is now passing into middle age, the financing of old-age benefits will require increasingly more money in the future from a smaller working population. In 1955, for example, there were 8.6 taxpayers per Social Security beneficiary; but, by 2005, the ratio will be 2.7 taxpayers per retiree. By 2035, the ratio will drop to about 1.9 taxpayers for every retiree. A future crisis in the financing and provision of services for the elderly in the United States appears certain.

These trends are important, because when people become very old they require a greater share of public services. In developed nations, the care of

TABLE 1–1   Percent of Total U.S. Population Age 65 and Over for Selected Years

	1900	1930	1950	1980	1987	2000 (PROJECTED)	2050 (PROJECTED)
Percent Age 65 and Over	4.0	5.4	8.1	11.2	12.3	13.1	21.8

Source: Based on U.S. Census Bureau data.

the elderly has generally shifted from being a family responsibility to being more of a societal responsibility. This change has come about for a number of reasons. One reason is the decline of the extended family, in which multiple generations of a single family continued to live with or near each other, and its replacement by the nuclear family, that is, a family consisting of one couple and their children. Other reasons include the high cost of health and nursing care, the type and degree of care required, and the increase in the number of persons needing such care. Although most old people will be relatively healthy in old age, there will come a time, particularly for the oldest of the old, when their health will fail, bringing about the requirement for extended care and greater public expenditures to meet this need.

With larger numbers of active, well-educated, affluent, and relatively healthy elderly people in society, there may also be an adjustment in normative expectations in social roles and values pertaining to aged persons. Negative stereotypes about the elderly that are common today (Baker 1985) may change and become more positive, because the prevailing stereotypes of the elderly as unhappy, in poor health, and lonely do not match the reality of life for the majority of older Americans (Spacapan and Oskamp 1989). An emphasis on youth in Western society may decline and greater value be placed on some feature of older age, such as having experience or looking distinguished. Work roles may change in which the aged are encouraged to remain longer in the work force because of a smaller population of younger workers; or conversely, the aged may retire earlier in order to take advantage of the added years of life expectancy. As sociologist Matilda White Riley (1987:9) observes, both the structure of society and the process of aging are mutable: they influence each other sequentially over time.

When the aged population of the United States was only 4 percent in 1900, the needs of the elderly were not as important in relation to the total population and could more easily be overlooked. But with one in every five Americans being aged in the twenty-first century, concerns of the elderly are going to be a major feature of social policy in America. The same circumstance exists in Western Europe, where the aged population is increasing even more so than in America. In 1980, for example, the median age (one-half of the population is younger than this age and the other half is older) in the United States was 30. In 1987, the median age for Americans had risen to 32.1. But in West Germany, the median age in 1985 had already reached 37.7, followed by 35.5 in Italy, 35.4 in Great Britain, and 33.6 in France.

SOCIAL GERONTOLOGY

With the increase in numbers and proportions of the aged, the study of gerontology, or aging, has correspondingly increased in scope and importance. Gerontology, at its current stage of development, is multidisciplinary, not a discipline by itself. However, those in the field tend to believe that a multidisciplinary approach is a major strength, for it attracts researchers from a variety of areas—medicine, biology, biochemistry, sociology, psychology, and the like. Social scientists tend to specialize in social gerontology, which is the study of aging as a social experience. Social gerontology is a rapidly growing subfield because of the demand for research that can be articulated into social policy and programs for the aged due to the increase in the elderly population. The intent of this book is to review the subfield of social gerontology, especially from the standpoint of work in sociology and social psychology.

A social science focus on aging is important because it allows for a more complete understanding of what it means to be old in society; it is not limited by explanations that are strictly biological, biochemical, or psychological. According to Riley and her associates (Riley, Foner, and Waring 1988), there is a plasticity to aging in which social processes interact with biological and psychological processes to influence the ways in which people change from childhood through adulthood and old age. Riley and her colleagues suggest that there is a diversity among individuals as they grow older that is dependent upon their socioeconomic position, their relationships with other people, and their concept of self. They conclude, along with others (Fennell, Phillipson, and Evers 1988), that understanding the process of aging is largely a sociological matter. It is not that biology and psychology are unimportant. Quite the contrary; aging is fundamentally a biological process with significant psychological implications for the individual. However, aging is also experienced socially, and to a large extent what it *means* be aged in society is a sociological phenomenon. This book, accordingly, will discuss the social aspects of aging.

WHAT CAUSES AGING?

For centuries, people have wanted to know what causes biological aging, but the answer remains a mystery. Aging is known to occur as a result of changes in the cells of the body, yet what makes these changes take place is not clear. The two most widely accepted theories of aging involve the idea that either (1) 'wear and tear' on the body over time causes it to break down and age, or (2) we have genetic clocks ticking away within us that are programmed to determine the manner and time at which we all age and die (Rosenfeld 1985).

The 'wear and tear' approach includes the notion that aging may be due in large part to deterioration in the integratory homeostasis that exists between cells of the same tissue and those of other tissues. Although the body's DNA is known to have a self-repair capability, this capability apparently declines over time, and when this happens we begin to age. Another 'wear and tear' perspective on aging is that it is due to a decline of immunity. That is, over time, the body loses some of its ability to recognize and attack disease-causing agents and may even attack healthy cells, resulting in autoimmune diseases like rheumatoid arthritis. When our immune system begins to wear down, the aging process may be accelerated.

The genetic clock approach maintains that aging is the result of some form of preset genetic program. In other words, as Albert Rosenfeld (1985:101) suggests, we all have some sort of built-in timer that sets off aging at a preselected point in time. All species appear to have a specific life span that sets limits on how long they are likely to live. For example, some tortoises may live for 150 years, and people, in developed nations, average about 75 years. Thus, aging may not just be a case of random wear and tear. Rather, a genetic clock may set certain limits beyond which no one is able to live. But where is this genetic clock? One view is that the clock is cellular, because normal cells have been found to have a finite life span; however, cancer cells have been found to be immortal. It is not clear why normal cells age and abnormal cancer cells do not; it may be that there is a cellular genetic clock that can be disrupted by abnormal cells. Another view is that the clock is at the base of the brain in the area housing the hypothalamus and the pituitary gland, which controls the release of hormones into the body. At some preset time, a hormone—currently unidentified—may be released into the body to produce aging. Or it may be that there is a relationship between cellular and brain triggers in the aging process, or there may be some combination of genetic clocks and the effects of 'wear and tear' on the body.

New evidence supporting the importance of hormones in the aging process was uncovered with the discovery by Daniel Rudman and his colleagues (1990) that the human growth hormone could reverse the effects of aging. In a clinical test involving 21 healthy men between the ages of 61 and 81, a genetically engineered version of the natural growth hormone reduced body fat, increased muscle bulk, and helped rebuild vital organs—such as the heart and kidneys—that shrink with age. Moreover, the men's skin regained a more youthful appearance and thickness. They looked more fit and in better overall physical condition. The results suggest that a decline in the body's production of growth hormone is a major factor causing fat to accumulate, muscles to wither, and organs to become smaller as a person ages. While the research by Rudman and associates is not conclusive, it strongly suggests that the growth hormone has a critical role in aging and can be used to help elderly people maintain muscles and increase strength.

Whatever the cause of aging, the interaction of various genetic and other biological factors is involved, and social-psychological influences, such as stress, also seem to be important. In addition, aging can be of a primary or secondary nature. Primary aging occurs over time; secondary aging is usually due to disease or psychological trauma, and is premature. The most obvious indication of aging is the appearance of a person's skin, which tends to dry out and wrinkle. The person's capacity for sight and hearing is reduced, and the brain begins to shrink from loss of cells. Muscles also shrink and become weaker, joints stiffen and swell, while the heart, lungs, kidneys, and bladder begin to operate at reduced levels of effectiveness, and the body's output of hormones begins to diminish. The body thus becomes increasingly susceptible to infection, injury, and degenerative diseases like coronary heart disease, cancer, and diabetes.

According to Donald King, Neela Pushparaj, and Kathleen O'Toole (1982), illness and disability in the elderly result from a programmed process of deterioration (a genetic clock), and death involves stresses (wear and tear) to the body that are better tolerated at younger ages. "Indeed," states King and his colleagues (1982:109), "when one looks at morbidity and mortality in the very old, one ironically finds that the leading causes of disability and death are those seen in the very young—infection and trauma." The difference is that younger people can cope with infection and trauma (injury) much better than older people. King and colleagues suggest that the oldest of the elderly should be viewed as resisting the genetic and environmentally derived pathologies that determine susceptibility to disease and death throughout the human life span. Genetically caused diseases are often responsible for death in the young, but if the individual survives early childhood, the years to about age 40 are comparatively healthy. Between ages 40 and 80, illness and mortality begin to increase, and King and associates surmise that environmental factors are most responsible for this trend—in particular, a detrimental personal lifestyle in previous years involving a lack of physical activity, smoking, heavy alcohol consumption, and poor diet. Such a lifestyle—especially if imposed upon genetic mechanisms that predispose a person to obesity, diabetes, heart disease, cirrhosis, cancer, or other problems—promotes death.

Therefore, King and colleagues maintain that those who survive well beyond the age of 80 are a select group by virtue of both genetic and environmental advantages. Nevertheless, the steady deterioration of the body, which seems part of a programmed process, ensures that any advantage in warding off signs of aging by the individual only acts as a deferment of the final and irrevocable outcome. Support for King and colleagues' thesis is shown in Table 1–2, which lists the death rates for the ten leading causes of death in the United States in 1984 for persons ages 55–64, 65–74, 75–84, and 85 and older. Essentially, the causes of death are the same for each of these four age-groups; the basic difference is that those who reach the older ages are those who have best been able to avoid or control these problems.

What separates aging from other biological processes is that physical aging (1) comes on gradually from within the organism instead of from the external environment, (2) has a negative effect on physical functioning, and (3) is universal in that the physical changes that take place happen to everyone (Strehler 1977). If any one of these three criteria is missing in regard to a physical change in an individual, then that change is not part of aging. For example, cancer can come on gradually from within the body and have a negative effect on physical functioning, but not everybody gets cancer, and the onset of cancer can be influenced by factors in the external environment (such as radiation, biochemicals, or, in the case of lung cancer, cigarette smoking). Although aged people may be more likely to get cancer, cancer is not automatic with aging.

Who lives the longest? Rosenfeld (1985) has found, while noting that most people in primitive societies age quickly and die young, that the greatest longevity is nevertheless among certain groups of people living in economically depressed mountain tribes. The Vilcabambans of Ecuador, the Hunzas on the border of China and Pakistan, and the Abkhasians in the southwest Soviet Union have people claiming to be 120 years of age and older. Whether these claims are valid is not known, although the proportion of persons over 100 years old in these tribes is unusually high. Whether their longevity is a result of genetics is not known. What is known is that they live a slow-paced rural life at high altitudes, work and exercise regularly even at old age, and eat a simple diet that is practically meat-free, omits sugar, and includes large amounts of fruits, vegetables, and yogurt. They also consume fewer calories (about 2,200 a day on the average) than Americans and West Europeans, whose diet often exceeds 3,000 calories daily.

The American claiming the longest life, according to Rosenfeld, is Charlie Smith, who arrived as a slave from Africa in 1854 and died in 1979 in Florida, supposedly at the age of 137. The longest life that has been documented in the world, however, is for an American woman, Carrie C. White, who was 115 years old in 1990 and lived in a Florida nursing home. She was born in 1874 when Ulysses S. Grant was president. The oldest man with a birth certificate proving his age was John Evans, a retired British coal miner, who died in 1990 at the age of 112. He was born in 1877, when Queen Victoria was on the British throne.

What people with longevity have in common is that they tend to come from families whose members typically live a long time. This suggests that longevity is inherited, but to what degree is not known. Nor is much else known about why certain people reach the oldest ages and others do not. Persons at the upper end of the socioeconomic scale tend to live longer than members of lower socioeconomic groups, but an affluent lifestyle, involving a rich diet, heavy smoking, and lack of exercise, can also be detrimental to a person's health. Poverty clearly decreases an individual's life chances because it enhances exposure to crowded living conditions, poor diet, inferior housing, violence, alcoholism and problem drinking, and drug abuse. People who are relaxed and not greatly affected by stress, and who have a family history of longevity and live a healthy lifestyle with respect to eating properly, getting enough rest, exercising, and avoiding practices like smoking, abusing alcohol, and taking drugs appear to be the most long-lived.

TABLE 1–2 Death Rates for the Ten Leading Causes of Death for Persons Age 55 Years and Over in Rank Order, by Age: United States, 1984

Rank	Age Span and Cause of Death	Number of Deaths per 100,000 Resident Population	Rank	Age Span and Cause of Death	Number of Deaths per 100,000 Resident Population
	55–64 years			**75–84**	
. . .	All causes	1,287.8	. . .	All causes	6,399.3
1	Diseases of heart	450.3	1	Diseases of heart	2,748.6
2	Malignant neoplasms, including neoplasms of lymphatic and hematopoietic tissues	448.4	2	Malignant neoplasms, including neoplasms of lymphatic and hematopoietic tissues	1,272.3
3	Cerebrovascular diseases	55.8	3	Cerebrovascular diseases	626.2
4	Chronic obstructive pulmonary diseases and allied conditions	46.0	4	Chronic obstructive pulmonary diseases and allied conditions	270.3
5	Accidents and adverse effects	36.0	5	Pneumonia and influenza	216.0
6	Chronic liver disease and cirrhosis	35.0	6	Diabetes and mellitus	126.1
7	Diabetes mellitus	24.6	7	Accidents and adverse effects	107.2
8	Suicide	17.3	8	Atherosclerosis	88.4
9	Pneumonia and influenza	16.8	9	Nephritis, nephrotic syndrome, and nephrosis	76.1
10	Nephritis, nephrotic syndrome, and nephrosis	9.2	10	Septicemia	51.7

	65–74 years		85 years and over	
. . .	All causes	2,848.1	All causes	15,223.6
1	Diseases of heart	1,102.7	Diseases of heart	7,251.0
2	Malignant neoplasms, including neoplasms of lymphatic and hematopoietic tissues	835.1	Cerebrovascular diseases	1,883.8
3	Cerebrovascular diseases	177.0	Malignant neoplasms, including neoplasms of lymphatic and hematopoietic tissues	1,604.0
4	Chronic obstructive pulmonary diseases and allied conditions	141.4	Pneumonia and influenza	883.2
5	Diabetes mellitus	59.4	Atherosclerosis	488.4
6	Pneumonia and influenza	53.7	Chronic obstructive pulmonary diseases and allied conditions	331.0
7	Accidents and adverse effects	50.3	Accidents and adverse effects	256.9
8	Chronic liver disease and cirrhosis	39.3	Diabetes mellitus	216.8
9	Nephritis, nephrotic syndrome, and nephrosis	26.8	Nephritis, nephrotic syndrome, and nephrosis	201.0
10	Septicemia	19.8	Septicemia	142.1

Source: U.S. National Center for Health Statistics, *Health Statistics on Older Persons*, United States, 1986, Series 3, No. 25 (Washington, D.C.: U.S. Government Printing Office, 1987).

AGING AND THE LIFE CYCLE

In the United States, age 65 has generally marked that point in life when a person is "officially" old. This is largely because of its arbitrary selection by the Social Security Administration in 1935 as the age of eligibility for old-age benefits. Except for its bureaucratic significance, however, being age 65 has no other particular relevance. This is because chronological age is an inconsistent indicator of the aging process. Just as physical and intellectual capabilities mature at different times in different people, so can aging be said to begin at different points in time for different people. It is possible to be a "young" 65 or an "old" 55.

Not only do individuals vary in relation to aging, but the concept of old age itself is relative and differs between societies. The more primitive a society, the earlier in life people are defined as being old (Cowgill 1986). Modern societies select a chronological age, like 65, as the point of old age, whereas less-developed societies tend to rely more on a particular event, such as becoming a grandparent, to mark a person as old.

One way to organize the social and psychological aspects of the aging experience is to categorize that experience into stages that denote the human life cycle. Although the stages of the life cycle are based on chronological age and do not account for variations among individuals, they are indicative of the general life course most people follow. Implicit in the idea of a life cycle is a common set of social experiences through which members of a society are expected to pass. For instance, childhood is the time when a person generally receives a primary education; adolescence and young adulthood are usually the time of courtship and marriage; the period of later maturity is typically the time of retirement.

Age is an important dimension of social organization, because the divisions of the life cycle are those prescribed by the culture of a society in order to lend stability and predictability to the typical sequence of life events. Implied in this arrangement is the idea that individuals also undergo a change in behavior as they pass from one stage of life into a subsequent stage. Infants, children, young adults, middle-aged adults, and older persons are all expected by other people to behave in a manner characteristic of their age-group; social judgments of their maturity depend on how closely their behavior approximates the corresponding age-related norm. Furthermore, at each stage of life, a person takes on new social roles and the responsibilities that accrue to those roles, and the person's status and relationships with other people are modified accordingly.

The typical stages of the human life cycle and the approximate ages they represent are shown in Table 1–3. Although a person can be regarded as aging from the moment of conception or from the moment the individual reaches full maturation (there is some disagreement on this point), for the purposes of our discussion, the stages of middle age, later maturity, and old age are most

TABLE 1–3   The Life Cycle

Stage	Approximate Age
Infancy	2
Preschool	2–5
Childhood	5–12
Adolescence	12–17
Early Maturity	17–25
Maturity	25–40
Middle Age	40–55
Later Maturity	55–75
Old Age	75

relevant. Although the life cycle is not necessarily experienced in neatly packaged phases by everybody, stage theories are useful in highlighting the general pattern of the life course.

According to Robert Atchley (1988), middle age (ages 40–55) is the period of life when a person initially becomes aware of the fact that he or she is aging. Middle age is the time when the person recognizes a reduction of energy and often begins to favor less strenuous activities. Usually the person's work career more or less reaches a plateau, and the great majority of a couple's children will have left home to lead their own lives. This is a time of life when parents or other older people close to the individual die. As Atchley explains, middle age is also when most people realize that they themselves are aging and that death is very real, not just something that happens to somebody else. Robert Kastenbaum (1971), for example, found that a characteristic of old age is a foreshortened time perspective. The older person avoids thought of the future because of the limited time left and instead dwells on the past. Kastenbaum suggests that a majority of people are past oriented by age 40 and virtually all people are by age 55.

Later maturity (ages 55–75) is characterized by a marked reduction in energy, vision, and hearing. Chronic health disorders are commonplace, and poor health can join with reduced income, retirement, and the deaths of friends and relatives to curtail social interaction. By the time they are in their midsixties, most women are widows. But, as Atchley notes, the period of later maturity can be a pleasant one for those people who plan for it, retain a good measure of physical vigor, and perhaps wish to enjoy a time of lessened responsibilities. Also, the aged individual may continue to be a highly productive member of society. Charles Bowden and Alvin Burstein (1974:212) point out, for example, that the "myth that age necessarily involves an inability to produce is challenged by the numbers of second careers and examples of influence maintained by prominent individuals late into their lives." Both Ronald Reagan and George Bush were elected president of the

United States while in their sixties; most members of the U.S. Supreme Court and many members of Congress serve in office while elderly.

Old age (75 and over), in contrast to other stages of life, is more likely to be a less pleasant period, for there is a higher probability of loneliness, boredom, and loss of self-esteem. Also, it can be a time when mental processes are diminished. Whereas it seems clear that the aged brain takes longer to respond to a stimulus and the recall of recent events may be impaired (probably because of the older person's tendency toward increased distractibility), remote memory of past events is usually quite good. If there is considerable memory loss, it can be a sign of organic brain damage. But it should be realized that although such brain damage may be likely to occur with increasing age, it does not occur in most elderly people. Besides reduced mental activity in very old age, another problem peculiar to the elderly is that of physical frailty and the possibility of being so disabled that physical mobility is highly restricted or denied.

Physical and mental infirmities and the reality of being tired, ill, and less able to cope with problems—all set in a framework of the recognition of impending death—can and do produce severe problems of adjustment and depression for the elderly. With reduced resources, the elderly person is less able to cope with stress and adapt to new conditions. Old age is thus a period in life many people fear and wish to avoid; yet, as in the period of later maturity, the key to success in old age is to maintain an optimal level of physical strength and mental awareness.

However, to be old in society often means assuming a devalued status. Despite the fact that a majority of aged persons are not sick, lonely, poor, insecure, or mentally deficient, some of them are, and the negative stereotype of the elderly that results from this situation is widespread and resistant to change.

Therefore, it needs to be pointed out that the transition from middle to old age is not always negative and that added years of life now mean added opportunities. Older people today differ markedly from the aged of earlier periods in that they are more healthy, alert, vigorous, and younger in outlook (Pifer and Bronte 1986). In modern societies, it is typically only after the age of 75 that most people begin to decline physically and some decline mentally, whereas others remain relatively healthy past the age of 75. James Fries (1980) claims that the average human life expectancy may be extended to 85 years in the near future. The years up to age 85 will essentially be healthy; but at age 85, people will run into a "wall" and everything will come apart at once. Thus, people may not be extremely sick or disabled, on the average, until the very end of their lives. Fries theorizes that if avoidable diseases and accidents were eliminated, 99 percent of all Americans would die between the ages of 73 and 97, with age 85 being the average. Whether this theory is correct or not awaits verification. But the fact remains that in the future, societies throughout the world will experience the largest population of elderly people in their history.

Consequently, there is now a blurring of the life-cycle periods between middle age and later maturity for many people, for it is becoming less apparent when middle age ends and later maturity begins. As Bernice and Dail Neugarten (1986) observe, it is a new historical phenomenon that a very large group of elderly are healthy, vigorous, financially secure, well integrated into the lives of their families and communities, and politically active. What seems to be emerging among the elderly are new divisions of "young-old (from approximately 65–75 years of age,)" "old-old (75–85 years)," and the "oldest-old (85 and over)," with the young-old being both active and youthful in their approach to life. The majority of the young-old would not be appreciably different from younger persons in the late maturity stage (55–75 years) of the life cycle.

According to Matilda White Riley and John Riley (1986), the implications of added years for the individual's life cycle are only now beginning to be comprehended. What increased longevity means for the individual, state Riley and Riley (1986:53), is that it (1) prolongs the opportunity for accumulating life experiences; (2) maximizes a person's opportunities to complete or change the roles of early and middle life—such as changing careers or marriage partners, or taking on new roles in the later years; (3) prolongs relationships with others—spouse, family, children, and friends, who also live longer; and (4) increases the potential complexity of a person's social networks—kinship, friendship, and community—as all members survive longer. As Riley and Riley (1986:53–54) explain: "All these consequences of longevity mean that people now have unprecedented opportunity to accumulate experience, to exercise new and expanded options, to respond to social change, and to influence it."

In the final analysis, although growing older means stability and can include the potential for personal growth, aging also means a period of physical and perhaps mental decline. Consequently, the last part of the life cycle is both a period of opportunity and a period in which death is an increasing reality.

SUMMARY

Social gerontology is the study of the social experience of aging. This field has gained in importance and scope in recent years because of the significant worldwide increase of aged persons during the twentieth century. In 1987, life expectancy had reached 75 years for Americans, and the elderly constituted over 12 percent of the population. By 2050, it is projected that over 20 percent of the population, or one in five Americans, will be age 65 or older. This trend is likely to bring important changes, because the aged population will not only be larger, but also healthier, better educated, and more affluent than comparable cohorts of elderly persons in the past.

Currently, it is not known what causes physical aging. The two most widely accepted theories are (1) that wear and tear on the body over time causes it to break down and age or (2) that all of us have genetic clocks ticking away within us that are programmed or preset to determine the manner and time at which we age and die. Either theory may be correct, or there may be some combination of wear and tear and genetic clocks that trigger aging. One way to view the social experiences associated with physical aging is to organize those experiences into stages denoting the human life cycle. Such stages are indicative of the general life course that people follow. The focus of this book is upon the stages of later maturity (ages 55–75) and old age (age 75 and over). However, in recent years there has been a blurring of life-cycle periods between middle age and later maturity. The ages from 65–75 are beginning to represent a category of "young-old" persons, because many people in this age-group remain relatively active and healthy. Old age is becoming both a period of increased opportunity and a time in which death is an increased reality.

The Demography of Aging

As discussed in the first chapter, the greatest change in the age structure of most societies in the twentieth century has been the growth of the population over the age of 65. Because of its strong social implications, this demographic trend is not something that younger people today can consider unimportant or irrelevant. The significant increase in numbers and proportions of older people will impact heavily on future patterns of employment, taxation, health care delivery, and other aspects of daily life. Unless there is a global war or some widespread natural disaster that takes millions of lives, the increase in elderly people will intensify in the twenty-first century. At present, the world's elderly population is growing at a rate of 2.4 percent annually, which is faster than the growth rate for the world population as a whole. If this rate continues, the U.S. Census Bureau (1987) estimates that there will be 410 million elderly worldwide by the year 2000 (compared with 290 million in 1985). Moreover, the increase in numbers of the aged will be taking place not just in the most advanced nations, but throughout the world. The result is that there will be a greater proportion of elderly people in the twenty-first century than ever before in human history.

In this chapter we will examine this situation by first discussing the demography of aging in the United States and then comparing the U.S. pattern with global projections. In order to place this discussion in perspective, it should be pointed out that large numbers of elderly persons are a very recent occurrence in human society. As Donald Cowgill (1986) explains, life expectancy in prehistoric times averaged only about 20 years per person; thus, old people were very rare during humankind's earliest periods. Longevity increased little during the time of ancient Greece and Rome, and actually declined somewhat after the fall of Rome. There was not a noticeable improvement until the seventeenth century in Europe, when the average life expectancy reached just under 30 years of age. Yet this modest increase was not enough, as Cowgill observes, to produce any significant change in the age structure of even the most developed countries at that time.

Consequently, for most of the history of the world, human populations have tended to consist largely of children and young adults. Relatively few persons reached middle age, and only the very few reached old age. It was not until the middle of the nineteenth century that the average life expectancy in a developed nation finally reached 45 years. The greatest extension of longevity has occurred in the twentieth century, especially since World War II, with the most advanced nations now showing life expectancies in the mid-70s or higher. In 1987, the highest mean for life expectancy in the world was 79.1 years for Japan. For the first time ever, large populations of old people are becoming common throughout the world.

DEMOGRAPHIC PATTERNS IN THE UNITED STATES

The demographic pattern of aging in the United States has followed a course similar to that of other major industrialized countries. Life expectancy for Americans, as noted in the last chapter, increased from 47.3 years in 1900 to 75.0 years in 1987. In 1900, persons 65 years of age and over in the United States numbered 3.1 million and constituted 4 percent of the total population; in 1987, some 29.8 million, or 12.3 percent, of all Americans were 65 or older. As shown in Figure 2–1, the proportion of the elderly is expected to increase even more significantly in the future. The growth of the older population will be relatively slow during the 1990s because of the decline in the birthrate during the Great Depression of the 1930s. From 29.8 million in 1987, Figure 2–1 shows that the number of older Americans will reach 34.9 million in the year 2000. However, the most rapid increase in the elderly population will take place in the twenty-first century; Figure 2–1 shows the aged population reaching 39.4 million in 2010, 52.1 million in 2020, and 65.6 million in 2030. By 2000, persons 65 years and older are expected to be 13 percent of the total population, and this percentage may reach 21.8 percent by 2050.

Declining mortality rates and the rise in life expectancy have also meant that the older population itself is getting older. Thus, it may not be unusual in the future to see 70-year-old daughters caring for their 95-year-old mothers. We see this potential in statistics like those for 1987, when the 65–74-year-old

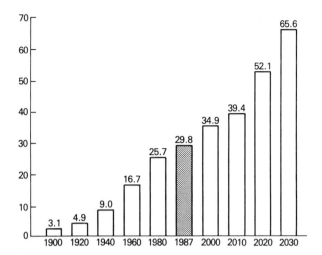

FIGURE 2–1   Number of persons age 65 and over, United States, 1900 to 2030

Source: Based on U.S. Census Bureau data.

age-group (17.7 million people) was eight times larger than in 1900, but the 75–84 age-group (9.3 million) was twelve times larger, and the age 85 and over group (2.9 million) was twenty-three times larger. The fastest growing segment of the aged population is the oldest-old—those persons age 85 and over. The oldest-old age cohort increased by 141 percent in the United States between 1960 and 1980, and Census Bureau projections indicate an additional increase of 117 percent between 1980 and 2000. In terms of actual numbers, the oldest-old will grow from 2.9 million in 1987 to 4.9 million in 2000 and to over 7.1 million by 2020; by 2040, the population 85 years and older will number about 13 million. From 1 percent of the American population in the late 1980s, the oldest-old will constitute over 5 percent of the population by the mid–twenty-first century, which is the largest gain of any age-group during this period.

Gender

Although the life expectancy of the elderly in the United States has increased significantly in the twentieth century, the greatest increase has been among women and whites. Females tend to live much longer than males, and this fact is true both in the United States and worldwide. Males exceed female death rates at all ages and for the leading causes of death, such as heart disease, cancer, stroke, accidents, and pneumonia. Women do suffer from illness and physical disability more often than men, but their usual health problems are not as serious or life threatening as those men typically encounter. Although later in life, women also die from the same illnesses as men, what distinguishes the sexes, as Lois Verbrugge (1985) observes, is the frequency of those problems and the pace of death. Men, for example, are 1.5 times more likely than women to die from cancer. Coronary heart disease is the leading cause of death for women after age 66, but becomes the number one killer of men after age 39. In sum, women are sick more often (with less serious health problems), but live longer; men, in contrast, are sick less often, but die sooner from more life-threatening diseases.

There is also evidence that women have a biological advantage in life expectancy over men from the earliest periods of life. Males have higher mortality rates than females from the prenatal and neonatal stages of life onward. Although percentages vary from year to year, males die at about a 12 percent greater rate than females during the prenatal stage, and rates are 130 percent greater during the neonatal (newborn) stage. Consequently, males appear to be weaker physiologically than females as the two sexes begin life, and this biological advantage seems to continue over the life span.

Social and psychological factors also play an important role in influencing life expectancy for males. Men are generally expected to be more aggressive than women in relation to their respective roles in society. At least this seems to be the case, for men have significantly greater participation in violent sports and exposure to high-risk occupations, such as motorcycle racing, structural steel workers, lumbermen, bank guards, munitions workers, coal miners, and police officers. More men than women are killed or injured in accidents. In addition, men and boys drink alcohol more frequently and consume more when they drink than do women and girls. High alcohol use has been identified as a risk factor for some diseases (such as cirrhosis of the liver) and deaths from automobile accidents. Another factor contributing to excess male mortality may be occupational competition and the pressure associated with a job. For instance, middle-age business executives and professionals who emphasize their career and display a strong drive toward success as part of their lifestyle are noted by insurance companies as a high-risk group for heart disease. This is particularly so if they smoke, are overweight, and tend to overwork. It would seem, therefore, that both the male sex role and the psychodynamics of male competitiveness have an effect on male longevity.

The result is that, as of 1987, the average life expectancy in the United States for females was 78.3 years compared with 71.5 years for males. Overall, women outnumber men in the United States 127 million to 121 million, with the greatest disparity at the oldest ages. United States Census figures for 1987 show that of the 29.8 million elderly persons in the United States, 17.7 million were women and 12.3 million were men, for a sex ratio of 146 elderly women for every 100 elderly men. For every 100 men in the 65–69 age-group, there were 120 women, but for every 100 men in the 85 years and older age bracket, there were 256 women.

What this pattern signifies for most women is a highly decreased likelihood of being married in old age. This situation is depicted in Figure 2–2, which shows U.S. Census Bureau statistics for unmarried adults in 1988. As Figure 2–2 indicates, for every 100 unmarried women, there were 114 unmarried men in the 18–24-year-old age-group, 127 men in the 25–29 age-group, 121 men at 30–34, and 104 men at 35–39. The figures are reversed, however, beginning at ages 40–44, where Figure 2–2 shows that for every 100 unmarried women, there were 75 unmarried men; at ages 45–64, there were 56 eligible men per 100 unmarried women; and, finally, for age 65 and older, there were only 27 male bachelors for every 100 unmarried women.

There is some evidence that the American population may be shifting toward greater equality in mortality between the sexes. If this is the case, the ratio of men to women at the oldest ages could change somewhat. This possibility is based on data, as Verbrugge (1985) explains, that shows sex differences for some major causes of death have either become stable, decreased, or only slowly widened. Considerable speculation exists with respect to the possible effects on female longevity posed by their increased participation in the labor force and changes in lifestyle, but it will be several years—until the present cohort of middle-aged and young adult women die—before these effects can be fully determined.

However, we are already seeing such changes as a decline in lung cancer among males because of reduced smoking, whereas lung cancer has increased significantly among women as a result of greater numbers of females taking up smoking in the 1940s. Between 1960 and 1983, death rates from lung cancer increased at an average annual rate of 6.2 percent for

FIGURE 2–2 Number of unmarried men per 100 unmarried women in 1988

Source: Based on U.S. Census Bureau data.

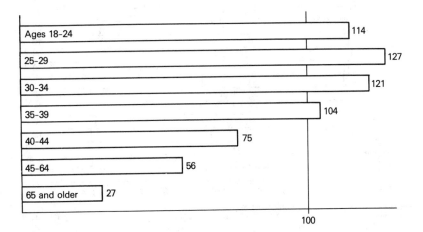

women. Lung cancer ranked eighth among cancer deaths for women in 1961, was second to breast cancer by 1979, and moved into first place as the leading cancer killer of women by 1986. Male death rates from lung cancer are still higher than those of women, but the dramatic increase in deaths from lung cancer for women has reduced the differences between the sexes for this cause of death. Patterns such as these may produce a greater balance in mortality between men and women in the future and may affect aging trends. For instance, life expectancy for men increased from 70.9 years in 1982 to 71.5 years in 1987, an improvement of six-tenths of a year; for women, life expectancy improved only one-tenth of a year (from 78.2 to 78.3) during the same period. But for the time being, the imbalance between males and females in overall mortality remains weighted heavily in favor of women.

This imbalance is reflected in the much greater proportion of elderly females than elderly males in the total population. Figure 2–3 shows the distribution by age and sex for the United States for 1980, 1990, and 2000. Figure 2–3 is a population pyramid, which is a method used to depict graphically the overall age structure of a society. Figure 2–3 shows that the largest proportions of people (as indicated by the greatest bulges in the pyramid) in 1980 were in age-groups spread between 15–34 years of age. In 1990, the shape of the pyramid had changed with the aging of the population;

FIGURE 2–3   Distribution of the U.S. population by age and sex, 1980, 1990, and 2000

Source: Based on U.S. Census Bureau data.

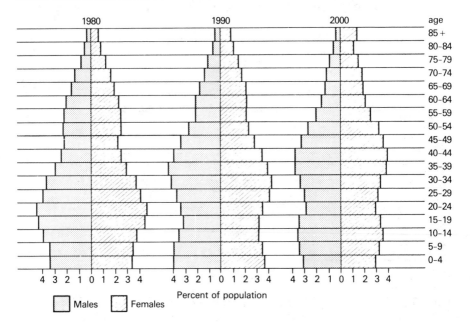

the bulges were greatest for age-groups between 25–44 years. For the year 2000, Figure 2–3 shows the shift in population continuing toward older age-groups, with the largest proportion of people located in the 35–49-year-old age brackets. Figure 2–3 also shows increasingly larger proportions of persons in the oldest age categories and an increasing preponderance of women at the oldest ages.

Race

An important reflection of social inequality in the United States is the difference in life expectancy between whites and blacks. Table 2–1 shows that life expectancy for both whites and nonwhites has significantly increased since 1900. By 1987, the average life expectancy of white females is shown in Table 2–1 to have increased to 78.9 years compared with 72.2 years for white males. For blacks, females had an average life expectancy of 73.6 years in 1987 compared with 65.2 years for males.

Although Table 2–1 shows that gender produces a strong difference in life expectancy, race is still important. The black female has a definite advantage in longevity over the black male, but white females outlive black females, black males, and white males by a wide margin. The most disadvantaged individual is the black male, whose life, on the average, is seven years less than that of the white male. Thus, despite the female advantage, life expectancy in the United States is strongly affected by racial background and the manner in which this background can be translated into a healthy life. Unfortunately, the conditions of poverty restrict the life chances of many racial minority persons. For a long life in the United States, it is best to be female and white.

TABLE 2–1   Average Number of Years of Life Expectancy in the United States by Race and Sex, Since 1900

LIFE EXPECTANCY AT BIRTH BY YEAR	WHITE MALES	WHITE FEMALES	BLACK MALES	BLACK FEMALES
1900	46.6	48.7	32.5[1]	33.5[1]
1950	66.5	72.2	58.9	62.7
1960	67.4	74.1	60.7	65.9
1970	68.0	75.6	60.0	68.3
1980	70.7	78.1	63.8	72.5
1987	72.2	78.9	65.2	73.6

[1] Includes all nonwhites.

Source: U.S. National Center for Health Statistics, *Health, United States, 1989* (Washington, D.C.: U.S. Government Printing Office, 1990).

In 1987, the overall racial composition of the population 65 years of age and older in the United States was about 90 percent white, 8 percent black, and 2 percent other races (namely, American Indians, Eskimos, Aleuts, Asians, and Pacific Islanders). Hispanics, whose racial origin may be either white, black, or Indian, constituted some 3 percent of the older population. For the future, the proportion of the elderly population that is black, Hispanic, or Asian is likely to increase, whereas the proportion of whites will decline somewhat, and the proportion of other races will remain about the same (Atchley 1988). However, in terms of total numbers, the elderly population in the United States will be predominantly white.

Socioeconomic Status

Age does not determine a person's socioeconomic position in American society. That is, simply being old in itself does not confer enhanced social prestige unless the individual is 100 years of age or older, which is generally viewed as an accomplishment (Baker 1985). Typically, an individual's income, level of education, and occupational prestige are the major determinants of his or her socioeconomic status (SES). Typically, the elderly do not have great incomes or high occupational status because they are retired. Also, in the past many elderly were not highly educated. Therefore, elderly persons have not generally filled roles associated with the highest socioeconomic status. There have been some exceptions, however, such as Ronald Reagan, who served as president of the United States from 1980–1988 while in his seventies. Yet Reagan's high status in society was determined by his role as president, not his age. But, with persons now surviving to the oldest ages with greater financial resources and higher levels of education than in the past, the socioeconomic position of the aged as a cohort needs to be reexamined.

The term *socioeconomic status* is a reflection of the work of the German sociologist Max Weber (1864–1920), who maintained that wealth alone does not determine a person's social standing, but rather it is a combination of social class position, status, and power that serves to mark an individual's position in society. It was Weber's (1958) contention that although social class is an objective dimension of social life, signified by how much money and property a person has, status is subjective in that it consists largely of how much esteem a person is accorded by other people. A person's status is derived particularly from his or her lifestyle, but also from educational attainment and occupational prestige. Persons belonging to the same status group share similar material circumstances, prestige, levels of education and occupation, and political influence and power; they also display the same lifestyle and the social perspectives associated with it.

Weber's influence on analyses of social stratification is seen mainly in the use of socioeconomic status as a variable to determine social position.

Typically, SES consists of measures of income, occupational prestige, and level of education. It not only reflects a person's economic situation, but also allows for status differences that are not necessarily based on wealth. A drug dealer, for example, can be wealthy but will have low socioeconomic status, whereas a university professor may not be wealthy but can have relatively high status because of his or her education and academic accomplishments.

As for the socioeconomic status of the elderly in American society, it is important to note that the aged are a diverse group from all walks of life. To be over the age of 65 does not automatically confer a low socioeconomic rank on an individual; the aged are found in every social class. The elderly may enjoy upper-class status because of their wealth, prestige, and power, or be lower class because of their relative lack of such attributes. Consequently, age alone does not cause an individual's level of social standing. Although old age is usually a negative factor in determining current status—wealth, power, and past statuses can be more important determinants. Nevertheless, some general statements are able to be made about the overall position of the elderly in society from the standpoint of income, occupation, and education.

Income. The median income (half of all persons have incomes higher than the median and half have incomes that are lower) in 1987 in the United States was $26,008 for men and $16,909 for women. Among the elderly, median incomes in 1987 were $11,854 for men and $6,734 for women. On an individual level, the incomes of aged men and women are less than half that of their younger counterparts. Among families generally, regardless of size, the median 1987 income was $30,853 ($32,274 was the median for whites, $20,306 for Hispanics, and $18,098 for blacks); among families headed by persons age 65 or over, the median 1987 income was $20,813 ($21,474 for whites, $14,377 for Hispanics, and $14,107 for blacks). Overall, families headed by an elderly person had incomes from one-fourth to one-third lower than that of families headed by younger persons.

The percent distribution of income among the elderly for 1987 is shown in Figure 2–4. For families headed by an elderly person, Figure 2–4 shows that 10.5 percent had an income of $50,000 or higher, and another 12.4 percent had incomes between $35,000 and $49,999. Conversely, some 31.5 percent of families headed by a person age 65 or older had incomes of less than $15,000. Figure 2–4 also shows that elderly persons living alone or with nonrelatives were likely to have low incomes in 1987, with 40.6 percent in income categories of less than $7,000. Only some 22.5 percent of this group reported incomes of more than $15,000.

The major source of income for older families and individuals in 1986 was Social Security (38 percent), followed by income from assets and earnings (26 percent), employment (17 percent), public and private pensions (16 percent), and other payments such as Supplemental Income Security, unemployment compensation, and veterans benefits (3 percent). In the 1960s,

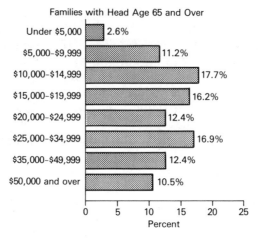

Families with Head Age 65 and Over

Income	Percent
Under $5,000	2.6%
$5,000-$9,999	11.2%
$10,000-$14,999	17.7%
$15,000-$19,999	16.2%
$20,000-$24,999	12.4%
$25,000-$34,999	16.9%
$35,000-$49,999	12.4%
$50,000 and over	10.5%

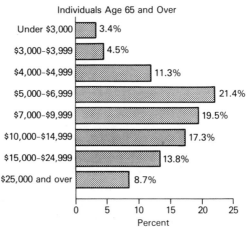

Individuals Age 65 and Over

Income	Percent
Under $3,000	3.4%
$3,000-$3,999	4.5%
$4,000-$4,999	11.3%
$5,000-$6,999	21.4%
$7,000-$9,999	19.5%
$10,000-$14,999	17.3%
$15,000-$24,999	13.8%
$25,000 and over	8.7%

$20,813 median for families with heads age 65 and over
$8,205 median for unrelated individuals age 65 and over

FIGURE 2–4   Percent distribution by income, United States, 1987

Source: Based on U.S. Census Bureau data.

about 60 percent of all elderly people lived solely on Social Security, but currently most retired people have some income in addition to Social Security from pension plans. However, for those persons age 65 and over with the lowest incomes, Social Security remains the single largest source of money. As shown in Table 2–2, 77 percent of the income for those elderly persons with less than $5,000 annual income in 1986 came from Social Security. In contrast, Table 2–2 shows that persons with incomes of $20,000 or more

TABLE 2–2   Sources of Income for Couples and Single People 65 or Older, United States, 1986

INCOME	EMPLOY-MENT	SOCIAL SECURITY	PENSIONS AND ANNUITIES	INCOME FROM ASSETS	PUBLIC ASSISTANCE	OTHER
Under $5,000	0%	77%	3%	4%	14%	2%
$5,000–$9,999	3	75	8	9	3	2
$10,000–$19,999	9	51	18	19	0	2
$20,000 and over	24	21	19	34	0	1
Total	17	38	16	26	1	2

Source: Based on U.S. Department of Health and Human Services data.

received only 21 percent of their income from Social Security. For this latter group, income from assets (34 percent) was much greater. Table 2–2 shows that the lower one's income, the greater that income is derived from Social Security and public assistance; the higher one's income, the greater that income is obtained from employment, pensions and annuities, and assets.

Some 3.5 million elderly persons lived below the poverty line in 1987, which ranged from $5,800 or less for one person to $23,000 for a family of nine. A family of four was considered poor with an income of $11,600 or less. Some 12.2 percent of persons age 65 or older lived below the 1987 poverty line compared with 10.8 percent of persons age 18–64. Another 2.3 million, or 8 percent, of the elderly lived just above the poverty line. Altogether, one-fifth, or 20 percent, of the aged population was poor or near-poor in 1987.

However, when considering only the poor (not the near-poor) living on or below the poverty line, the elderly's figure of 12.2 percent for 1987 is not disproportional when it is recognized that the proportion of all Americans living in poverty that year was 13.5 percent, or 32.5 million. Furthermore, 12.2 percent is a vast improvement over 35.2 percent, which was the percentage of elderly persons living below the poverty line in 1959. Although poverty remains a serious problem for many aged Americans, it is clear that the trend is toward lessened numbers of the elderly in the ranks of the poor.

Yet it should be noted that there are groups within the older population who still confront very high rates of poverty. One of every ten (10 percent) elderly whites was poor in 1987, compared with about one-third (34 percent) of elderly blacks and over one-fourth (27 percent) of elderly Hispanics. Older women had a higher poverty rate (15 percent) than older men (9 percent), whereas older persons living alone or with nonrelatives were much more likely to be poor (24 percent) than elderly persons living in families (7 percent). The highest rates of poverty for the elderly are found in the South, where the percentage of elderly living below the poverty line is greatest in Mississippi (34 percent); followed by Alabama, Arkansas, and Louisiana (28 percent); Georgia (26 percent); South Carolina and Tennessee (25 percent); North Carolina (24 percent); and Kentucky (23 percent).

Occupation.   In 1987, some 3.1 million elderly persons, representing 11 percent of the total population age 65 years or older, were in the labor force, either working or actively seeking employment. Some 1.9 million men (16 percent of all elderly men) and 1.2 million women (7 percent of all elderly women) constituted the aged labor force; these persons represented some 2.6 percent of the entire U.S. labor force. About half (52 percent) of these workers were employed part-time. Some 775,000, or 25 percent, of all older workers in 1987 were self-employed, and three-fourths of them were men. Because most elderly persons (89 percent) are not employed or seeking work, the prestige of one's current occupation is not a major factor in determining the socioeconomic status of the aged. However, the prestige associated with their former occupation can still be important.

Education.   The educational level of the elderly has been consistently increasing. The median level of education for the aged in 1987 was 12.0 years compared with 8.7 years in 1970. The median level of education for elderly whites in 1987 was 12.1 years, whereas the median for blacks was 8.4 years and for Hispanics was 7.4 years. In addition, the percentage of the older population who had completed high school was 51 percent in 1987, which represents a major increase over the 1970 figure of 28 percent. Moreover, about 10 percent of the elderly in 1987 were college graduates, and it is projected by the U.S. Census Bureau that 20 percent of the aged will hold college degrees by the year 2010. The trend is clearly toward higher levels of educational attainment for future generations of the aged.

Overall, it would appear that the elderly are becoming more affluent and reaching old age with higher levels of education than in the past. As a group, it would appear that the socioeconomic status of the elderly in society is improving because the aged have more money and education. Consequently, the loss of socioeconomic status in general that old age brings may not be so pervasive in the future.

This does not mean that being old now enhances one's socioeconomic status. Older persons still tend generally to have lower status than younger persons in the same socioeconomic group because of the effects of retirement on income and occupational prestige. However, Robert Atchley (1988) reminds us that these changes do not necessarily bring lessened status among the elderly themselves. According to John Henretta and Richard Campbell (1976), factors like education and occupation that determine income in retirement are the same ones that determined income before retirement. Those elderly with high incomes before retirement tend to have relatively higher incomes during retirement, even though everybody may "take a pay cut." Therefore, among the elderly, a person's preretirement socioeconomic status usually carries over into retirement among his or her age peers. The elderly may lose status in socioeconomic terms in the wider society, but among themselves their former status tends to be preserved.

It should be noted that, as Gordon Streib (1984) points out, research on social stratification and aging in the latter part of the life cycle requires a shift in analytical perspective. Typically, such research focuses on social mobility and status attainment. In the case of the aged, it is highly unlikely that they will be upwardly mobile; rather, they will tend to maintain their status, especially among their age peers, or will be downwardly mobile. Moreover, Streib points out that biological factors associated with aging complicate patterns of stratification among older people. The physical and mental decline of the aged can have a major effect on their social status—regardless of their income, education, power, lifestyle, or former occupation. Status is altered significantly if a person is physically or mentally disabled as well as old. Streib suggests that instead of employing the same stratification rankings, such as occupational prestige, that apply to younger persons, perhaps new concepts and measures to determine the status of those beyond the working years should be developed.

Marital Status

With women living to old age in greater proportions than men, it is not surprising that in 1987 there were five times as many widows (8.1 million) as widowers (1.6 million) in the United States. Figure 2–5 shows that 41 percent of all elderly women in 1987 were married, 49 percent were widowed, 5 percent had never married, and 4 percent were divorced. For elderly men, Figure 2–5 shows that 77 percent were married, 14 percent were widowers, 5 percent had never married, and 4 percent were divorced. The notable difference between aged men and women in relation to marital status is that men are significantly more likely (nearly twice as likely) to be married in old age than are women.

Living Arrangements

Most elderly Americans, about 95 percent, live in a noninstitutionalized environment. The remaining 5 percent, some 1.3 million out of a total older population of 29.8 million in 1987, live in nursing homes or homes for the aged. The idea that most aged persons are institutionalized is clearly a myth, for the great majority live in ordinary households. However, the percentage of older people living in long-care facilities for the elderly increases with age;

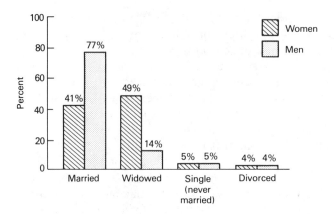

FIGURE 2–5   Marital status of persons age 65 and over, United States, 1987

Source: Based on U.S. Census Bureau data.

and over the life course, about 20 percent of those over age 65 will eventually live in a long-term care facility.

For 1985, about 2 percent of all persons in the 65–74-year-old age-group were institutionalized, but the percentage for the 75–84 age-group was 7.7, and for 85 years of age and older was 24.4 (Longino 1986). For the oldest-old (those over 85), one in four are institutionalized. It has been suggested that because the oldest-old are the fastest growing segment of the population, there will be a dramatic increase in the need for space in nursing homes and old-age homes in the future (Manton and Soldo 1985).

Most elderly, as noted, live outside institutions in family settings. United States Census data for 1987 show that, for the approximately 28.5 million noninstitutionalized aged, 82 percent of older men and 57 percent of older women lived either with their spouse or other relatives. More specifically, 75 percent of the men lived with their spouse and 7 percent with other relatives, whereas 39 percent of the women lived with their spouse and 18 percent lived with other relatives. These living arrangements are depicted in Table 2–3, which also shows that 16 percent of older men and 41 percent of

TABLE 2–3   **Living Arrangements of Noninstitutionalized Persons Age 65 and Over, United States, 1987**

	MEN	*WOMEN*	*OVERALL*
Living alone	16%	41%	30%
Living with spouse	75	39	55
Living with other relatives	7	18	13
Living with nonrelatives	2	2	2

Source: Based on U.S. Census Bureau data.

older women lived alone. The remaining 2 percent of noninstitutionalized men and women lived with nonrelatives. Living alone in old age is much more common for women.

Geographic Distribution

Table 2–4 shows the distribution of the elderly by state in the United States for 1987. In terms of numbers, California has the largest number of aged persons (nearly 3 million), followed by New York and Florida with over 2 million. About half (49 percent) of all elderly persons are concentrated numerically in eight states, with California, New York, and Florida followed by Pennsylvania, Texas, Illinois, Ohio, and Michigan. When it comes to percentage of the total state population, a higher percentage of elderly persons (17.8 percent) live in Florida than any other state. The elderly population in Iowa, Pennsylvania, Rhode Island, Arkansas, and South Dakota ranges from 14 to 14.9 percent, and the proportion of the aged in West Virginia, Nebraska, and Missouri is between 13.8 and 13.9 percent.

As for the greatest increase in the older population by state for the years between 1980 and 1987, Table 2–4 shows that Alaska had the highest gain (63.3 percent), followed by Nevada (61.7 percent), Hawaii (43.2 percent), Arizona (40.0 percent), New Mexico (29.4 percent), South Carolina (27.6 percent), Florida (26.8 percent), Utah (26.0 percent), Delaware (25.9 percent), and North Carolina (25.1 percent). In addition, Table 2–4 shows the percentage of the elderly living below the poverty line for 1979, the most recent figures available. As previously discussed, the highest proportion of the aged living in poverty is in the South. The percentage of the elderly in the total population for each state and the change in the percentage of the aged by state for 1980 to 1987 is illustrated in Figure 2–6.

When it comes to living in urban areas as opposed to rural settings, most elderly (73 percent) live in an urban environment. For 1987, U.S. Census data indicate that 31 percent of all elderly lived in large cities and 42 percent lived in suburbs; the remaining 27 percent lived in rural areas. Elderly persons are somewhat more likely than persons under the age of 65 to live in rural areas, but the difference is not great. The elderly are also less likely to change their residence than other age-groups, but when they do move, the majority have moved from the Northeast and Midwest to the South or West.

Median Age

In 1988, Americans reached their highest median age ever—32.3 years. The median age is the midpoint for age; it means that half the country is older than this age and half younger. When the median age increases, the population as a whole is getting older. In 1950, the median age was 30.2; it rose to 32.1 by 1987. The increase in median age is due to the maturing of the large

TABLE 2–4   United States Population Age 65 and Over by State, 1987

STATE	NUMBER (000's) 1987	PERCENT OF ALL AGES 1987	PERCENT INCREASE 1980–87	PERCENT BELOW POVERTY LEVEL 1979[1]
U.S., total	29,835	12.3	16.8	14.8
Alabama	505	12.4	14.7	28.4
Alaska	19	3.6	63.3	14.2
Arizona	430	12.7	40.0	12.2
Arkansas	348	14.6	11.4	28.2
California	2,944	10.6	21.9	8.3
Colorado	305	9.2	23.3	12.8
Connecticut	429	13.4	17.6	8.8
Delaware	75	11.6	25.9	13.6
District of Columbia	77	12.3	3.1	18.9
Florida	2,140	17.8	26.8	12.7
Georgia	623	10.0	20.5	25.7
Hawaii	109	10.1	43.2	10.5
Idaho	115	11.5	22.7	16.0
Illinois	1,405	12.1	11.3	11.9
Indiana	670	12.1	14.5	12.7
Iowa	421	14.8	8.6	13.3
Kansas	336	13.6	9.7	14.2
Kentucky	457	12.3	11.6	23.3
Louisiana	481	10.8	19.0	27.7
Maine	159	13.4	12.5	16.4
Maryland	486	10.7	22.9	12.7
Massachusetts	800	13.7	10.2	9.7
Michigan	1,058	11.5	16.0	12.2
Minnesota	534	12.6	11.3	14.8
Mississippi	318	12.1	10.0	34.3
Missouri	703	13.8	8.5	17.4
Montana	101	12.5	19.9	14.4
Nebraska	220	13.8	7.1	15.5
Nevada	106	10.6	61.7	10.7
New Hampshire	121	11.5	18.0	12.3
New Jersey	994	13.0	15.6	9.9
New Mexico	150	10.0	29.4	21.1
New York	2,309	13.0	6.9	11.6
North Carolina	754	11.8	25.1	23.9
North Dakota	90	13.3	11.4	17.0
Ohio	1,346	12.5	15.1	12.6

(*continued*)

TABLE 2–4   *(continued)*

STATE	NUMBER (000's) 1987	PERCENT OF ALL AGES 1987	PERCENT INCREASE 1980–87	PERCENT BELOW POVERTY LEVEL 1979[1]
Oklahoma	418	12.8	11.0	21.0
Oregon	373	13.7	22.9	11.8
Pennsylvania	1,764	14.8	15.3	11.9
Rhode Island	145	14.7	14.0	12.8
South Carolina	367	10.7	27.6	25.4
South Dakota	100	14.0	9.4	20.2
Tennessee	602	12.4	16.3	25.1
Texas	1,627	9.7	18.7	21.2
Utah	138	8.2	26.0	11.8
Vermont	65	11.9	12.1	13.8
Virginia	623	10.6	23.3	17.3
Washington	536	11.8	24.1	11.3
West Virginia	264	13.9	11.1	18.5
Wisconsin	633	13.2	12.3	9.6
Wyoming	44	8.9	17.8	14.0

[1] Below poverty level figures reflect most recent information available.
Source: Based on U.S. Census Bureau data.

Baby Boom generation born after World War II. As this cohort ages, it raises the nation's median age because there are fewer people in the generations that follow them.

Table 2–5 shows the median ages by state as of July 1, 1988. Florida has the oldest population, with a median age of 36.4, followed by New Jersey, with a median age of 34.5, and Pennsylvania and Connecticut at 34.4. Nebraska and North Carolina, with median ages of 32.3, are in the middle. The youngest population is found in Utah, where the median age is 25.7. As the United States moves into the twenty-first century and the aged population continues to increase, the median age is expected to rise.

DEMOGRAPHIC PATTERNS WORLDWIDE

In order to put demographic patterns of aging into a global perspective, the remainder of this chapter will discuss aging patterns worldwide. Each nation of the world is part of an interdependent system linked together with other countries through trade, banking and finance, communications systems, and international politics. Thus, human society appears to be moving more than ever before toward becoming a single social system (Giddens 1989). This globalization of society does not necessarily mean growth in world unity, but

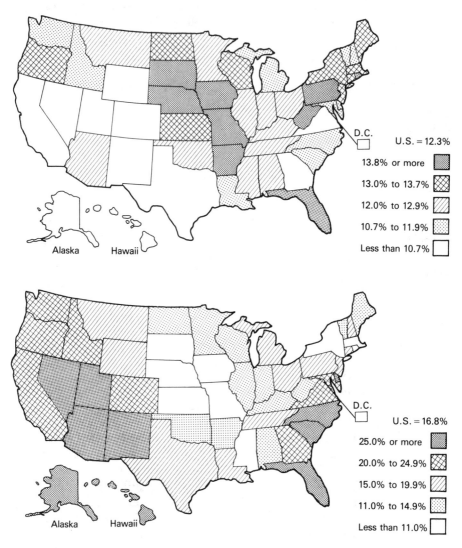

FIGURE 2–6 *Top:* persons age 65 and over as percentage of total population, United States, 1987. *Bottom:* percentage change in age 65 and over population, United States, 1980 to 1987

Source: Based on U.S. Census Bureau data.

TABLE 2–5   Median Ages by State, United States, 1988

STATE	AGE	STATE	AGE	STATE	AGE
Florida	36.4	Illinois	32.4	Oklahoma	31.8
New Jersey	34.5	Kansas	32.4	South Dakota	31.8
Connecticut	34.4	Virginia	32.4	Alabama	31.7
Pennsylvania	34.4	Washington	32.4	Arizona	31.7
New York	33.8	Nebraska	32.3	Vermont	31.6
Rhode Island	33.7	North Carolina	32.3	Colorado	31.4
Massachusetts	33.5	Montana	32.2	North Dakota	31.3
Dist. of Col.	33.3	Nevada	32.2	South Carolina	30.9
Oregon	33.3	Minnesota	32.1	Georgia	30.8
West Virginia	33.3	N. Hampshire	32.1	Idaho	30.7
Iowa	33.0	Wisconsin	32.1	New Mexico	30.4
Maine	33.0	Delaware	32.0	Texas	30.1
Missouri	33.0	Indiana	32.0	Mississippi	30.0
Arkansas	32.7	Hawaii	31.9	Louisiana	29.9
Maryland	32.7	Kentucky	31.9	Wyoming	29.8
Tennessee	32.7	California	31.8	Alaska	28.7
Ohio	32.6	Michigan	31.8	Utah	25.7

Source: Based on U.S. Census Bureau data.

rather that the daily lives of people are increasingly influenced by events and trends happening elsewhere in the world. This situation is particularly true when it comes to aging. Older populations are increasing on a global basis; therefore, the issues and problems associated with aging are worldwide.

The aged, by virtue of their 2.4 percent annual population increase, are growing, as previously noted, much faster than the rest of the world's population as a whole. For example, in 1985, in only a few countries of Western Europe—namely, Norway, Sweden, Denmark, Great Britain, West Germany, Austria, Italy, and Greece—was the proportion of the elderly 13 percent or higher in the total population. However, for the year 2025, the U.S. Census Bureau (1987) estimates that the proportion of elderly constituting 13 percent or more of a nation's total population will have significantly increased. Australia and the world's entire northern tier of countries, including Canada and the United States, all of Western Europe (less Turkey), Eastern Europe and the Soviet Union, and Japan, will have at least 13 percent of their populations age 65 or older.

To illustrate further the worldwide increase in elderly persons, Table 2–6 shows that in 1985, 23 countries had aged populations of 2 million or more people, but by 2025, some 50 nations will have reached this level. China and India currently have (as seen in Table 2–6) and will continue to have the largest number of elderly of any nations on earth. This is because both

TABLE 2–6   Countries with More Than 2 Million Elderly in 1985 and 2025

Countries with More Than 2 Million Elderly in 1985
(numbers in thousands)

COUNTRY	POPULATION 65 AND OVER	COUNTRY	POPULATION 65 AND OVER
China	52,889	Poland	3,484
India	32,698	Bangladesh	3,119
United States	28,609	Pakistan	2,818
Soviet Union	25,974	Mexico	2,797
Japan	12,125	Canada	2,651
Germany (Fed. Rep.)	8,812	Argentina	2,610
United Kingdom	8,466	Vietnam	2,393
Italy	7,443	Nigeria	2,307
France	6,748	Germany (Dem. Rep.)	2,217
Indonesia	5,901	Romania	2,155
Brazil	5,828	Turkey	2,093
Spain	4,274		

Countries with More Than 2 Million Elderly in 2025
(numbers in thousands)

COUNTRY	POPULATION 65 AND OVER	COUNTRY	POPULATION 65 AND OVER
China	178,150	Phillippines	7,687
India	118,968	Korea (Rep.)	7,230
United States	58,771	Spain	7,217
Soviet Union	54,641	Egypt	7,050
Japan	26,842	Iran	6,422
Indonesia	23,663	Canada	6,240
Brazil	22,844	Burma	5,354
Germany	15,175	Argentina	5,227
Mexico	11,849	Yugoslavia	4,638
France	11,273	Colombia	4,256
Italy	11,221	Romania	4,252
Pakistan	10,614	South Africa	4,221
United Kingdom	10,437	Ethiopia	4,104
Nigeria	9,865	Australia	3,585
Bangladesh	9,386	Zaire	3,466
Thailand	7,799	Korea (Dem. People's Rep.)	3,272
Poland	7,736	Netherlands	3,258
Vietnam	7,725	Morocco	3,155
Turkey	7,724	Peru	3,100

(continued)

TABLE 2–6   *(continued)*

Countries with More Than 2 Million Elderly in 2025
(Numbers in thousands)

COUNTRY	POPULATION 65 AND OVER	COUNTRY	POPULATION 65 AND OVER
Czechoslovakia	2,945	Tanzania	2,437
Venezuela	2,927	Chile	2,193
Algeria	2,904	Kenya	2,188
Sri Lanka	2,875	Iraq	2,166
Malaysia	2,529	Hungary	2,017
Sudan	2,498		

Source: U.S. Census Bureau, *An Aging World* (Washington, D.C.: U.S. Government Printing Office, 1987).

countries have larger overall populations than other nations and both have experienced lower birth and death rates than in the past. Consequently, the aged population in China and India will increase dramatically between 1985 and 2025. In 2025, Table 2–6 shows, China will have over 178 million elderly (up from nearly 53 million in 1985), and India over 118 million (from nearly 33 million in 1985). The United States will be a distant third in 2025, with over 58 million elderly, followed by the Soviet Union with over 54 million. Japan will be in fifth place in the number of elderly in 2025, with over 26 million. Overall, the greatest increase in absolute numbers of the aged will be in Asia.

Figure 2–7 shows the percent increase in the elderly populations of selected countries between 1985 and 2025. By 2025, the percentage of older persons will more than triple in Guatemala, Singapore, Mexico, the Philippines, and Indonesia. What is indicated in Figure 2–7 is that the expansion of the world's elderly population is going to be greatest in developing nations. In none of the developed nations will the proportion of the elderly increase by 200 or 300 percent. Figure 2–7 shows that the proportion of elderly in Canada will increase by 135 percent by 2025, but this percentage (the highest for a developed nation shown in Figure 2–7) is far below the 357 percent projected for Guatemala or even the 201 percent for Bangladesh. In fact, the elderly populations of many developing Asian countries—Singapore, the Philippines, Indonesia, India, China, Hong Kong, and Bangladesh—will more than double between 1985 and 2025. Although not shown in Figure 2–7, the lowest increases, overall, will be recorded in Africa; but there are some exceptions to this trend, particularly for Kenya, where the aged population is also expected to nearly triple by 2025. In the year 2000, some 41 percent of the world's elderly will live in developed nations and 59 percent in developing countries; by 2025, only 31 percent will live in developed nations compared with 69 percent for the developing nations. By the first quarter of the twenty-

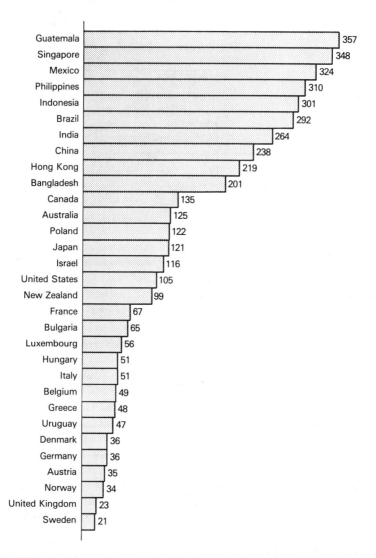

FIGURE 2–7 Percent increase in elderly population, selected countries, 1985 to 2025

Source: U.S. Census Bureau, *An Aging World* (Washington, D.C.: U.S. Government Printing Office, 1987).

first century, more than two-thirds of the world's old people will reside in developing areas.

Although the greatest increases in the percentage of older persons will be in developing nations, the greatest percentages of elderly in relation to the total population are currently found in developed nations. For example, Figure 2–7 shows that the percentage of the elderly will increase in Guatemala by 357 percent and in Sweden by only 21 percent between 1985 and 2025, but Figure 2–8, showing percentages of the elderly for 1985, indicates that only 2.9 percent of Guatemala's population is elderly compared with 16.9 percent for Sweden. Sweden is the world's "oldest" country, because its 1985 percentage of 16.9 percent is the highest proportion of elderly for any single nation. Sweden also has, as shown in Figure 2–8, the highest proportion (3.5 percent) of persons 80 years and older. In addition, Figure 2–8 shows that the United States, with 12 percent of its population 65 years of age or over in 1985, ranks lower than all of the Western European countries shown and Hungary in the percentage of its aged. The lowest percentages depicted in Figure 2–8 for 1985 are for the developing nations, which, in the future, as previously discussed, will experience the greatest expansion in numbers and proportions of older people.

The region of the world with the highest percentage of elderly is Western Europe. Although Asia has the most older persons in terms of absolute numbers and is expected to show the greatest increases in both numbers and percentages of the elderly by 2025, Western Europe has the highest percentages of elderly at present. However, Europe's aged population will increase only modestly percentage-wise in the immediate future. There will be some exceptions, such as the Soviet Union, where the older population will jump from 9 to 13 percent, and Germany, where the increase will be from 14 to 19 percent between 1985 to 2005. Yet elsewhere in Europe, where the populations in the Scandinavian countries and Great Britain are already among the world's oldest, there will be little change in the proportion of the aged in society.

Between 1985 and 2005, for example, Sweden's older population will increase from only 16.9 percent to 17 percent. By 2025, Sweden will have an older population of 22.2 percent, which will still be the highest percentage of older people in any one country in the world. But other countries will be catching up. Japan, with only 10 percent of its population age 65 and over in 1985, will see its proportion of the elderly increase to 20.3 percent by 2025. This increase will occur because the aging of the population in Japan is taking place more rapidly than in any other nation in the late twentieth century. Between 1985 and 2005, the 65–74-year-old age-group in Japan is expected to experience an average annual growth rate of 2.7 percent, and the 75 years and older age-group will average a 2.9 percent annual increase. Japan will have literally doubled (from 7 to 14 percent) the proportion of its older population in just 25 years between 1970 and 1995. It will take the United States 66 years (1944–2010) to increase its aged population from 7 to 14 percent and took France 115 years (1865–1980) to accomplish the same thing. In 1985, as noted, the elderly constituted 10 percent of Japan's population. By 2005, they will reach 16.5 percent, and by 2025 the elderly population will have increased to 20.3 percent—one of the world's highest percentages.

In the twenty-first century, however, China is likely to age faster than

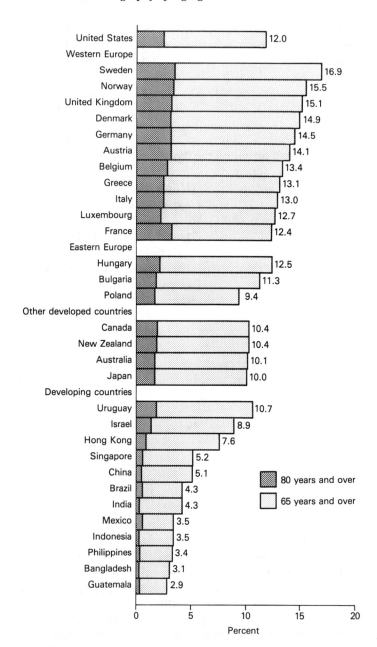

FIGURE 2–8   Elderly population, by age, selected countries, 1985

Source: U.S. Census Bureau, *An Aging World* (Washington, D.C.: U.S. Government Printing Office, 1987).

any other country. China has an official policy of one child per married couple; this policy decreased birthrates through the 1970s and 1980s. This policy has resulted in fewer children relative to the adult population; and if it continues into the twenty-first century, projections are that some 40 percent of the population will be 65 or older by the mid–twenty-first century.

According to Linda Martin (1988), Asia has been the most successful region of the world in reducing fertility. Reductions in fertility reduce the proportions of younger people and raise the proportions of older people. Consequently, Asian nations will be the first among the developing nations to have to accommodate large elderly populations, including highly developed Japan. By 2025, several Asian countries—Japan, Singapore, Hong Kong, China, Sri Lanka, and South Korea—will have more than 10 percent of their population age 65 or over. Therefore, as Martin points out, Asia is beginning to view aging as not just a concern of the West but as its own problem as well.

Life Expectancy

Japan has the highest overall life expectancy of any nation in the world. As seen in Table 2–7, depicting the average number of years a person in thirty-three developed countries in 1987 would be expected to live from birth, Japan has the highest average, with 79.1 years. No other country, including those not shown in Table 2–6, outranks Japan in longevity. Switzerland has the second highest life expectancy in the world; Table 2–7 shows the Swiss living, on the average, some 77.6 years. The United States shows a life expectancy of 75.0 years for 1987, which places it thirteenth among developed countries. At the bottom in life expectancy among developed countries are the Soviet Union and the nations of Eastern Europe. The Soviet Union is second from the bottom, with an average life expectancy of 69.8 years, and Hungary is last at 69.7 years. Just ahead of the Soviet Union were Romania, Yugoslavia, Poland, and Czechoslovakia. However, some African nations south of the Sahara, which are not shown in Table 2–7, have the lowest life expectancies in the world. These are countries like the Central African Republic (43 years), Ethiopia and Somalia (41 years), Gambia (36 years), and Sierra Leone (35 years).

In virtually every developed nation, women live longer than men. In North American and most European countries, women outlive men some seven years on the average. Only in a few developing nations of South Asia and the Middle East, where females have low social status and strong preferences exist for male offspring, is there a somewhat higher life expectancy for males at birth. In fact, in all of the countries of South Asia except Sri Lanka, the usual sex differential in mortality is reversed, and life expectancy is slightly higher for men than women. In countries like Bangladesh, India, Nepal, and Pakistan, men outlive women. In India, for example, the differential is not great, because men lived, on the average, 55.6 years in 1985

TABLE 2–7   Ranking of Life Expectancy
in Thirty-Three Developed
Countries, 1987

1. Japan 79.1
2. Switzerland 77.6
3. Iceland 77.4
4. Sweden 77.1
5. Spain 76.6
6. Canada 76.5
6. Greece 76.5
6. Netherlands 76.5
7. Australia 76.3
7. Norway 76.3
7. United Kingdom 76.3
8. France 75.9
9. West Germany 75.8
10. Italy 75.5
11. Israel 75.2
12. Austria 75.1
13. United States 75.0
14. Denmark 74.9
15. Finland 74.8
15. Malta 74.8
16. Belgium 74.3
17. New Zealand 74.2
18. Luxembourg 74.1
18. Portugal 74.1
19. Ireland 73.5
20. East Germany 73.2
21. Bulgaria 71.5
22. Czecholslovakia 71.0
22. Poland 71.0
22. Yugoslavia 71.0
23. Romania 69.9
24. Soviet Union 69.8
25. Hungary 69.7

Source: Based on U.S. Center for Disease
Control data.

compared with 55.2 years for women; but in Pakistan, the average in 1985 was
two years, with men averaging 51 years and women 49 years. According to
Martin (1988), nutritional deprivation and differing access to health care for
women are among the possible reasons for this reversal of the usual female
superiority in life expectancy.

Table 2–8 shows life expectancy at birth and at age 65 for males and
females in 1986 in selected countries. The clear leader in life expectancy in
each category is Japan. Japanese men in 1986 had an average life expectancy
of 75.5 years at birth and typically had 16.1 years of life remaining at age 65.
Greece ranked second in longevity for males, followed by Sweden, Hong

Kong, Switzerland, Israel, Spain, the Netherlands, Canada, and Australia. In each of these countries, Table 2–8 shows, male life expectancy at birth was 73 years and higher. The United States is ranked twentieth, with an average male life expectancy of 71.3 years in 1986 and 14.7 years left at 65 years of age. The lowest life expectancy for males is the Soviet Union, with 64.2 years.

Life expectancy for women in 1986 at birth and at age 65 is also shown in Table 2–8. Japanese women, like men, have the highest life expectancy in the world. In 1986, the average Japanese woman lived 81.6 years; at age 65, Japanese women had approximately 20 years of life remaining. Women in Sweden, France, and Switzerland had 80 years or more of longevity as well; the average life span for women in Norway, Canada, the Netherlands, Spain, and Australia was just below 80. The United States was ranked fifteenth, with a female life expectancy at birth in 1986 of 78.3 years and 18.6 years remaining at age 65. Romania is ranked last in female life expectancy in Table 2–6, with an average of 72.7 years.

Overall, Table 2–8 shows that Japan and Western nations have the highest life expectancy, whereas the Soviet Union and the countries of Eastern Europe have the lowest. Undoubtedly, this situation reflects general disparities in diet, living conditions, lifestyles, and medical care. Not shown, however, are averages for men and women in developing nations like those in Africa south of the Sahara, such as Gambia, Ethiopia, and Somalia, where, as noted, life expectancy is the lowest in the world—around 40 years.

Gender

With females outliving males in practically all countries, it is not surprising that elderly women greatly outnumber elderly men. Therefore, as a population grows older, the usual pattern is for the percentage of women in each age cohort to become larger. This is especially true in developed nations, where a majority of the oldest-old are women (Rosenwaike 1985; Suzman and Riley 1985). For instance, in Germany, elderly women outnumber elderly men 2 to 1, and a similar imbalance exists in Austria. Of those persons between the ages of 65 and 69 in West Germany in 1985, 62 percent were women, and at 80 years of age and older, 70 percent were women. High male war losses are responsible for this situation, along with the female advantage in life expectancy common in developed nations. Anton Amann (1981) notes that in 1980, for every 100 women in Austria 75 years of age and older there were only 44 men, and in West Germany there were 45 men per 100 women in that same age bracket. In France, where fewer men were killed in World War II than in Germany and Austria, and in Switzerland, which was neutral in the war, there were 60 men per 100 women at 75 years of age and older for 1980. An exception to the disparity in numbers between elderly men and women in Western Europe is found in Greece. In 1985, 55 percent of all Greeks between ages 65 and 69 were women, whereas at 80 years and older

TABLE 2–8 **Life Expectancy at Birth and at Age 65, According to Sex: Selected Countries, 1986**
(Data are based on reporting by countries)

COUNTRY	AT BIRTH 1986[1]	AT 65 YEARS 1986[1]	COUNTRY	AT BIRTH 1986[1]	AT 65 YEARS 1986[1]
Male	Life expectancy in years		Female	Life expectancy in years	
Japan	75.5	16.1	Japan	81.6	20.0
Greece	74.1	15.4	Switzerland	80.6	19.4
Sweden	74.0	14.9	Sweden	80.2	19.0
Hong Kong	73.8	14.9	France	80.0	19.2
Switzerland	73.8	15.1	Norway	79.9	19.0
Israel	73.4	14.9	Canada	79.9	19.3
Spain	73.2	15.2	Netherlands	79.8	18.9
Netherlands	73.1	14.1	Spain	79.8	18.7
Canada	73.1	15.0	Australia	79.6	18.9
Australia	73.0	14.9	Hong Kong	79.2	18.2
Norway	72.9	14.5	Finland	78.9	17.7
Cuba	72.7	15.8	Greece	78.9	17.7
England and Wales	72.6	13.9	Italy	78.9	17.7
Costa Rica	72.0	14.2	Federal Republic of Germany	78.5	17.7
Denmark	71.9	14.1	United States	78.3	18.6
Federal Republic of Germany	71.9	13.8	England and Wales	78.3	17.9
Kuwait	71.9	13.9	Denmark	77.8	18.1

Country			Country		
France	71.8	14.7	Austria	77.8	17.3
Italy	71.3	13.7	Belgium	77.7	17.8
United States	71.3	14.7	New Zealand	77.5	17.8
New Zealand	71.1	13.9	Puerto Rico	77.2	17.3
Northern Ireland	71.1	13.0	Northern Ireland	77.2	16.9
Austria	71.0	14.0	Trinidad and Tobago	77.2	17.3
Singapore	71.0	13.4	Portugal	77.1	17.3
Belgium	70.9	13.6	Israel	77.0	16.4
Ireland	70.8	12.4	Costa Rica	76.6	17.1
Finland	70.6	13.5	Ireland	76.4	16.0
Puerto Rico	70.2	15.0	Singapore	76.4	16.5
Portugal	70.2	14.1	Scotland	76.3	16.4
Trinidad and Tobago	70.2	15.0	Cuba	76.1	17.4
Scotland	70.1	12.6	German Democratic Republic	75.4	15.3
German Democratic Republic	69.5	12.4	Chile	75.4	16.5
Chile	68.9	13.3	Poland	75.1	15.9
Bulgaria	68.6	12.7	Kuwait	74.9	15.4
Czechoslovakia	67.3	11.7	Czechoslovakia	74.8	15.0
Romania	67.1	12.8	Bulgaria	74.7	14.9
Poland	66.7	12.3	Hungary	73.3	15.1
Hungary	65.3	11.9	U.S.S.R.	73.3	15.8
U.S.S.R.	64.2	12.3	Romania	72.7	14.7

[1] Data for Chile, the German Democratic Republic, Hong Kong, Italy, and Puerto Rico are for 1985; data for England, Wales, and Northern Ireland are for 1987; data for Romania and Spain are for 1984; data for the U.S.S.R. are for 1985–1986; and data for Trinidad and Tobago are for 1983.

Source: U.S. National Center for Health Statistics, Health, United States, 1989 (Washington, D.C.: U.S. Government Printing Office, 1990).

the percentage of women was only slightly higher, at almost 59 percent. Overall, however, there is a preponderance of women at the oldest ages in Western Europe, and this is especially true of the most developed countries in that region.

In the United States, only 55 percent of the persons between 65 and 69 years of age were women in 1985, but at 80 years of age and older the proportion of women soars to 68 percent because of the lessened life expectancy of males. China shows a similar pattern in that only some 52 percent of persons 65–69 years of age in 1985 were women; however, by 80 years of age and older, the ratio is nearly 66 percent women to 34 percent men. In Japan, the sex differential is not as extreme because the Japanese have the highest life expectancy for both men and women; yet there is still a slight gender gap, for 57 percent of persons between 65 and 69 were women in 1985, and at 80 years of age and older, women constituted about 63 percent of the population. In Asia generally, as in North America and Europe, there is a relative surplus of women at the oldest ages. Exceptions are found in South Asia, where the sex ratio is more balanced in the elderly population and in some countries is reversed because, as noted, men have a somewhat higher life expectancy than women. In India, for example, in the 65–69-year-old age-group, some 49.6 percent were women and 50.4 percent were men in 1985; for ages 80 and older, there was little change, with 50.5 percent women compared with 49.5 percent men.

In most developing nations, other than in some countries in South Asia and the Middle East, older women outnumber men, and the differential increases sharply with age. And, in the majority of developing states, the female proportion of future older populations is expected to increase even further. Therefore, when the world as a whole is considered, there are significantly more older women than older men. According to U.S. Census Bureau (1987) projections, the disparity between numbers of older men and women typically widens as people grow older. The difference can be striking, as in the United States and China, or relatively minor, as in Greece and Japan. Widowhood is a fact of life for a majority of women worldwide after the age of 65. Most elderly men, in contrast, are married, because women usually live longer than men and men often marry younger women, which increases the likelihood of the wife's outliving her husband.

Living Arrangements

Historically, the family has provided for the needs of its aged members. With life expectancy relatively low until the nineteenth century, family assistance for the aged was typically of short duration. In modern society, conditions for the care of the elderly have clearly changed, with people living longer and the elderly increasingly requiring support, especially medical treatment, which is beyond the capability of families to perform themselves. Moreover, urbanization and modern economic development have contributed to the decline of the extended family, with its large network of mutually supporting relatives, and promoted the rise of the nuclear family consisting only of an adult couple and their children. The nuclear family is less able to sustain long-term care of the elderly, and the importance of the aged in such a family is also diminished, because adult children typically will not be living in the same household with their elderly parents or grandparents. Consequently, living alone is becoming more common for the elderly in developed countries; and, in developing nations, family support for the aged is beginning to erode as the need for long-term care for the oldest-old becomes increasingly necessary.

In the United States, as previously discussed, about 30 percent of all Americans 65 years of age and older (41 percent of all older women and 16 percent of older men) lived alone in 1987. Half of all women age 75 and over in the United States lived alone. In Western Europe, the proportion of elderly people living alone is much higher. In Great Britain, for example, some 80 percent of all women age 75 and older lived alone in 1985. In Austria, Amann (1981) indicates over two-thirds of some 660,000 one-person households were inhabited by people over 60 years of age, and the great majority were women. In Vienna, over 111,000 women over the age of 65 lived alone, and nearly 55,000 women over age 75 did likewise.

A major exception to this pattern in developed nations is found in Japan, where less than 10 percent of the elderly lived alone in 1985. Nearly 75 percent of all elderly Japanese lived with relatives, and over half lived in three-generation households. If elderly Japanese do live alone, however, women are more likely than men to be by themselves. In 1980, as Martin (1988) indicates, some 11.2 percent of elderly Japanese women lived alone compared with 4.3 percent of elderly men. In developing nations, few elderly live alone. In 1985, only 2 percent lived alone in the Philippines and 6 percent in Singapore. Consequently, the family still provides most of the support for the aged in developing nations, where the norm is still for the parent or parents to live in an offspring's home in old age. Martin suggests that, in Asia, this norm may be changing somewhat because of migration, urbanization, and increased female labor force participation, which may mean that generations of the same family may live apart or female caregivers may not be available for full-time care of elderly family members. However, Martin also explains that, given the traditional role of the family in Asia in the care of the elderly, institutionalization of older persons is seen as undesirable and infeasible. Homes for the aged in Asia have a bad reputation because they are primarily homes for the aged poor. At present, families play a larger role in caring for the elderly in developing countries than in developed nations, and this is especially true in Asia.

SUMMARY

The focus of this chapter has been to describe demographic patterns of aging in the United States and worldwide. The pattern of aging in the United States is much like that of other developed nations in that the proportion of the aged in society is significantly increasing. Life expectancy for Americans rose from 47.3 years in 1900 to 75.0 years in 1987, and the percentage of elderly in the total population increased from 4 percent to 12.3 percent in the same period. By 2050, the percentage of older Americans may reach as high as 21.8 percent, or one-fifth of the entire population. The largest increase in the elderly population has been among women, whites, and the oldest-old (85 years and older). Women currently outnumber men three to two in the United States, with the greatest disparity at the oldest ages.

Being elderly does not confer enhanced social status on an individual by virtue of his or her age alone (unless the person is 100 years of age or older). Rather, a person's position in society is determined by his or her socioeconomic status or attributes: income, occupational status, and level of education. The elderly are at a particular disadvantage in this regard because they are most likely to have a reduced income and be retired. However, with the significant increase in numbers of elderly persons who are more affluent and better educated than older generations in the past, the status of the aged appears to be improving somewhat in American society. The percentage of elderly living below the poverty line in 1987 was 12.2 percent. The largest proportions of elderly living in poverty are found in the South in such states as Mississippi, Alabama, Arkansas, and Louisiana.

As for living arrangements, most older Americans (95 percent) live in ordinary households. The idea that a majority of aged persons are institutionalized is a myth. Most elderly men (75 percent) live with their spouse, whereas 39 percent of the women live with their spouse and 41 percent live alone. Elderly women are much more likely than elderly men to live by themselves. In recent years (1980–1987), states like Alaska, Nevada, Hawaii, and Arizona have seen the greatest gains of any states in elderly residents. The state with the largest proportion of elderly is Florida (17.8 percent).

On a worldwide basis, the aged population is increasing some 2.4 percent annually, which is much faster than the rest of the world's population as a whole. Western Europe has the greatest proportion of elderly at present. Sweden is considered the world's oldest country, with 16.9 percent of its population age 65 or older. However, in the future, the greatest increases in both absolute numbers and percentages of older people will take place in developing countries—especially in Asia. China and India have the largest populations in the world, and these two countries will see the greatest gains in numbers of the aged. Although developed nations currently have the greatest proportions of the elderly, this will change in the future as the proportions of aged increase in developing nations. In the year 2000, some 41 percent of the elderly will live in developed countries and 59 percent in developing nations; by 2025, only 31 percent will live in developed nations, compared with 69 percent for developing countries. Some 40 percent of China's population, potentially the largest of any country, may be age 65 and older by mid–twenty-first century.

At present, the proportion of older persons in Japan is expanding more rapidly than in any other country and is projected to reach 20.3 percent by 2025. Sweden will still have the highest percentage of elderly (22.2 percent) at that time. Japan also has the highest overall life expectancy in the world (77.1 years). Both males and females live longer in Japan than in any other country; Sweden is in second place in each gender category. Women outlive men on a worldwide basis and do so in practically every nation, with the exception of a few countries in South Asia and the Middle East. Thus, elderly women outnumber elderly men in the world, and elderly women are significantly more likely to live alone. Unlike developed nations, families in developing nations are more likely to be responsible for the care of older family members and to have those family members as part of the household.

Social Theories of Aging

This chapter will examine selected theories intended to explain aging as a social experience. Theories specify relationships between concepts and provide a framework for explaining why certain things happen the way they do. When it comes to the social aspects of aging, no single theoretical approach is dominant. Social gerontology is a relatively new field that marks its beginning in the late 1940s. The development and testing of theoretical statements have largely taken place only since the 1960s. Nevertheless, a considerable amount of theoretical work has been accomplished, and several viewpoints have emerged to provide the field with a variety of theories and a solid foundation for the future.

The objective of this chapter will be to review those theories in social gerontology that have been the most influential to date in explaining the relationship between society and the aging process. The theories are (1) disengagement, (2) activity, (3) continuity, (4) age stratification, and (5) modernization. Two other important theoretical approaches, symbolic interaction and conflict theory, whose potential for studying aging has not been realized, will also be discussed.

DISENGAGEMENT THEORY

Disengagement theory is based on the structural-functionalist perspective in sociology, especially the work of France's Émile Durkheim (1858–1917) and America's Talcott Parsons (1902–1979). Disengagement theory was attractive to many sociologists concerned with explaining the social aspects of aging, because structural-functionalism was a particularly important theoretical approach in sociology in the mid-1950s and 1960s when social gerontology was developing into a specialized field. Disengagement theory also had the merit of providing a link to classical sociological theory, because its orientation could be traced to such major works in structural-functionalism as Durkheim's *The Division of Labor in Society,* originally published in 1893, and Parsons' *The Social System,* which appeared in 1951. Consequently, disengagement theory had a strong claim to academic legitimacy when it was initially proposed and was readily accepted by sociologists who were advocates of structural-functionalism in general and the work of Parsons in particular. This section will therefore begin with a brief introduction to structural-functionalism, for it provides the theoretical foundation for disengagement theory.

The Structural-Functionalist Perspective

Structural-functionalism, often called simply functionalism, portrays society as a self-regulating system made up of interdependent parts operating together to generate stability and social order. The components of this system consist of various social institutions such as religion, the family, medicine, the economic system, politics, and the like, which function to maintain society in a state of harmonious balance or equilibrium. Because functionalist theorists perceive social systems as composed of these various interconnected parts, they argue that changes, decisions, and events that take place in one part of the system inevitably affect to some degree all other parts of the system. What makes social life possible is the expectation that people will typically behave in accordance with the norms and values common to their particular social system. This process is "functional" because it results in social harmony and counterbalances dysfunctional processes, like crime and mental illness, that disrupt the social order. Functionalist theory thus provides a view of society that emphasizes stability, integration, and order.

When social problems arise, they are handled within the system as society's various components adjust to the dysfunctional situation in order to control, reduce, or eliminate it. Individuals are pressured by society to conform to the prevailing norms, with punishment and/or isolation from the social mainstream falling to those who are found deviant. For example, for those who are criminals, society develops a criminal justice system intended to apprehend, bring to trial, and remove to prisons those persons who disrupt social order by breaking laws. Medicine, as Parsons (1951) observes, is also an institution of social control in that the mentally and physically ill are likewise sent to hospitals; this institutionalization lessens their dysfunctional impact on society. Generally, society distinguishes between criminals and the sick by punishing law breakers and providing therapeutic care for the ill. But both processes require the intervention of social agencies, law enforcement, or medicine, in order to control deviant behavior and maintain social stability and cohesion.

The tendency of a society toward self-maintenance through equilibrium is very similar to the biological concept of homeostasis, in which the human body attempts to regulate physiological (internal) conditions within a relatively constant range in order to maintain bodily functioning. A person may suffer from indigestion, migraine headaches, or a broken leg and still be generally healthy. Likewise, a social system is viewed in the functionalist perspective as maintaining social functioning through the regulation of its various parts within a relatively constant range. A social system may have problems with crime, delinquency, and mental illness, but still be "healthy" because of its overall capacity to function effectively.

Functionalism was a dominant theoretical perspective in sociology until the late 1960s, when its influence was significantly curtailed. Conflict theorists (Dahrendorf 1959), whose intellectual roots are in Marxist theory, argued that functionalism was too conservative in its emphasis upon stability and order. Conflict theorists insisted that functionalism failed to explain adequately such important processes in society as social change, conflict, and alienation. Symbolic interactionists (Blumer 1969), whose focus is upon small-group processes, objected to the functionalist view that individual human behavior is largely determined by society. These theorists claimed that human beings determine their own behavior by defining their particular social situation and acting on the basis of that definition, instead of always acting in a certain way simply because society requires it. Functionalist theory, in their view, needed to give more credit to the individual's ability to think and decide on his or her own course of behavior.

Nevertheless, functionalist theory still maintains some merits. The theory can explain why various components of a social system exist and why they persist (because they provide certain functions for society that result in certain consequences). Functionalism also provides insight into how large-scale social processes can create situations in which people are more or less forced to respond to conditions not of their own choosing. Being required to disengage from society through retirement, not because of choice but because of age, is an example of the latter.

The Disengagement Perspective

Disengagement theory is an application of functionalism to the study of aging. According to its proponents, Elaine Cumming and William Henry (1961), disengagement theory has three basic propositions: (1) a process of mutual withdrawal of aging individuals and society from each other is natural; (2) this process of withdrawal is inevitable; and (3) it is also necessary for "successful" aging. Disengagement theory tells us that although all people eventually die, society's institutions need to survive if they are to maintain social stability. It follows then that it is necessary to have an orderly means of transferring power from older members of society to the younger. Disengagement theory supports the notion that it is to society's benefit to phase out those individuals whose deaths would disrupt the smooth functioning of the social order. The process of phasing out older people from the mainstream of society thus becomes institutionalized as stable and routine norms are developed to indicate which individuals should be disengaged and what forms of behavior should occur at this time. Accordingly, societies develop norms requiring that an individual retire from work at a certain age, and a rite of status passage—usually a retirement ceremony—often marks the occasion. When the ceremony is over, the person honored sees his or her status change from being employed to being retired. However, disengagement is typically not a single event, but is instead a gradual process that involves the separation of the individual from several of his or her regular social roles and activities over time.

Disengagement theory is consistent with the Kingsley Davis and Wilbert Moore (1945) functionalist theory of social stratification. Davis and Moore held that to attract the best qualified people to compete for the positions that meet society's most important needs, it is necessary to offer such people society's greatest rewards and inducements (money, power, status, and prestige). Differential rewards are therefore required as a means of ensuring that essential tasks are accomplished. The extent of the rewards is related to the social importance of a particular position and the relative availability of qualified persons to fill that position. The greatest rewards are associated with those roles that (1) have the greatest importance for society and (2) require the greatest training or talent.

Disengagement theory extends the Davis-Moore thesis by explaining that the work of people in key positions must also continue uninterrupted if the social order is to be preserved. Society must be able to replace people whose ability to perform adequately in an important position becomes questionable as a result of old age. Therefore, the continuous functioning of social institutions can be enhanced through a disengagement process. Such a process allows for an orderly transition of younger persons into the positions of older persons, while avoiding the disruptions that might occur if all workers stayed in their jobs until they died. Of course, the disengagement of elderly people is more likely in a developed, industrialized society where a continuous replacement of older workers by younger ones is needed to maintain modern work skills. In developing societies, the aged do not typically disengage from society as much, because the elderly are more likely to continue to work and remain as the head of the family.

Yet the disengagement of society from the individual is only half of disengagement theory. The other half of the theory is that individuals themselves select to withdraw from particular social roles when they become old. The more roles an older person withdraws from, the less involved that person is in mainstream activities. He or she no longer is preoccupied with work, career, raising children, and the like. The disengaged person is thus able to fill a particular social role (the retired person) that allows him or her to become increasingly more self-centered and focused on personal interests, such as hobbies, clubs, travel, and sports like fishing and golf.

There are, however, some important shortcomings to disengagement theory. The theory assumes that people will desire to be disengaged in order to pursue their own interests and does not explain what happens if this is not the case. Paul Roman and Philip Taietz (1967), for example, studied a group of university professors several years ago who were given the opportunity to continue their work after retirement. They found that most chose to continue in their preretirement activities of teaching, research, administration, or public service. Roman and Taietz concluded that the assumption of disengagement theory that people naturally want to disengage as they get older is not necessarily true of everyone. Some people may disengage only because an institution's rules and regulations force them to or because of poor health. But with the opportunity, means, and continued capacity for work, they might well choose to continue. Furthermore, disengagement does not seem to occur in all social institutions. United States Supreme Court justices, for example, are appointed for life, and the majority continue in the position when they are elderly. If disengagement were a functional necessity for society, it should apply to everyone—including members of the Supreme Court. Consequently, disengagement theory does not apply to all people, nor all situations. As Alfred Lindesmith and his colleagues explain:

> The theory does not account for the "nondisengaging" behaviors of certain groups and of certain individuals. Elderly rural Americans, for example, are still commonly absorbed into the fabric of the extended family; those persons who do not leave the labor market at age 65 often have been observed to lead healthy, involved, and politically influential lives into their late 80s. Both Charles de Gaulle and Winston Churchill were in their mid-80s when they died; Pablo Casals was 93, and Picasso was 86.[1]

1. Alfred R. Lindesmith, Anselm L. Strauss, and Norman K. Denzin, *Social Psychology*, 6th ed. (Englewood Cliffs, NJ: Prentice-Hall, 1988), 351.

In a review of twenty years of research findings, Robert Atchley (1988) determined that disengagement is not natural or inevitable. Most cases of disengagement were found to result from a lack of opportunity for continued involvement. Gordon Streib and Clement Schneider (1971) noted earlier that disengagement, if it occurred, was more likely to be partial than total. Older people may withdraw from some activities because of age, but may maintain or simply decrease participation in other things they do.

Why then is disengagement theory important? Chiefly because it is able to describe the social processes that occur when older people withdraw from their usual roles as a result of age. The theory is particularly applicable to situations of forced disengagement according to predetermined rules of an institution or organization and to situations of mutual disengagement, where both society and the individual define disengagement as positive. The strength of disengagement theory lies in the realization that at some point in time the interests of society intersect with the role performance of older people in their positions, and the result is often the disengagement of that older person. By setting a specific age, usually sixty-five, as the time of retirement, disengagement becomes institutionalized, orderly, and inevitable—just as aging itself is inevitable. Some degree of disengagement appears to be inherent in the aging process for many (perhaps most) people, and disengagement theory helps to explain what happens when this is the case. As Atchley (1988:273) points out, "Disengagement is *not* what most older people want. It is, however, what many older people get."

It is precisely for this reason, the transition from work to retirement, regardless of the desires of the individual, that disengagement theory remains important. Many elderly people are forced to retire, whether they want to or not, and disengagement theory explains why this happens in modern societies.

ACTIVITY THEORY

Another important theory is activity theory. As formulated by Robert Havighurst (1963), activity theory is primarily an action theory for successful aging. It has three basic premises: (1) that the majority of normally aging people will maintain fairly constant levels of activity; (2) that the amount of engagement or disengagement will be influenced by past lifestyles and socioeconomic factors, rather than by some inevitable process; and (3) that it is necessary to maintain or develop substantial levels of social, physical, and mental activity if the aging experience is to be successful.

What constitutes successful aging? According to Havighurst, the norms for old age are the same as those for middle age; therefore, successful aging is based on how close an elderly person approximates the norms and activities of middle-aged persons. In other words, activity theory is an approach to understanding the social behavior of elderly people in terms of how well they deny the fact that they are elderly. Successful aging consists of being or behaving as much as possible like a middle-aged person. If certain roles are lost because of retirement or poor health, Havighurst points out that other activities could be substituted in their place so the individual remains active.

There is research that supports the basic propositions offered by activity theory. In a longitudinal study carried out at Duke University over a ten-year period, Erdman Palmore (1968, 1969) found that older men tended to show almost no overall reduction in their activities or in life satisfaction, whereas older women tended to have a small but statistically significant reduction in both activities and life satisfaction. Temporary decreases in activities due to illness were usually followed by subsequent increases so that there was little or no overall change.

Palmore noted that his data were obtained from people who were relatively healthy, and, therefore, disengagement may be more typical of the less healthy. His point was, however, that disengagement by the elderly is not an inevitable result of aging. The respondents showed consistently high levels of activity throughout the ten-year period of the study. Furthermore, it was found that activity was strongly related to high morale and life satisfaction. The more active a person was, the more likely that person was to be happy. Palmore concluded that continued engagement rather than disengagement was typical of the normal, healthy older person, and the amount of that person's activity was consistent with his or her past lifestyle. If disengagement occurred, it usually did so only just prior to death.

In another study, Andrea Fontana (1977) investigated what it meant to the individual to grow old among a group of elderly persons at a senior citizens center in a small, affluent community in southern California. Fontana found that activity was strongly related to high morale and life satisfaction. The more active a person was, the more likely that person was to be happy. Fontana found that these persons tended to deny that they themselves were old, although they were more able to give reasons why someone else might be old. Among many of these aged individuals, a person had to be at least 80 years old to be considered beyond middle age. The respondents indicated that to keep active was to stay young and that to become passive and relinquish one's activities and associations was to become old. Thus, successful aging was to be active and to be active was to be young. Fontana concluded:

Americans may have succeeded in freeing themselves from the work ethic, but the dying monster has sprung many new heads: activities. Work no longer provides the central identification of life for many, but activities do. Thus, older individuals find new ways to give their lives meaning, by being a bridge player, a canasta-club member, a shuffleboard contestant, going fishing, watching television, writing postcards, or walking in the woods. Not only do activities provide meaning, but they are seen as the panacea to cure the plague of old age: to be active is to keep old age at bay.[2]

What activity theory essentially tells us is that most people do not disengage from society when they become old. If they do retire from their occupational role, they compensate for it by substituting some other type of activity that provides satisfaction. Bernice Neugarten (1971), for example, cites the case of a 75-year-old schoolteacher who made the most money of his life selling insurance after retirement. This is not to forecast, however, that most elderly persons seek a second career, but rather that they are likely to remain active in some fashion if their past lives were characterized by being active.

Yet, as a theory explaining the social behavior of the aged in general, activity theory suffers from two basic inadequacies. First, it rests on the assumption that older people judge themselves according to norms common to middle-aged activity and behavior, but it does not explain what happens when the elderly do not subscribe to such norms. And second, it does not explain what happens to those older people who cannot, for physical, mental, or socioeconomic reasons, maintain a middle-aged standard of living regardless of how they judge themselves. The older a person gets, the more difficult it is to be active according to middle-aged standards. Activity theory does account for the manner in which some (perhaps a majority) of the aged cope with aging through activity, but, like disengagement theory, it cannot explain the behavior of all elderly.

Also, it should not be presumed that being active prolongs an older person's life. Activity may promote life satisfaction among the aged, but there is no conclusive evidence that activity also leads to a longer life. In an eight-year study of a population of Mexican-American and non-Hispanic elderly in Texas, David Lee and Kyriakos Markides (1990) attempted to determine whether there is a significant relationship between being active in old age and living longer. The popular notion that an active life among the elderly leads to extended longevity was not supported. Whether a person was active or inactive in old age made little or no difference in living longer. Activity theory's strength rests in its assertion that elderly people generally desire to be active when they are old, and, if this is possible, they feel better about themselves and their lives as a result.

2. Andrea Fontana, *The Last Frontier: The Social Meaning of Growing Old* (Beverly Hills, CA: Sage, 1977), 176.

CONTINUITY THEORY

Continuity theory is based on the premise that people retain a high degree of consistency in their personality over the various stages of the life cycle. As a person grows to maturity and passes on into old age, continuity theory holds that the individual develops rather stable values, attitudes, norms, and habits that become an integral part of his or her personality. The manner in which an individual will react to the aging process will thus be influenced by that person's personality traits and predispositions. Successful aging is thought to occur when people are able to maintain or continue having the traits, interests, and behaviors they have always had while aging.

Continuity theorists do recognize, however, that predispositions to act in certain ways are subject to change or modification because of the ongoing and sometimes complex forms of interaction people have with others and their social environment during all stages of the life cycle. Although there will be a tendency toward consistency, continuity theory admits that people also change by adapting to new situations. For instance, a person who looked forward to retirement might not like it after all, and might instead be forced to accommodate to an unwelcome situation and adjust his or her expectations and behavior. Continuity theory thus maintains that a wide range of reactions to the aging experience is possible, but, on balance, the aged person will generally respond to situations in a manner consistent with his or her basic personality over the life cycle.

According to Neugarten (1964), continuity theory is based on two central propositions: (1) people tend to maintain their own particular personality over time; and (2) the only major internal dimension of the personality that changes with age is the tendency to experience greater introversion by turning one's attention and interest inward on the self. Other studies support the notion that a person's personality tends to remain stable after middle age as mature adults typically respond to situations in a consistent manner and deal with their social world in habitual ways (McCrae and Costa 1982; Streib and Schneider 1971). According to Vern Bengston and his associates (Bengston, Reedy, and Gordon 1985), there is a global aspect to the personality which is stable and reflects a person's general character throughout life. Beneath this global orientation, there can be changes in certain features of someone's personality, without inducing an overall personality change.

Continuity theory contributes to our understanding of the aging process by showing that the personality of people in old age tends to be much the same as it was in middle age. This finding is of great use in predicting the behavior of old people and provides both practical and theoretical insight to researchers studying how aging is experienced. However, continuity theory is not a full-blown theory in the research literature on aging, because it is concerned with only one particular and limited aspect of aging, that of personality effects.

However, compared with the previous social theories of aging discussed in this chapter—disengagement and activity theory—continuity theory presents a micro, rather than a macro, orientation. Macro-level social theories explain how large-scale social processes, like disengagement and a normative emphasis on activity, influence individual behavior. Micro-level views, like continuity theory, allow us to see how individuals, not the wider society, construct their own behavior. What continuity theory tells us is that people tend to respond to social situations in their old age in a fashion that is consistent with their past adult personality. Although there is much more to the aging process than simply its effect on the personality, continuity theory nevertheless provides an important perspective on behavior among the elderly.

AGE STRATIFICATION THEORY

Age stratification theory is a relatively recent theory based largely on the work of Matilda White Riley (1971, 1987; Riley, Johnson, and Foner 1972; Riley, Foner, and Waring 1988). It takes the position that society is stratified into various age cohorts. Each age cohort has both life course and historical dimensions. The life course dimension refers to stages of the life cycle. People belong to a particular age-group depending on how long they have lived, and as a result, they share similar social roles and experiences. At approximately the same point in their lives, they have all been children, students, workers, perhaps parents and grandparents, were retired, and so forth. Thus, they have had similar roles in their respective pasts, are occupying similar roles in the present, and are likely to have similar roles in the future as members of the same age cohort moving through the life cycle. As they grow older, everyone else grows older as well, and younger people fill their former roles, while they move on with others of their age to assume roles consistent with their age cohort. As Anne Foner (1974, 1986) notes, people of similar ages have similar roles and confront similar life cycle circumstances that foster common attitudes and interests. Belonging to a particular age cohort is not only a characteristic of a person beginning at birth, but also has consequences for that person at every age.

The historical dimension pertains to the fact that people experience distinct periods of history together and share particular events on the basis of age. For example, the Vietnam War is likely to have had a different meaning for Americans who were children at the time, or who were eligible for military service, or who were older and had experienced World War II and the Korean War. Each shared an event, but brought a different perspective to it that was influenced by age.

Riley (1987) argues, however, that different age cohorts also age differently as the societies they live in change. That is, both similarities and differences can be found between age cohorts. Similarities stem from younger people replacing older people in the same roles, whereas differences emerge not only because of historical events but because society itself changes over time. Riley explains:

> People who were young earlier in this century learned from the age norms and patterns of behavior prevalent in that period; most learned from their parents that only a few years of schooling suffice for most jobs; and from their grandparents that old age can be bleak. But now that these people have themselves grown old, they have outdistanced the world for which they were initially prepared. Similarly, cohorts of people who are young today are perceiving the entire occupational ladder as it is now—before it has time to be further transformed by fast-breaking technological innovations and accompanying changes in the age structure of the future. These young people will not be old in the same society in which they began. In short, while individuals within a particular cohort are aging, the society is changing around them.[3]

But age stratification theory holds that not only are new patterns of aging caused by social change, they also contribute to it. That is, at every level of the social system, society and the process of aging influence each other sequentially over time. The link between the aging of individuals and the larger society, in Riley's view, is the flow of age cohorts. Cohort flow affects the numbers and kinds of people in a particular age strata, as well as the capacities, attitudes, and activities of people in that strata. Riley (1987:4) points out that as society moves through time, the age structure and people within that structure are altered. People in a particular age strata are no longer the same people in that they have been replaced by younger people with more recent life experiences as they themselves have replaced older people. Various roles, institutions, and norms, in the meantime, may have been affected as changes in retirement age, patterns of leisure for older persons, the composition of the work force, and perhaps even tax burdens for younger people take place. Riley states:

> In response to social change, millions of individuals in a cohort begin to develop new age-typical patterns and regularities of behavior (changes in aging); these behavior patterns then become defined as age-appropriate norms and rules, are reinforced by "authorities," and thereby become institutionalized in the structure of society (social change); in turn, these changes in age norms and social structures redirect age-related behaviors (further changes in aging). Through such a dialectical sequence, the members of each cohort, responsive to social change, exert a collective force for further change as they move through the age-stratified society: they press for adjustments in social roles and social values, influence other people throughout the age strata, contribute to continuing alterations in both aging and social structure.[4]

3. Matilda White Riley, "On the Significance of Age in Sociology," *American Sociological Review* 52 (1987): 5.

4. Riley, "On the Significance of Age in Sociology," 4–5.

Consequently, age stratification theory provides a view that emphasizes a continuing interplay—generated by cohort flow—between social change and individuals as they age. Though interdependent, the processes of aging and social change are not synchronized. People follow a predictable and sequential life cycle, but social change moves along its own axis of historical time and according to its own rhythm. Some periods of history witness greater social change than other periods, but people follow the same life course. As a result, the degree of difference between age cohorts because of social change can vary from great to small.

In sum, Riley claims that society is composed of successive cohorts of individuals who are aging and continually forcing older cohorts into and out of particular social roles. "This flow of cohorts," states Riley (1987:5), "forms the channel that connects the two dynamisms of aging and social change: it ties them both to the forces of history, creates the asynchrony between them, and presses for still further alterations." The larger society, institutions, groups, social networks and strata, and individuals are all affected by the aging process of particular cohorts, as these cohorts are affected, in turn, by them.

Age stratification theory does offer a method by which most characteristics of age cohorts can be analyzed. An age cohort can be seen as a particular generation in relation to other living generations and one that brings its own attitudes, beliefs, and values to bear on situations held in common. Individuals can also be seen as members of a generation living within the context of particular historical circumstances. People can, accordingly, be viewed as living in a world already constructed for them and as active participants in shaping that world to meet their needs. Aging is not passive; the individual's aging process is influenced at the "macro" level by the wider society and at the "micro" level by other people and the person's own characteristics and personality. Age stratification theory is attractive because it is logical, appears comprehensive, and points the way toward which a researcher can analyze the interplay between macro- and micro-level social processes as they relate to aging.

Unfortunately, this theory is somewhat difficult to operationalize for testing and empirical research because of its complexity. Moreover, an important critique of age stratification theory by Gordon Streib and Carroll Bourg (1984) calls attention to the need for some additional considerations. Streib and Bourg seriously question whether age stratification theory actually qualifies as a theory of stratification, because it does not account for social inequality. Rather, they maintain that differences within age cohorts, especially those pertaining to socioeconomic differences, can be as great or greater than differences between age cohorts. The Vietnam War, for example, would have been experienced differently by people not only on the basis of age, but also (and perhaps of just as much or even more importance) in relation to their socioeconomic situation. Socially and economically disadvantaged young adult males were much more likely than their affluent counterparts to serve in the war, especially in combat units. Parents in low-income families were likewise more likely to have their sons drafted for military duty or volunteer as a means to escape poverty. More advantaged young adult males could gain deferments from military service if they were in good standing as college or university students; thus, affluent families had a different experience with the war than the less affluent, even if they belonged to the same age cohort.

Streib and Bourg thus reject the notion that a person's experience of historical events is so strongly determined by age. Although age clearly constitutes a major division of society and biological aging is the principal force behind the aging experience, other variables, like socioeconomic status, affect responses to aging in powerful ways. A weakness of age stratification theory is that differences within, not just between, age cohorts are not given sufficient consideration. Besides socioeconomic factors, gender, race, and ethnicity may also shape the aging experience within cohorts, and age stratification theory does not account for such differences. However, despite its critics, like Streib and Bourg (1984) and others (Cain 1987), age stratification theory remains a highly influential theoretical perspective.

MODERNIZATION THEORY

Modernization theory is a macro-level theory of global social change in sociology that has been adapted by Donald Cowgill (1986) to explain aging. As a theory of social change, modernization theory takes the position that underdeveloped societies will gradually be transformed by industrialization to resemble North America and Europe. The theory depicts the world as divided into either wealthy industrial nations (about one-fifth of the world) or poor preindustrial countries (the remaining four-fifths), with poor countries in various stages of evolution toward modernity. According to Walt Rostow (1978), there are four stages to modernization: (1) the traditional stage, in which mortality and population growth decline and life expectancy increases as a result of improved health care and living conditions; (2) the takeoff stage, consisting of growth in a market economy and an increased achievement orientation among the population; (3) the drive to technological maturity, which includes a growing industrial economy, urbanization, and mass education; and (4) the high mass consumption stage, in which a wide range of consumer goods and services appear.

Modernization theory has been a popular theory in sociology and is consistent with the foreign policy of industrial nations with respect to providing assistance for economic development and introducing Western culture. However, the theory has some important criticisms: (1) it tends to view technological advances as positive only; (2) it has only one path to modernization; (3) it is largely ahistorical; (4) foreign aid is seldom simply a case of altruism on the part of developed nations (they want something in return); and (5) the causes of poverty in developing nations are not found just in underdeveloped regions of the world, nor are solutions to these problems found only among industrialized countries. Many nations have experienced modernization as suggested by modernization theory, but the theory remains controversial because it seems to favor a privileged position for developed societies as a model in the world economy and overlooks issues of conflict and exploitation.

How then does modernization theory explain aging? According to Cowgill (1986; Cowgill and Holmes 1972), there is a systematic relationship between aging and modernization. Cowgill explains that the concept of old age is relative to a society's degree of modernization: people in primitive societies, as compared to modern ones, are classified as old at earlier chronological ages, have the onset of old age determined more by an event (such as becoming a grandparent) rather than age, and live shorter lives but have higher status and are more likely to hold positions of political and economic power. In modern societies, in contrast, the elderly are likely to live longer but have low status and hold less important positions in society. Therefore, the aged have relatively high status in developing societies where they are able to continue useful and valued functions, but have low status in technologically advanced societies where the most important work is done by younger people. Moreover, there can be differences within countries; for example, old men in Turkey living in provinces characterized by low urbanization and industrialization are more likely to head a household and hold a job than elderly men living in industrial centers (Gilleard and Gurkan 1987). Even modern education appears to promote devaluation of the elderly. As Cowgill explains:

> Certainly one of the most salient aspects of modernization relative to the status of aged is the development of specialized institutions of formal education. These, along with libraries, voluminous printed material, and recent revolutionary techniques for storing and retrieving information, have all but completely abolished a formerly highly significant role of older people—that of repositories and transmitters of vital information to the younger generation. Schools, both general and technical, are always viewed as an essential part of any modernization effort. But the main targets and beneficiaries of mass education efforts are the young. One consequence of such efforts is that very shortly the younger generation has command of more information, especially technical information, than the elderly. Certainly the elderly no longer have a monopoly on such information, as they have in nonliterate societies, and with the loss of that monopoly, they lose a vital status-according role.[5]

With a lessened position in education and the workplace, combined with urbanization and the decline of the extended family, modernity appears

---

5. Donald O. Cowgill, *Aging Around the World* (Belmont, CA: Wadsworth, 1986), 197.

to have adversely affected the status of the aged. Retirement, notes Cowgill, is a modern invention and is found chiefly in modern high-productivity societies. A system of retirement based on age has been adopted by all industrialized societies and is a means to ensure that younger and more recently trained workers have jobs available. Consequently, the basic premise of the modernization theory of aging is that the processes that cause societies to change from a rural and agrarian system to an urban and industrial economy also change the roles of the elderly and reduce the status and esteem they are accorded. A tendency toward disengagement of the aged, states Cowgill, appears to accompany modernization.

Therefore, modernization would seem to be an especially negative process for the status of old people. Yet Cowgill suggests that this is not necessarily the case in the mature modern state. He cites research (Palmore and Manton 1974) showing that whereas the status of the aged is generally low in modernized societies, the trend in the most modernized countries is toward somewhat higher status. That is, among modern nations, the most advanced accord greater esteem to the elderly than do the less advanced. Other research (Pampel 1981), for example, shows considerable improvement in the quality of life available to older people in the United States. Cowgill suggests that perhaps modern societies were unprepared for large numbers of elderly persons, and it is not surprising that there were temporary dislocations— including an overvaluation of youth. The most modern societies, according to Cowgill (1986:200), "are now beginning to come to terms with their aged populations and are achieving appropriate cultural and institutional adaptations." James Dowd (1984) likewise agrees that the status of older people is higher in modern societies than it was earlier, and cites the extension of old-age pensions and benefits in the late twentieth century as evidence of this change.

There are critiques of the modernization perspective on aging, such as the fact that a concept of retirement for aged workers is not new and can be found in some premodern societies (Quadagno 1982), or that the theory does not adequately account for differences in gender and socioeconomic status in the aging of modern populations (Dowd 1980; Williamson, Evans, and Powell 1982). Furthermore, when it comes to the effects of modernization on aging, culture appears to be an important intervening variable. Japan is one of the most modern and industrialized nations in the world, yet the status of the aged has remained quite high. Elderly Japanese tend to remain strongly integrated into both family and community life in a manner consistent with Japanese culture in particular and Asian culture in general (Palmore 1975a, 1975b, 1985; Morgan and Hirosima 1983). The effects of modernization on the status of the aged may therefore be strongly influenced by culture.

SYMBOLIC INTERACTION THEORY

One promising theoretical approach in sociology that has not seen extensive use in studies of aging is symbolic interaction. This is surprising, because symbolic interaction is a major theoretical perspective and has considerable potential for aging research, especially in regard to explaining the self-concepts and social relationships of the elderly.

The symbolic interactionist perspective views society from the micro-level standpoint of the individual person, not in terms of personality but in the nature of the interaction that person has with other people. It regards the individual as a creative, thinking entity able to choose his or her behavior instead of reacting more or less mechanically to the influence of large-scale social forces, as implied by functionalist theories. Central to the symbolic interactionist's conception of human behavior is the assumption that all behavior is self-directed on the basis of symbolic meanings that are shared, communicated, and manipulated by interacting human beings in social situations (Denzin, 1970a). The process of such interaction between people forms behavior in a creative fashion, rather than being merely a means by which behavior is expressed. Therefore, society is seen as a human product and people are seen as a social product, because both are formed in a continuing dialectical process in which human beings and their social environment act and react toward each other (Berger and Luckmann 1967).

Although the symbolic interactionist tradition in sociology can be traced to the ideas of William James, John Dewey, William I. Thomas, and Charles Cooley at the beginning of the twentieth century, George Herbert Mead (1863–1931) is generally regarded as the individual most responsible for its development. Mead, an American philosopher who taught social psychology at the University of Chicago between 1894 and 1931, published little; yet his book *Mind, Self, and Society* (1934), based upon student notes from his courses and unpublished manuscripts, is a sociological classic. A major interpretation of Mead's work, however, is found in the writings of Herbert Blumer, one of Mead's students, who has drawn together much of the material that is the basis of contemporary symbolic interactionist thought.

Blumer (1969), for example, explains Mead's analysis of social action by denoting its five central features: (1) the self, (2) the act, (3) social interaction, (4) objects, and (5) joint action. Mead believed that the *self* of a person is formed and developed as a result of social interaction and experience with other people; thus, the self is a social product derived from a person's relationship with others in society. In this context, the human being is able to perceive, have conceptions of, communicate with, and act toward himself or herself as a social object in relation to other people. Second is Mead's concept of the *act*. Mead insisted that human beings do not just respond more or less automatically to a given social influence but are able to interpret and define their own particular situation and organize their behavior to meet their circumstances. Blumer states:

> In order to act the individual has to identify what he wants, establish an objective or goal, map out a prospective line of behavior, note and interpret the actions of others, figure out what to do at other points, and frequently spur himself on in the face of dragging dispositions or discouraging settings.[6]

Third is the concept of *social interaction,* which consists of two forms, the nonsymbolic and the symbolic. Nonsymbolic interaction is essentially the stimulus-response paradigm in which a person makes a nonthinking response to a certain stimulus, such as stepping back from a growling dog or raising a hand to catch a baseball. Symbolic interaction, in contrast, is a situation in which human beings interpret and define actions and objects based upon symbolic meanings shared with other people. Fourth is the notion of the *object,* which maintains that objects do not possess inherent meaning but become what they are defined as by human beings interacting with each other. Thus, human beings act toward an object on the basis of the meaning that object has for them. Humans define gold as valuable and act toward it accordingly. Yet there is nothing intrinsic to gold that makes it valuable; the social meaning of gold depends upon how humans define it. Fifth is the *joint act,* which is the focal point by which symbolic interactionists judge group behavior. Each participant in a social gathering brings his or her own individual social act or line of behavior to a situation. By fitting together all of these separate acts or lines of behavior into a single collective or joint act involving each person present, it is possible to ascertain the overall direction of group behavior. The result is that group activities are socially constructed by individual people coming together and interacting with each other in respect to the overall group enterprise. Joint actions may be open to many outcomes; once started they may be interrupted, abandoned, modified, or continued as expected. What happens depends upon what those involved decide to do and how they act upon their decisions.

Joint acts contribute a sense of stability to social situations, because they require a participant to identify that activity and orient himself or herself in that direction prior to engaging in behavior that is appropriate to the scene. Blumer (1969:71) states, "Thus, to act appropriately, the participant has to identify a marriage ceremony as a marriage ceremony, a holdup as a holdup, a debate as a debate, a war as a war, and so forth." However, as pointed out by Norman Denzin (1970b), it is necessary to go beyond the surface of social

---

6. Herbert Blumer, *Symbolic Interaction* (Englewood Cliffs, NJ: Prentice-Hall, 1969), 64.

situations and extend analysis of the joint act to the more subtle nuances of social relationships between people, for example, those verbal and nonverbal acts and gestures between two persons that signify particular interpretations of a situation.

We can see in the above analysis of social action that human behavior is regarded as an ongoing process of definition, interpretation of, and calculated response to the actions of others and the conditions of the environment. *Reality is therefore socially constructed as it emanates from the perceptions and actions of those involved.*

The merit of symbolic interaction for aging studies is its capability to analyze micro-level, or small-scale, forms of human interaction. Symbolic interaction theory is unique in its ability to explain the subjective meaning of social experiences and the manner in which reality is socially constructed between individuals. But in general, symbolic interactionists have tended to ignore aging. Existing work, however, includes analysis of the formation of a "sisterhood" by elderly women living in a housing project (Hochschild 1973), the self-feelings of widows in relation to the social support provided them by their adult children (Mutran and Reitzes 1984), and the impact of bereavement on the self-concepts of elderly surviving spouses (Lund, Caserta, Dimond, and Gray 1986).

The housing project study by Arlie Hochschild (1973) took place in San Francisco. Hochschild discovered that the widowed residents formed sibling bonds (i.e., a sisterhood) that provided support and a social life independent of the family. This was a positive adjustment to an old-age situation where social isolation and loneliness were the alternative. The study by Elizabeth Mutran and Donald Reitzes (1984) involved a nationwide survey investigating the forms of support provided by adult children to their widowed mothers. Receiving help from their children was found to be an important factor in allowing the widows to feel positive about themselves. In Salt Lake City, Dale Lund and his colleagues (1986) studied the self-concepts of older persons whose spouses had died. They found that the surviving spouses expressed significantly lower levels of social anchorage; that is, the death of their spouses deprived them of their identity as part of a "couple." Thus, they had not only lost a spouse, they had also lost part of their sense of self.

A limitation of symbolic interaction theory, however, is in linking individual and small-group behavior to the larger social order. Micro-level theories like symbolic interaction often do not adequately acknowledge the influence of larger social structures and organizations or account for relationships between them. The strength of this approach, on the other hand, lies in the capability of explaining how people perceive situations, events, and people, and define a course of action. It also helps to explain individual variations and the role of culture in providing symbolic meanings.

CONFLICT THEORY

Conflict theory has sometimes been used to help explain the disadvantaged situation of older people in relation to employment problems and retirement, but it has not seen extensive application in studies of aging in Western society. As the name indicates, conflict theory views society as a social system characterized by inequality and conflict. Conflict theory traces its intellectual origins to Karl Marx (1818–1883), the nineteenth-century German philosopher and founder of communism. Marx argued that social relationships between people are determined by their relative positions in regard to the means of economic production common in their society. These relationships were characterized historically as a class struggle between various groups of "haves" and "have nots" until eventually a classless society based upon economic, political, and social equality evolves from the conflict. Class consciousness (an awareness of common interests with others in the same socioeconomic circumstances) is viewed by Marx as the key element in how a person interprets reality and organizes his or her behavior.

Marx focuses on how particular social relationships and means of production, during specific historical periods, allowed the economically and politically powerful to shape the social order to their advantage. The poor, of course, would be disadvantaged; their social reality would tend to be alienating and oppressive. Class struggle and revolution would eventually lead to socialism, which would evolve into communism and bring about improved conditions for those persons at the bottom of society. In the meantime, the disadvantaged would remain in an exploited state.

For workers, scientific and technological advances under a capitalist system would not improve their lives. Workers would find themselves in an even more marginal economic position as new machinery and automation took the place of human labor. Those that remained employed would be subjected to greater stresses as they became tied to machine production and inflexible schedules. In this situation, older persons would be more likely to be fired and least likely to be hired. For example, William Graebner (1980) found in his study of retirement in the United States that many older workers were phased out of their jobs or simply fired when speed of production became a central feature of factory work in the late nineteenth and early twentieth centuries. In the printing business, for example, Graebner describes how older workers at the turn of the century were phased out for younger ones with better eyesight, speed, and endurance. Age limits in hiring became commonplace, and some firms were willing to take the more unpopular action of simply releasing older employees. Laying off workers once they became old was a clear case of age discrimination, and, until retirement programs were established on a widespread basis in the 1920s and Social Security benefits were authorized in 1935, many workers found themselves destitute in old age.

A Marxist view of the situation of people considered too old to be effective in the workplace places the blame for their circumstances on the general problems of capitalist society. Exploitation by the capitalist system through low wages or layoffs would produce a sense of alienation, not only among older workers, but among workers generally as they found little satisfaction in their lives and felt individually powerless to deal with the situation. The centrality of work in a person's life rests in the Marxist claim that work is the means through which people come to realize themselves in relation to others. According to Vicente Navarro (1986:34), it is obvious that "in our consumer society today what *you have* depends on what *you do,* but even more important, that one's psychological framework—which determines one's level of expectations—is very much determined by one's work." But under capitalism, work is controlled by the upper class and organized to protect their socioeconomic advantage. This situation promotes alienation, and Marx maintained that the more alienated people are from their work, the less able they are to conceive of themselves as other than they are in the present (Lichtman 1982).

All of this points toward a particularly disadvantaged situation for the elderly, as they are less in demand as workers and their status as unemployed or retired places them in a highly marginal and devalued position in a capitalist society. However, Bryan Turner (1987) points out that there are some difficulties with this perspective. For instance, being socially and economically disadvantaged when old is not peculiar just to capitalism, but is found throughout human history in various types of societies. Marxism also underestimates the capability of the elderly to mobilize for political action in capitalist nations and bring reform. Furthermore, Turner notes that evidence from socialist societies describes attitudes toward the old that are not especially different from the negative stereotypes that prevail in capitalist countries.

Consequently, a conflict theory explanation grounded in Marxism has serious limitations and appears confined to the manner in which work affects the elderly. Yet work is a major determining factor in the quality of life available to an individual, and a thorough analysis of aging from a Marxist perspective has yet to be accomplished. One contemporary approach to conflict theory in the United States has been to move away from notions of class struggle and concentrate instead on competition among interest groups such as those representing labor, management, geographical regions, political parties, and professional and other organized pressure groups, including agencies within the government itself (Akers and Hawkins 1975). Laws and government regulations, as well as social and economic advantages, are viewed as outgrowths of power struggles among interest groups. In this context, the elderly clearly qualify as an interest group in American society and have organized effective political action groups, like the American Association of Retired Persons, the National Committee to Preserve Social Security and Medicare, the Gray Panthers, and local senior citizen's groups. Analysis of these organizations from a conflict theory perspective is a highly promising line of inquiry that awaits research.

SUMMARY

To date, it would appear that the most influential approach to theories of aging in social gerontology is structural-functionalism. Three of the five theoretical positions in social gerontology—disengagement theory, activity theory, and modernization theory—are all clearly grounded in a functionalist perspective. That is, each provides a macro-level view of the aging process in which older individuals are subject to norms requiring them either to disengage, to remain active, or to cope with reduced status because of modernization, while the larger society remains functional and relatively unaffected by large numbers of the elderly. Continuity theory has a micro orientation, but is limited to explaining personality adjustments in old age. The remaining major approach, age stratification theory, has also been identified as a functionalist approach in that it is essentially a macro theory of aging depicting the orderly flow of age cohorts through society (Estes, Wallace, and Binney 1989).

This does not mean that a functionalist perspective is the best theoretical approach in social gerontology; rather, functionalism was highly influential in sociology when social gerontology was first being developed in the 1950s. Other theoretical paradigms so far have provided little that is relevant in explaining aging. Particularly lacking is a broad micro-level approach such as that found in symbolic interaction. Symbolic interaction theory is especially oriented toward explaining the subjective meaning of social experiences and the manner in which reality is socially constructed between interacting individuals. But, in general, symbolic interactionists have conducted few studies in aging. Another theory that has potential is conflict theory in regard to explaining the situation of devalued older workers, or how the elderly, as an interest group, compete for resources in society. To date, conflict theory has also been underutilized in social gerontology.

Of the functionalist approaches, disengagement theory and activity theory remain the most widely utilized theories at present in social gerontology. Disengagement theory views old age as a distinct phase of life decidedly different from middle age; it is a time when specific social and psychological forces come to bear upon the person to make him or her aware of a reduced ability to function in society. Furthermore, disengagement theory suggests that disengagement of the elderly from society's important functions is beneficial not only for society, but also for the elderly person, who is freed from the stresses of the preretirement role. Although an overall decrease in social activity is generally observable in old age, disengagement theory does not account for the fact that many older people remain active (engaged) in some fashion and that such activity is significantly related to life satisfaction. So it is not at all clear that disengagement is inevitable, nor is it as personally satisfying an experience as the theory would suggest.

Activity theory, on the other hand, strongly supports the notion of a positive relationship between activity and life satisfaction. Yet its weakness lies in not explaining what happens to people who cannot be active or who do not believe that being active is the only way to keep happy in old age. The proposition that higher levels of activity are necessary for "successful" aging has not been conclusively demonstrated. And, of course, older people can finally reach a point where it is difficult or impossible to be active. Age stratification theory is highly promising. It describes the manner in which age classes develop their own class "consciousness" and relate to other age-groups, and discusses how individual behavior is affected by large-scale (macro) processes in the aging experience. However, age stratification theory does not deal extensively with small-scale (micro) processes, nor does it fully account for differences within age cohorts, such as socioeconomic status and gender, that impact on the social experience of aging. Finally, there is modernization theory, which helps us to understand the status of the aged in modern society but, again, does not explain the effects of socioeconomic differences in aging. Moreover, there are cultural variations, such as seen in Japan, where modernization theory does not adequately apply.

It is obvious that all of these theories in social gerontology are still in the formative stage. There are two major reasons for this situation. First, social gerontology is a relatively new field. As such it awaits the accumulation of an extensive body of research data that can come only with a considerable amount of work in the field. Second, research concerning the aging experience should include longitudinal or long-term studies of people as they age if social gerontology is going to be able to explain and perhaps to predict the changes in behavior that come with aging. Such research not only is expensive, but, if done correctly, is going to take several years of data collection on aging cohorts before adequate theories can be formulated.

Health of the Aged

The single most important determinant of the quality of an elderly person's life is health. Older people who are unhealthy lead relatively shorter and less satisfactory lives than older people who are healthy, feel good, and have the physical capability to pursue their chosen activities. Especially among the elderly, health matters affect all other areas of life, including social roles.

Moreover, positive feelings about one's health in old age go a long way toward determining whether or not an individual is happy. Although it might be thought that happiness declines with age more or less automatically because of a decrease in social activities and a failure to measure up to prevailing (youthful) standards of physical attractiveness, this does not appear to be the case. David Witt and his colleagues (1980) analysed national opinion polls in the United States for a thirty-year period and found that happiness does not decline with age and perhaps never did. Popular opinion often maintained that being old meant being unhappy because no one really wanted to be old. When older people themselves were asked about old age by researchers, many confirmed this view. But what was misleading, as noted by Witt and his associates, is that most of the studies conducted during the mid-twentieth century did not go far enough in asking about various factors that might influence personal happiness in old age, such as health, finances, and social relationships.

The key difference, states Witt and his colleagues, turns out to be the *perception* of one's health. Although money, self-esteem, and other factors are important, what really seems to matter the most is how the elderly person perceives his or her health. Those elderly who believe themselves to be healthy for their age are clearly the happiest among older persons. This finding is true for recent studies as well as for those studies conducted in the 1940s and 1950s that correlated health with happiness. With increasing numbers of persons reaching old age in a healthy condition, it had appeared to some researchers that the aged population as a whole was happier than in the past. But actually, the healthy aged were generally happy all along, as Witt and his colleagues concluded. The difference is that today there are significantly more of them, and this gave the false impression that being happy and old was something new.

PERCEIVED HEALTH STATUS

Because perceived health status is so important in determining the happiness of an elderly person, and because research such as that by Witt and his colleagues finds a high level of happiness among older people, it would appear that aged individuals in the United States tend to perceive their health in a positive fashion. But how can this be, for health deteriorates with age? Several studies have investigated this situation and found examples of both institutionalized and noninstitutionalized elderly rating their health status as very good (Cockerham, Sharp, and Wilcox 1983; Ferraro 1980; Fillenbaum 1979; Myles 1978). In fact, studies of the old-old have found them assessing their health even higher than do the young-old (Ferraro 1980; Linn and Linn 1980).

The question thus arises as to whether or not such self-assessments are accurate measures of a person's health. Self-ratings of health have been criticized as subjective and unreliable. But John Ware (1986) points out that their subjectivity is their strength because they reflect personal evaluations of health not captured by other measures. Ware states that there should be no doubt that self-perceptions of health are reliable measures. A number of studies have found that self-ratings of health among elderly adults are also valid measures of the respondent's objective health status and match up as well or better than physician evaluations (Ferraro 1980; Fillenbaum 1979; LaRue et al. 1979; Maddox and Douglass 1973; Mossey and Shapiro 1982). Moreover, research in Canada (Mossey and Shapiro 1982) and Israel (Kaplan, Barell, and Lusky 1988) has found that elderly persons who rate their health high have tended to live longer than those who rate their health less positively. Although research continues to improve methods for health self-assessments for the elderly (Liang 1986; Wolinsky et al. 1983), the existing literature is clear that such ratings to date have been valid and reliable.

It may seem incongruent that in spite of the fact that health declines with age, many older people tend to rate their health positively. But the fact remains that often older people perceive themselves as being in good health for their age. The reason for this appears to be that judgments concerning one's health by aged individuals are relative. That is, self-assessments of personal health by elderly persons are often based upon how they compare themselves with peers of their own age and sex, and perhaps also upon the expectations others have of their health. The tendency of aged persons to rate their health in this relative fashion most likely is rationalized in two ways.

First, simply surviving to old age in a condition reasonably free of serious illness or severe disability would be evidence of relatively good health. Only among the last few generations has survival to old age without severe health problems become fairly common. With increasing numbers living past age 65, many people in the older age categories are able to feel that their health has indeed been good. Eleanor Stoller (1984) suggests, for example, that older persons may expect a decline in their health as they age, but when the deterioration does not take place at the rate or to the extent they had anticipated, they may begin to assess their health above the rating they would assign to their age peers. Other research has found that health status and functional capacity are important in the self-esteem of the aged (Gubrium 1975; Hochschild 1973), leading Stoller (1984:267) to surmise that "perhaps as people become older, they tend to devalue the health of others as a way of increasing their own status." Nevertheless, it seems clear that the fact that they have survived to old age in a relatively healthy condition, when others have not, encourages them to feel that they can be positive about their health (Cockerham et al. 1983; Stoller 1984).

Secondly, as John Myles (1978) reminds us, subjective responses to a health problem tend to be a function of how much of a person's life is disrupted by the condition. The extent of the potential disruption is determined by the level of physical and mental functioning required in a particular social environment. Usually, elderly people are not required to maintain a highly active level of functioning and thus find it easier to perceive their health as good enough to meet their needs. As for the aged in institutions, who are likely to have the poorest objective levels of health, it should be kept in mind that institutions for the elderly are designed to minimize the effects of illness and disability. "If they are successful in this effort," states Myles (1978:518–519), "we should expect this to be reflected in their clients' subjective experience of illness." Therefore, as long as the institutional environment is able to buffer the effects of old age, including illness and disability, elderly individuals may be able to maintain the view that their health is adequate or even good for their surroundings. Being alive and able to function adequately apparently promotes the subjective impression that one's health in old age is relatively good.

This situation is depicted in research conducted by the author and his colleagues (Cockerham et al. 1983) in Illinois. A statewide random sample of persons over the age of 18 rated their health in comparison with others their age. The responses, shown in Table 4–1, indicate that people begin to define their health as much better than others their age after they enter the sixth decade of life. Table 4–1 shows that persons aged 18 to 60 show similar patterns in their self-assessment of health. About one-fourth of all respondents in each of the age categories below age 60 rated their health as much better than others their age, another one-fourth viewed their health as somewhat better, and another 40 percent saw their health as about the same as others their age.

Table 4–1 shows, however, that 42.2 percent of those aged 61 to 70 rated themselves as much better in health than their peers. This level of response is similar to those persons aged 71 to 80 and 81 and over. Consequently, the proportion of people who feel their health is much better than others their age is almost twice as high among people age 60 and over than for those under age 60. There is not a significant difference across age-groups for the response "somewhat better"; rather, the major difference in responses by age is in the category of "much better" and is characteristic only of the older age-groups.

Multivariate analysis of the data in the Cockerham and colleagues study showed that education and number of illness symptoms experienced were especially important influences on self-assessments of health. The more education a person had, the more likely health was perceived in a positive fashion. Perhaps those persons with more education considered themselves

TABLE 4–1   Percentage of Responses to the Question "Compared with Others Your Age, How Would You Rate Your Health?"

	AGE GROUPS						
RESPONSE	*18–30* *(N = 183)*	*31–40* *(N = 154)*	*41–50* *(N = 95)*	*51–60* *(N = 99)*	*61–70* *(N = 83)*	*71–80* *(N = 51)*	*OVER* *81* *(N = 19)*
Much better	24.0	25.3	27.4	24.2	42.2	41.2	36.8
Somewhat better	25.7	26.6	25.3	22.2	28.9	19.6	26.3
About the same	47.0	42.2	38.9	44.4	26.5	37.3	31.6
Somewhat worse	3.3	5.2	6.3	8.1	1.2	2.0	5.3
Much worse	0.0	0.7	2.1	1.0	1.2	0.0	0.0

Source: William C. Cockerham, Kimberly Sharp, and Julie Wilcox, "Aging and Perceived Health Status," *Journal of Gerontology* 38 (1983): 352.

more healthy relative to others because they felt their social environment was more conducive to maintaining good health than members of less educated and, most likely, less affluent groups. As one would expect, number of symptoms was significant in that those persons who experienced the fewest symptoms of illness tended to rate their health the highest.

The results of the Cockerham and colleagues (1983) study in Illinois are consistent with the findings of several other studies, including research conducted in northeastern New York (Stoller 1984), North Carolina (Maddox and Douglass 1973), and nationwide (Ferraro 1980). One study conducted in central Wisconsin, however, produced different results (elderly respondents rated their health worse than middle-aged persons) and concluded that "if elderly people do report more health optimism that younger individuals perhaps it is only when asked to compare themselves with their age peers" (Levkoff, Cleary, and Wetle 1987:118). This conclusion raises an important point. When younger people are asked to compare their health with others their age, the evaluation is likely to be "about the same"; elderly people, as discussed, appear more likely to rate their health higher than that of their peers. In old age, health differences between people become more obvious. Therefore, as Stoller (1984) explains, comparison with peers is of major importance in health self-assessments by the elderly, and it may be that such a comparison is a primary factor in influencing relatively high self-ratings. When asked to compare themselves with younger persons or with people generally, the aged may not rank their health as highly as they seem to do when comparing themselves with others in their age-group.

Therefore, as David Mechanic and Ronald Angel (1987) suggest, the elderly appear to adjust their perceptions of their health as they modify their expectations with age. That is, as people become older, they change their definition of what it is to be healthy in order to fit their circumstances. If they have survived to old age in reasonably good condition and can function relatively well in their environment, health self-assessments tend to be very positive when the elderly compare themselves with their peers. Mechanic and Angel found in a study of low back pain, for example, that older people in a nationwide sample complained of less pain than expected in comparison with other age-groups. Mechanic and Angel concluded:

> Subjective evaluations of health, we believe, are not absolute but on the contrary, are made in a context of self and other comparisons, and are always relative to some degree. As people age, they may attribute some of their discomforts to the aging process and are more likely to normalize bodily discomforts. Moreover, they may feel that they are doing relatively well compared to their reference groups and the physical demands of their life regimen. Indeed, there may be less requirement for them to engage in the types of activities that exacerbate their discomforts.[1]

1. David Mechanic and Ronald J. Angel, "Some Factors Associated with the Report and Evaluation of Back Pain," *Journal of Health and Social Behavior* 28 (1987): 138.

PHYSICAL HEALTH

Of course, the health of elderly people on the whole is not actually better than that of young adults in general. This is apparent when age differences in overall physical condition, stamina, hand and eye coordination, hearing and vision, and capacity for healing from disease and injury are considered. Although there are exceptions, older people generally cannot pursue a highly active physical lifestyle to the same extent as someone much younger. Rather, it is that the health of many older people is quite good for their age. The health of other older people, however, may be poor. The fact remains that health does deteriorate with age, and this occurs later in some people than in others. But eventually everyone's health declines if one lives long enough. The key to a positive quality of life in old age appears to be that of maintaining one's health as long as possible and as close as possible to the time of one's death. In this section, we will discuss the general situation of the aged in American society with respect to physical health.

Health Services Utilization

The two age-groups using health services the most are the elderly and young children, but it is the elderly who have the poorest health and are hospitalized more often than other age-groups. The general literature on health care utilization in the United States, including studies in Rhode Island (Monteiro 1973; Kronenfeld 1978), Los Angeles County, (Galvin and Fan 1975), five New York and Pennsylvania counties (Wan and Soifer 1974), Cleveland (Coulton and Frost 1982), St. Louis (Wolinsky et al. 1983) and nationwide (Wolinsky, Mosely, and Coe 1986), substantiates the supposition that elderly people are more likely to visit a physician than are young adults. Studies of the utilization of health services by the aged indicate that such use is determined more by actual need for care than any other single factor (Coulton and Frost 1982; Wan 1982; Wolinsky et al. 1983).

One of the clearest indicators of the public's contact with the medical profession is the proportion of the population who visit physicians. In 1985, the average number of physician visits per person in the United States was 5.3; for persons age 65 and older, however, the average number of visits was 8.7. According to a national survey conducted by the National Center for Health Statistics (1986a) in 1984, four out of five people 65 years of age and older living outside of institutions had seen a physician within the previous year. Another 6 percent had seen a physician within two years, 12 percent had not visited a doctor at all for more than two years despite their being at an age when the need for medical care is great. But most older people did have contacts with a physician. Nearly 60 percent (59.5 percent) of them, however, had only 1–6 contacts over a year's time, suggesting that many received relatively routine medical care. Only 8 percent had 13 or more contacts.

As for hospitalization, some 20.5 percent of all elderly persons had been hospitalized one or more times during the preceding year. Only 18 percent of those 65–74 years of age were hospitalized compared with 29 percent of those 85 years and over. Although there is not a striking contrast between the young-old and the old-old (age 85 and over) in number of physician contacts, the old-old are hospitalized significantly more often.

Health Characteristics of the Aged

In the United States, as in other developed countries, there has been a reduction in infectious diseases and an increase in chronic health disorders. These chronic disorders—namely, heart disease, cancer, hypertension, diabetes, and the like—are the most important problems of physical health facing older people today (Kart, Metress, and Metress 1988; Ory and Bond 1989). For example, Table 4–2 shows that the leading causes of death (in order) in the United States in 1900 were influenza and pneumonia, and tuberculosis. In 1988 these disorders had been replaced by heart disease, cancer, cerebrovascular disease or stroke, and accidents as the major causes of death in an increasingly urban, industrialized, and aging society. Improvements in living conditions and medical technology had all but eliminated disorders such as tuberculosis, gastroenteritis, and diphtheria as major threats to life in 1988; but smoking, excessive consumption of calories and animal fats, stress reactions, and inadequate physical activity had helped promote other health problems, such as heart disease and other cardiovascular disorders like cerebrovascular diseases and arteriosclerosis.

Although heart disease is America's leading killer, since the mid-1960s there has been a decline in deaths from the disease for both men and women. About 308 of every 100,000 persons in the general population died from heart

TABLE 4–2   The Ten Leading Causes of Death in the United States, 1900 and 1988

1900	1988
Influenza and pneumonia	Heart Disease
Tuberculosis	Cancer
Gastroenteritis	Cerebrovascular diseases
Heart disease	Accidents
Cerebral hemorrhage	Pulmonary diseases
Chronic nephritis	Influenza and pneumonia
Accidents	Diabetes
Cancer	Suicide
Diseases of early infancy	Cirrhosis of liver
Diphtheria	Atherosclerosis

disease in 1950 compared with a rate of 183.6 persons per 100,000 in 1984. The decline in mortality from heart disease is but one example pointing toward improved health for older people.

The healthiest of the aged are those who live in community settings, rather than in institutions such as old-age homes and nursing homes. Only about 5 percent of all elderly are institutionalized; thus, the overwhelming majority (95 percent) live outside of an institutional environment, and their health is typical of most aged persons. Data from the 1984 National Center for Health Statistics (1986a) study depicting some of the health characteristics of these noninstitutionalized elderly are shown in Table 4–3. The sample consisted of 5,982 persons over the age of 65 who were representative of the estimated 26 million elderly living outside institutions. Table 4–3 shows the findings for those persons (1) 65–74 years of age and (2) 75 years and older; the oldest age-group, age 75 and over, has been subdivided into two groups of 75–84 years and age 85 and older to provide data on the oldest-old. The majority of people in all age-groups of older persons shown in Table 4–3 were in good health on each of the three measures of health status: perceived health status, days spent in bed, and limitation of activity. There was, however, a shift toward poorer health with increased age.

Table 4–3 shows that 67 percent of all older people comprising the sample rated their health as good or better: approximately 16 percent as excellent, 19 percent as very good, and 32 percent as good. Some 21 percent were in fair health, and about 12 percent were in poor health according to the individual or some other person interviewed who was most likely to know about them. These self-ratings of health do not appreciably change across age-groups. The results are almost identical for the ages between 65–74 and 75–84, and there is only a slight increase in the categories of fair or poor health for the 85 years and over group.

There also was not a great deal of difference between the elderly with respect to bed days per year. Overall, some 62 percent had not been confined to a bed for a single day during the previous year. Some 13.8 percent had spent less than a week in bed, 7.1 percent had spent 7–13 days, and 6.6 percent 14–27 days. Of the remainder, 8.9 percent indicated 28–365 bed days the previous year, and 1.4 percent were always confined to their bed. The highest percentage of bed days for any specific age-group was for those 85 years and over; even so, 55.8 percent of them had no bed days.

In addition, Table 4–3 shows that almost 60 percent of all persons age 65 and over had no limitations on activity; 15.2 percent had limitations on outside (outside the home) activities, 13.6 percent had limitations on certain kinds or amounts of activities, and 11.4 percent were unable to perform usual activity. For those 85 years and over, slightly less than 40 percent had no limitations on activity, and some 22 percent were unable to perform their usual activity. Figure 4–1 depicts selected activities in 1984 for which various proportions of the elderly are dependent. Shopping, bathing, light house-

TABLE 4–3 Percent Distribution of People Age 65 and Over Living in the Community by Selected Health Characteristics, According to Age and Sex: United States, 1984

HEALTH CHARACTERISTIC	TOTAL	65–74 YEARS			75 YEARS AND OVER			75–84 YEARS	85 YEARS AND OVER
		BOTH SEXES	MEN	WOMEN	BOTH SEXES	MEN	WOMEN		
Sample (number)	5,982	3,731	1,625	2,106	2,251	822	1,429	1,803	448
Estimated population (number in thousands)	26,290	16,227	7,048	9,178	10,063	3,685	6,378	8,073	1,990
Total (percent distribution)	100.0	100.0	100.0	100.0	100.0	100.0	100.0	100.0	100.0
Perceived health status[1]									
Excellent	15.6	15.5	16.3	14.8	15.8	16.3	15.4	15.9	15.4
Very good	19.2	19.6	19.2	20.0	18.6	17.7	19.0	18.3	19.6
Good	31.9	32.5	31.2	33.5	30.8	30.2	31.2	32.0	26.3
Fair	21.4	21.4	20.6	22.1	21.3	21.3	21.2	20.8	23.0
Poor	11.5	10.6	12.5	9.2	13.0	13.8	12.5	12.4	15.3

Bed days in year

0	62.2	63.5	64.4	62.8	60.2	61.6	59.4	61.3	55.8
1–6 days	13.8	14.5	13.9	15.0	12.7	11.8	13.2	12.9	12.1
7–13 days	7.1	6.7	6.8	6.6	7.7	7.3	7.9	7.4	8.7
14–27 days	6.6	6.5	6.1	6.7	6.9	7.0	6.8	7.0	6.3
28–365 days	8.9	7.8	7.8	7.8	10.7	10.8	10.6	9.9	13.9
Always	1.4	1.0	1.0	1.0	1.9	1.5	2.2	1.6	3.4
Limitation of activity									
None	59.8	61.5	60.0	62.6	57.0	59.3	55.6	61.3	39.6
Outside activities only	15.2	14.5	14.2	14.8	16.2	20.2	13.9	16.8	13.8
Kind or amount of activity	13.6	12.4	9.9	14.4	15.6	10.7	18.5	13.4	24.6
Unable to perform usual activity	11.4	11.6	15.9	8.2	11.2	9.8	12.0	8.6	22.0

[1] Health status was unknown for 0.5 percent.

Source: National Center for Health Statistics, "Aging in the Eighties, Preliminary Data from the Supplement on Aging to the National Health Interview Survey, United States, January–June 1984." Advance Data from Vital and Health Statistics, No. 115 (U.S. Department of Health and Human Services, 1986).

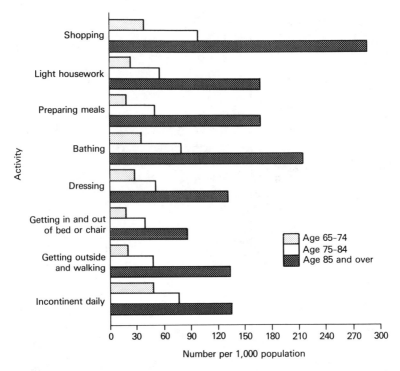

FIGURE 4–1   Proportion of persons age 65 and over dependent in selected activities by age-group: United States, 1984

Source: National Center for Health Statistics, "Physical Functioning of the Aged, United States, 1984," *Vital and Health Statistics,* Series 10, No. 167. (U.S. Department of Health and Human Services, 1989).

work, and preparing meals were the activities reflecting the greatest degree of dependency. The clear trend shown in Figure 4–1 is that the proportion of dependent elderly increases with age. For those 85 years of age and over, more than one-fourth (286 per 1,000) were dependent in bathing and more than one-sixth (170 per 1,000) were dependent in light housework and preparing their own meals.

The National Center for Health Statistics (1986a) summarizes its findings by pointing out that the health of older Americans is generally good, including those age 85 and over. Some 62 percent of all elderly had no bed days that preceding year, 60 percent had no limitations on their activity, and 67 percent rated their health as good or better. For the oldest-old, age 85 and over, some 55 percent had no bed days the preceding year, nearly 40 percent had no limitation of activity, and over 61 percent rated their health as good or better. However, it was also noted that this situation is partially because healthy older people are more likely to remain in the community than those in extremely poor health. The latter are much more likely to be institutionalized. Therefore, it should not be concluded that the health of the *total* elderly population is good. Rather, the health of the majority of older people who live outside of institutions is relatively good. But for the oldest-old at 85 years of age and older, there are more health problems and a much greater likelihood of becoming a patient in a nursing home. And the health of people in nursing homes is generally poor.

Data compiled on nursing home residents by the National Center for Health Statistics (1987a) shows that such residents typically are very old (45 percent are age 85 and over and 39 percent are between the ages of 74 and 85); they also tend to be female (75 percent) and white (93 percent). Only some 6 percent of all nursing home residents are black, and 1 percent are either Asians, American Indians, or native Alaskans. Because of the preponderance of very old residents in nursing homes, many are in poor health and need assistance in performing basic activities of daily living, such as bathing (91 percent), dressing (78 percent), using the toilet or moving from a bed or chair (63 percent), and eating (40 percent). Loss of independence among nursing home residents is most likely to occur in bathing and least likely in eating. The trend in nursing homes is toward *greater* functional dependence for the residents, as compared with the past, because of the increasingly larger proportion of the old-old in such institutions.

Two health problems that are particularly discomforting for the elderly are hearing and vision impairment. The National Center for Health Statistics (1986b) has compiled data, shown in Table 4–4, indicating that hearing problems are quite frequent among the elderly. For noninstitutionalized men in 1984, Table 4–4 indicates that some 30 percent between the ages of 65 and 74 had a hearing impairment. The proportion increases with age: hearing loss was attributed to some 32.7 percent of men between the ages of 75 and 84 and 58.3 percent of those age 85 and over. For women, Table 4–4 shows that hearing loss affected 17.5 percent of the females between the ages of 65 and 74 and increased to 28.2 percent of those between ages 75 and 84; among women age 85 years and over, some 44.3 percent had a hearing impairment.

As for blindness in one or both eyes or any other trouble seeing, some 12.8 percent of all noninstitutionalized older persons are shown in Table 4–5 to have this problem. Some 94.8 percent of all elderly wear eye glasses, and the majority (nearly 70 percent) report that they have no trouble seeing with glasses. But vision impairment, as in all other health problems, increases with age. Among the age 85 and over age-group, Table 4–5 shows that 26.8 percent have impaired vision, 37.9 percent (compared with 19 percent of all elderly) have cataracts, and 21.2 percent (compared with 5.4 percent of all elderly) report a lot of trouble seeing even with glasses. About 44 percent of those age 85 and over indicate they have no trouble seeing with glasses. The frequency of visual impairments generally among the aged is similar in both men and women, except that women have significantly more problems with cataracts.

TABLE 4–4 Percent Distribution of People Age 65 Years and Over Living in the Community by Selected Hearing Characteristics, According to Age and Sex: United States, January–June 1984

HEARING CHARACTERISTIC	TOTAL	65–74 YEARS			75–84 YEARS			85 YEARS AND OVER		
		BOTH SEXES	MEN	WOMEN	BOTH SEXES	MEN	WOMEN	BOTH SEXES	MEN	WOMEN
Sample (number)	5,982	3,731	1,625	2,106	1,803	690	1,113	448	132	316
Estimated population (number in thousands)	26,290	16,227	7,048	9,178	8,073	3,111	4,962	1,990	574	1,417
Total[1] (percent distribution)	100.0	100.0	100.0	100.0	100.0	100.0	100.0	100.0	100.0	100.0
Hearing impairment										
No	72.2	77.0	70.0	82.5	67.3	60.1	71.8	51.6	41.7	55.7
Yes	27.8	23.0	30.0	17.5	32.7	39.9	28.2	48.4	58.3	44.3
Deafness										
No deafness	87.1	89.8	86.7	92.1	85.4	81.0	88.0	71.7	61.5	76.2
Deafness in one ear	7.5	6.7	8.5	5.4	7.6	9.8	6.4	12.9	18.5	10.3
Deafness in both ears	5.2	3.3	4.5	2.5	6.7	8.7	5.4	14.5	19.2	12.4

Any other trouble hearing

No	81.5	84.6	79.4	88.4	77.9	72.1	81.2	68.9	69.2	68.8
Yes	18.3	15.3	20.5	11.5	21.8	27.1	18.7	30.0	30.8	29.7

Use hearing aid

No	92.0	94.4	93.0	95.5	88.9	85.2	91.1	84.0	76.6	87.2
Yes	8.0	5.6	7.0	4.5	11.0	14.8	8.8	15.8	23.4	12.4

Describe hearing (with hearing aid)

No trouble	61.1	66.9	59.2	72.8	55.0	47.7	59.4	37.5	33.9	39.1
Little trouble	33.3	29.8	36.6	24.6	38.0	41.9	35.7	43.2	43.9	43.0
Much trouble	5.5	3.2	4.1	2.5	6.8	10.1	4.8	19.1	22.3	17.7

¹ Figures may not add to total because of unknowns and rounding.

Source: National Center for Health Statistics, "Aging in the Eighties, Impaired Senses for Sound and Light in Persons Age 65 Years and Over," No. 125 (U.S. Department of Health and Human Services, 1986).

TABLE 4–5 Percent Distribution of People Age 65 Years and Over Living in the Community by Selected Visual Characteristics, According to Age and Sex: United States, 1984

VISUAL CHARACTERISTIC	TOTAL	65–74 YEARS			75–84 YEARS			85 YEARS AND OVER		
		BOTH SEXES	MEN	WOMEN	BOTH SEXES	MEN	WOMEN	BOTH SEXES	MEN	WOMEN
Sample (number)	5,982	3,731	1,625	2,106	1,803	690	1,113	448	132	316
Estimated population (number in thousands)	26,290	16,227	7,048	9,178	8,073	3,111	4,962	1,990	574	1,417
Total[1] (percent distribution)	100.0	100.0	100.0	100.0	100.0	100.0	100.0	100.0	100.0	100.0
Visual impairment										
No	87.2	90.5	90.3	90.6	84.0	83.3	84.4	73.2	75.0	72.5
Yes	12.8	9.5	9.7	9.4	16.0	16.7	15.6	26.8	25.0	27.5
Blindness										
No blindness	95.6	97.3	96.6	97.8	94.2	92.9	95.0	88.1	87.7	88.3
Blindness in one eye	3.2	2.2	2.9	1.6	4.4	5.9	3.6	[2]6.9	[2]5.4	[2]7.6
Blindness in both eyes	1.0	[2]0.5	[2]0.4	[2]0.6	[2]1.3	[2]1.1	[2]1.4	[2]4.8	[2]6.9	[2]3.8
Any other trouble seeing										
No	89.7	92.1	92.4	91.9	87.4	87.1	87.7	77.6	82.0	75.7
Yes	10.2	7.9	7.6	8.1	12.3	12.3	12.3	21.4	[2]17.2	23.2

Cataracts

No	79.5	86.1	89.5	83.5	71.2	75.4	68.6	59.0	66.9	55.5
Yes	19.1	12.9	9.6	15.4	27.0	22.3	29.9	37.9	31.5	40.8
Operation for cataracts										
No	89.5	92.9	93.2	92.8	84.6	84.9	84.4	80.3	81.0	80.0
Yes	10.5	7.0	6.8	7.3	15.2	14.9	15.4	19.7	[2]19.1	20.0
Use eyeglasses										
No	5.2	5.1	6.4	4.1	4.4	5.3	3.8	9.3	[2]12.5	[2]7.9
Yes	94.8	94.9	93.6	95.9	95.6	94.7	96.2	90.7	87.5	92.1
Describe vision (with glasses)										
No trouble	68.9	75.3	76.7	74.2	60.7	62.0	60.0	47.4	55.0	44.1
Little trouble	25.6	21.9	20.8	22.7	32.1	31.9	32.3	30.9	25.8	33.1
Much trouble	5.4	2.8	2.6	3.0	7.0	6.0	8.0	21.2	[2]18.3	22.4

[1] Figures may not add to total because of unknowns and rounding.

[2] Less than 30 persons with visual characteristic in age-sex subgroup.

Source: National Center for Health Statistics, "Aging in the Eighties, Preliminary Data from the Supplement on Aging to the National Health Interview Survey, United States, January–June 1984." Advance Data From Vital and Health Statistics, No. 115 (U.S. Department of Health and Human Services, 1986).

By the year 2000, it is estimated that the population of visually impaired elderly will be larger, older, and more predominantly female than in the 1980s (Kirchner 1986). The vision-impaired elderly are expected to increase some 36 percent (from 23 million to 32 million persons) between 1977 and 2000.

National Center for Health Statistics (1986a) data for noninstitutionalized older persons in 1984 show that 90 percent indicated they thought they were doing a good job of taking care of their health. Some 24 percent stated they thought they were doing an "excellent" job, 32 percent said "very good," and 34 percent replied "good." Of the remaining 10 percent, most indicated they were doing a fair job; very few felt they were doing poorly in taking care of their health. The majority felt they had control over their health, with 35 percent stating they had very good control and 46 percent stating they had some control. Only 8 percent indicated they had little control, and 7 percent felt they had no control. A sense of control over one's health has been found to be significantly related to the number of physician visits in that those elderly persons with a strong sense of control tend to seek out doctors less often, even during times of stress (Krause 1988). Living with other people, who are able to help the aged deal with their daily activities, has likewise been found to reduce the need for health services (Cafferata 1987).

Overall, the health of older persons does appear to be relatively good. Greater numbers of people are living to reach old age. But greater numbers of elderly persons also means greater numbers with health problems and an increased demand in the future for health care delivery services to treat the problems of aging.

Stress and the Aged

Another important factor in considering the health status of an individual, not just those past the age of 65, is exposure to stress. Stress can be defined as an emotional-psychophysiological state in a person that occurs in a situational context, involving stimuli that serve as cues to elicit fear or anxiety responses (Janis 1958). Usually stress occurs when people are faced with situations where their usual modes of behavior are not adequate and the consequences of not adapting to the situation are perceived as serious. When an individual is subject to stress, the body responds primarily through the autonomic nervous system (which controls heart rate, blood pressure, and gastrointestinal functions) and the neuroendocrine system (which controls the secretion of hormones from the adrenal and pituitary glands, the parathyroids, and elsewhere). A number of studies have shown that an individual's ability to deal with stress and control stress-induced physiological changes in the body can promote heart disease, hypertension, ulcers, muscular pain, compulsive vomiting, asthma, migraine headaches, and other health problems (Cockerham 1989).

Of course, individuals who are highly stressed and develop serious health problems as a result are not as likely to live long lives. Stress, for example, is considered a major factor in early deaths from heart attacks among people who tend to be hard driving, overaggressive, and obsessed with meeting deadlines. Stress is, however, not absent from the lives of the elderly as they cope with the death of a spouse, retirement, loss of income and status, and the like. Research on elderly persons experiencing the loss of a spouse and other negative life events shows a decline in perceived health status (Fenwick and Barresi 1981; Weinberger et al. 1986). Yet Kenneth Ferraro (1989) points out that aged women, even though they may suffer emotionally, are more psychologically prepared to lose their spouse because widowhood is relatively common. But this does not mean that women escape the stress of the event; rather, it means they typically adjust more quickly. When it comes to experiencing grief over the death of a spouse, however, other research by Dale Lund and his associates (Lund, Caserta, and Dimond 1986) finds that there are more similarities than differences between elderly men and women in the bereavement process. They are both hit hard by the loss.

As for retirement, there is little evidence that this event has a negative health effect on the individual—again, because it is an expected and normative transition for most people (Markides and Cooper 1987, 1989). This is not to say that the elderly are not affected by stress. Rather, it appears that older age-groups respond much the same as younger groups. Social networks of family and friends significantly buffer and counterbalance the effects of stress on older individuals, as they do for younger persons, by providing social support in the form of love, affection, concern, and assistance (Cohen, Teresi, and Holmes 1985; Krause 1986; George 1989). People who lack this form of support tend to fare worse in coping with stress. Extensive research on health and stress among the elderly is just beginning, but both are important topics for future research because of the insight provided into the effects of stress on people over the life course (Markides and Cooper 1989).

Health of the Elderly Poor and Minorities

To be poor is, by definition, to have less of everything in life, including health. Lower socioeconomic groups have the poorest health, and this is true in both capitalist and socialist countries (Cockerham 1989). Persons living in poverty have greater exposure than more affluent individuals to physical (dust, dampness, extreme temperatures), chemical and biochemical (diet, pollution, smoking, alcohol and drug abuse), biological (bacteria, viruses), and psychological (stress) risk factors that produce ill health.

Those at the bottom of the socioeconomic scale, therefore, appear to be especially disadvantaged in regard to health. This disadvantage extends not only to communicable diseases associated with unhealthy living conditions, but also to chronic health problems like heart disease that are prevalent in modern, industrialized countries and that are strongly affected by how one lives. Lifestyle and social/environmental conditions, along with preventive health measures, primarily determine health status. A healthy lifestyle includes the use of good personal habits such as eating properly, getting enough rest, exercising, and avoiding practices like smoking, abusing alcohol, and taking drugs. The type of lifestyle that promotes a healthy existence has been more typical of the upper and middle classes who have the resources to support a healthy lifestyle, but there is evidence that participation in healthy lifestyles has begun to spread across class lines in the United States and Western Europe (Cockerham, Kunz, and Lueschen 1988). Nevertheless, crowded living conditions, poor diet, inferior housing, low levels of income and education, enhanced exposure to violence, alcoholism, and problem drinking, and drug abuse all combine to decrease the life chances of the poor. This situation is reflected in the tendency of the poor generally (Cockerham et al. 1988) and the aged poor in particular (Mutran and Ferraro 1988) to rate their health worse than do the more affluent.

Consequently, the poor are less likely to reach the oldest ages and, for those that do, surviving longer can be a constant struggle. In the United States, as noted in the last chapter, about 20 percent of the elderly lived on or near the poverty line in 1987. The greatest problem affecting the health of these persons the most is not access to health care. Americans age 65 and over are eligible for Medicare, the nation's publicly funded health insurance program that pays for most medical services provided to older people. Rather, the central problem is living in an environment of poverty as an aged person and coping with the health disadvantages that such an environment promotes on a daily basis.

As for racial minority groups, the last chapter also disclosed that nonwhites have a lower life expectancy in general than whites. United States government figures for 1984 show that some 74.4 percent of white males survive from birth to age 65, compared with a much lower rate of 62.2 percent of all nonwhite males. For females, 85.5 percent of white females survive from birth to age 65 compared with 77.4 percent of nonwhite females. Despite the fact that nonwhites have made significant gains in life expectancy in the United States during the twentieth century, they still lag behind their white counterparts.

Black Americans.   Of all the American minorities, blacks have the worst health profile and highest overall mortality rates. For example, although blacks constitute 11.5 percent of the American population, they have 20 percent of the diagnosed hypertension. Hypertension is the leading cause of deaths from kidney failure and is a major contributor to deaths from end-stage renal disease, heart disease, and stroke. Black men who suffer from hypertension have nearly twenty times more kidney failure than white males 25–44 years of age, and ten times more at 45–64 years of age. Diabetes has also been increasing among the black population from a rate of 11.7 per 1,000 in 1963 to 35.9 per 1,000 in 1985. When it comes to mortality rates, blacks rank at the top for all causes of death and in major categories like heart disease and cancer. This is substantiated in a 1985 U.S. Department of Health and Human Services study on black and minority health, utilizing data from 1979–1981, which found blacks to have higher death rates from all causes and many specific diseases than whites, Native Americans, and Asian/Pacific Islanders.

More recent data for 1987, showing direct comparisons between blacks and whites, are presented in Table 4–6 on selected causes of death in the United States. Table 4–6 shows that for all causes, the age-adjusted mortality rate for black males was 1,023.2 per 100,000 resident population, whereas the rate for white males was 668.2 per 100,000. The death rate for black females was 586.2 per 100,000 compared with 384.1 for white females. For heart disease, the death rate for black males was 287.1 per 100,000, as contrasted with 225.9 for white males; black females, in turn, had a mortality rate of 180.8 compared with 116.3 for white females. For cancer, Table 4–6 shows the 1987 death rate for black males was 227.9 per 100,000 compared with 158.4 for white males; black females showed a rate of 132.0 compared with 109.7 for white females. The same general pattern (higher rates for blacks

TABLE 4–6   Age-Adjusted Death Rates for Selected Causes of Death, According to Sex and Race: United States, 1987

	DEATHS PER 100,000 RESIDENT POPULATION			
	WHITE MALES	WHITE FEMALES	BLACK MALES	BLACK FEMALES
All causes	668.2	384.1	1,023.2	586.2
Heart disease	225.9	116.3	287.1	180.8
Cerebrovascular diseases	30.3	26.3	57.1	46.7
Cancer	158.4	109.7	227.9	132.0
Pulmonary disease	27.4	13.7	24.0	9.5
Pneumonia and influenza	16.8	9.7	26.4	12.2
Liver disease and cirrhosis	12.1	5.1	22.0	9.1
Diabetes	9.5	8.1	18.3	21.3
Accidents	49.7	18.6	66.8	21.0
Suicide	20.1	5.3	12.0	2.1
Homicide	7.7	2.9	53.8	12.3
AIDS	8.3	0.6	25.4	4.7

Source: National Center for Health Statistics, *Health, United States, 1989* (Washington, D.C.: U.S. Government Printing Office, 1990).

than whites) is also shown to be the case in Table 4–6 for deaths from cerebrovascular diseases (stroke), pneumonia and influenza, liver disease and cirrhosis, accidents, homicide, and AIDS. Besides heart disease and cancer, black males have especially high death rates from homicide and AIDS. Whites, on the other hand, show higher death rates in two categories: pulmonary (lung) disease and suicide.

Data such as these clearly point to lessened life expectancy for blacks in comparison with whites. The black male, according to preliminary 1988 figures compiled by the U.S. National Center for Health Statistics (1990), with a life expectancy of 65.1 years, will typically live 7 years less than the white male, whose life expectancy is 72.1 years, and 13.8 years less than the white female, who has the highest life expectancy of all at 78.9 years. The black female, with a life expectancy in 1988 of 73.8 years, lives about 5.1 years less on the average than the white female. Excess mortality for black adults in the United States appears to be largely attributable not only to risk factors like smoking, cholesterol, high blood pressure, excess weight, alcohol intake, and diabetes, but also to the social, psychological, and physical environment associated with a low income (Otten et al. 1990). Given the socioeconomically disadvantaged position of many blacks in American society, they may be less prepared to deal with potentially fatal diseases and are therefore more likely to die early from such afflictions (Markides and Mindel 1987; Markides 1989).

However, when it comes to the oldest-old, those persons age 85 and over, the remaining years of life expectancy are higher for blacks than whites. U.S. National Center for Health Statistics (1986a) data for 1984 show, for instance, that black males had a life expectancy of 5.8 years at age 85 compared with 5.1 years for white males. Black females age 85 had 7.3 years, whereas white females of the same age had 6.5 years left on the average. According to Kyriakos Markides and Charles Mindel (1987) and others (Manton 1980), the greater longevity of blacks at age 85 is known as the racial mortality crossover phenomenon. Markides and Mindel explain that the racial mortality crossover may be misleading in that an advantage in life expectancy may be imputed to blacks. Instead, they point out that the existence of crossover actually signifies that a much greater proportion of blacks do not make it to advanced old age. A minority of blacks survive to very old age; most die much younger, and their deaths do not significantly reduce the life expectancy available to the relatively few blacks left alive at age 85. A much greater proportion of whites reach the oldest ages, and those who die early in old age reduce the average years of life expectancy computed for the longest lived whites surviving well past age 85. Thus, the average black person has more years of life left statistically at age 85 because there are not as many blacks left to lower the computations for life expectancy.

Overall, it would appear that blacks generally have poorer health than do whites, but the differences are not great at the oldest ages (Markides 1989; Manton 1980; Ferraro 1988). That is, among old people, blacks and whites have about the same level of health, but there is a significantly smaller proportion of surviving blacks.

Hispanic Americans.   Adverse differences in health are not limited to blacks, but also include Hispanic Americans. Health data on Hispanic Americans are limited because, until 1976, federal, state, and local agencies usually included Hispanics with non-Hispanic whites in the white category. The existing information indicates, however, that Hispanics have higher rates of influenza, pneumonia, and tuberculosis than do non-Hispanic whites; they also have a shorter life expectancy. Hispanics are thought to have lower rates of heart disease and cancer (although these diseases are still major killers), but this may be because many Hispanics do not reach the older ages where these diseases are most prevalent. Health problems like influenza and tuberculosis among Hispanics are typically associated with poverty, and a large proportion of Hispanics have low incomes in the United States. Moreover, the percent of male Mexican-American smokers ages 55–74 is higher than the percent for the general United States population (National Center for Health Statistics, 1987b). In 1985, about 40 percent of male Mexican-Americans between ages 55 and 74 smoked, as did 20 percent of the female Mexican-Americans in this age bracket. With mortality rates for lung cancer increasing in the United States, smoking is an area of special concern for the health of Hispanics.

Among the elderly, Hispanics are more likely than non-Hispanic whites to have some type of physical impairment, and the onset of health problems generally appears to take place much earlier among Hispanics (Becerra and Shaw 1984). Overall, Hispanics are found to have poorer health than non-Hispanic whites but somewhat better health than blacks in general (Markides and Mindel 1987; Markides 1989). However, Hispanics are the racial minority group with the greatest likelihood of not having health insurance. One-fourth (25.7 percent) of all Hispanic Americans under the age of 65 are not covered by health insurance, with the greatest proportion of Mexican descent (Cockerham 1989). Language barriers can also be an important problem for the Hispanic elderly in securing help from health care professionals and welfare agencies (Applewhite 1988).

Native Americans.   Native Americans, consisting of American Indians and native Alaskans, have shown a dramatic improvement in their overall level of health in the last few years. Infant mortality rates dropped from 82.1 deaths per 1,000 live births in 1950 to 9.5 per 1,000 births in 1984, which is about the same as that of whites (9.4 per 1,000 births in 1984). Life expectancy for Native Americans was 60 years in 1950, but had climbed to 71.1 years by

1981. American Indians and native Alaskans have the lowest rates of cancer in the United States. Mortality rates from heart disease are also lower than the general population, but heart disease is still a significant cause of death. However, American Indians have the highest mortality rates from diabetes, and the complications of diabetes take a further toll by increasing the probability of kidney disease, blindness, and heart disease. American Indians also suffer more dysentery, strep throat, and hepatitis than do other Americans.

Other significant health problems include widespread ear infections (chronic otitis media) among children, which produce hearing problems, as well as extensive alcoholism, dietary deficiencies, and cirrhosis of the liver among adults. Alcoholism remains a major health problem for American Indians. More Indians also die from accidents, primarily automobile accidents, than any other racial group in American society, and the death rate from suicide is about 20 percent higher than that of the general population (Cockerham 1989). Therefore, although Native Americans have experienced a general improvement in their overall level of health, significant problems remain. Considerably smaller proportions of Indians than whites survive to reach old age.

Asian Americans.   In striking contrast to other racial minority groups, the health and longevity of Asian Americans rank among the best in the country. Asian Americans have the highest levels of income, education, and employment of any racial/ethnic minority group in the United States, often exceeding levels achieved by whites. Consequently, it is not surprising that the lowest age-adjusted mortality rates in the United States are those of Asian Americans. Asians and Pacific Islanders in the United States showed an age-adjusted mortality rate in 1979 to 1981 of 449.8 per 100,000, which was the lowest at that time of any racial/ethnic group in the nation. Heart disease is the leading cause of death for Asians, but mortality from this disease is less than that of whites and other minorities. Asians have very low rates of death from infant mortality, homicide, suicide, and health problems associated with alcoholism. Overall, Asians and Pacific Islanders tend to be the healthiest racial group in American society.

Asians also have a tradition of strong family relationships and respect for the aged. It is more common in Asian families than in other families in American society for elderly parents to live with their children. However, this is not to say that older Asian Americans do not have problems. Many older Asian Americans, especially those who live in inner-city "Chinatowns," speak little or no English, face cultural barriers in daily living and in securing health services, are in poor financial circumstances, have poor health, and live in isolation from the more affluent Asian community (Markides and Mindel 1987; Markides 1989).

MENTAL HEALTH

The National Institute of Mental Health (1987) points out that the acceleration in the number and percentage of elderly persons in American society has profound consequences for the mental health delivery system. The nationwide trend toward greater longevity signifies an increased demand for mental health services by aged patients. This does not mean that elderly persons will have more mental disorder in the future than will younger persons. Rather, it means that with more elderly persons in the general population, there will also be an increase in the number of the elderly needing psychiatric care.

Mental Hospital Admissions

Persons age 65 and over accounted for 7 percent of all admissions to inpatient psychiatric services in the United States during 1980, the most recent year data were available as this book goes to press. The extent to which this percentage will increase in the future has not been determined to date, but it is certain that the percentage will increase and the practice of geriatric psychiatry (psychiatry for the aged) will become more important. The increase in elderly psychiatric inpatients is likely to be greatest in nonfederal general hospitals. At least, this is what is suggested by Figure 4–2, where 1980 admissions data show that 59 percent of all elderly admissions were in nonfederal general hospitals, followed by 20 percent in state and

FIGURE 4–2 Percent distribution of admissions age 65 and over to selected inpatient psychiatric services: United States, 1980

Source: National Institute of Mental Health, *Mental Health, United States, 1987* (Washington, D.C.: U.S. Government Printing Office, 1987).

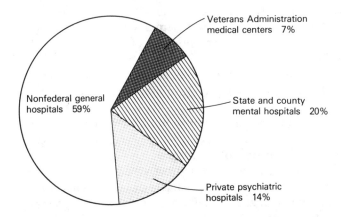

Veterans Administration medical centers   7%

Nonfederal general hospitals   59%

State and county mental hospitals   20%

Private psychiatric hospitals   14%

county mental hospitals, 14 percent in private psychiatric hospitals, and 7 percent in Veterans Administration medical centers.

Patients admitted to psychiatric care in nonfederal general hospitals do not typically remain on a long-term basis; rather, chronically ill or incurable patients are more likely to be found in state and county mental hospitals. In 1980, the average hospital stay for elderly patients was 122 days in state and county mental hospitals, 64 days in veterans hospitals, 40 days in private hospitals, and 34 days in nonfederal general hospitals. For patients age 85 and over, the average stay was 184 days in state and county mental hospitals, 88 days in veterans hospitals, and 42 days in private and nonfederal general hospitals.

Data on the age, sex, and race of elderly psychiatric inpatients in 1980 are presented in Table 4–7. Table 4–7 shows that within each type of hospital the largest percentage of elderly admissions was for persons between the ages of 65 and 74, with the percentage decreasing steadily by age. Of the 99,715 admissions for persons age 65 and over, Table 4–7 shows that 67.4 percent fell in the 65–74-year-old age-group. In future years, as noted, this may change somewhat as the percentage of oldest patients (85 years and over) increases. Nearly 90 percent (89.9 percent) of the elderly patients were white, and about 55 percent (54.6 percent) were female. Whites comprised the largest percentage of admissions within each hospital type. Females had the highest admission rates to nonfederal general hospitals and private psychiatric hospitals, whereas males were more likely to be admitted to state and county mental hospitals and veterans hospitals.

Comparisons of admission rates of elderly patients per 100,000 of the general United States civilian population within each hospital type indicate some significant differences. Table 4–7 shows not only that the admission rate in state and county mental hospitals was higher for elderly males than females (105 versus 60 per 100,000), but also that the rate for elderly persons from races other than white was twice the admission rate for whites (148 versus 71 per 100,000). Consequently, elderly males and nonwhites were most likely to be admitted to state and county mental hospitals that feature long-term, custodial care and often are the hospital of last resort for the psychologically disturbed poor.

Figure 4–3 shows the percent distribution of admissions of patients age 65 and over by selected primary diagnosis for 1980. Four major categories of mental disorder are shown: (1) alcohol and drug-related disorders; (2) organic mental disorders, which require evidence of an identifiable pathology within the central nervous system through laboratory tests, physical or neurological examinations, or the patient's history of health problems *and* are typically associated with aging or substance abuse; (3) affective disorders, in which some form of anxiety is the main characteristic; and (4) schizophrenia, which is a disturbance in mood, thinking, and behavior manifested by distortions of reality that include delusions (disturbance in thought) and hallucinations

TABLE 4–7 Number, Percent Distribution, and Rate per 100,000 Civilian Population of Admissions Age 65 and Over to Selected Inpatient Psychiatric Services, by Age, Sex, and Race: United States, 1980

AGE, SEX, AND RACE	TOTAL	INPATIENT PSYCHIATRIC SERVICES			
		STATE AND COUNTY MENTAL HOSPITALS	PRIVATE PSYCHIATRIC HOSPITALS	NONFEDERAL GENERAL HOSPITALS	VA MEDICAL CENTERS
			Number		
Total, 65 and over	99,715	20,056	13,916	59,254	6,489
Age					
65–74	67,184	13,248	9,169	39,438	5,329
75–84	27,203	5,789	3,855	16,787	772
85 and over	5,328	1,019	892	3,029	388
Sex					
Male	45,268	10,913	4,899	23,163	6,293
Female	54,447	9,143	9,017	36,091	196
Race					
White	89,607	16,512	12,842	54,260	5,993
All other races	10,108	3,544	1,074	4,994	496
			Percent distribution		
Total, 65 and over	100.0%	100.0%	100.0%	100.0%	100.0%
Age					
65–74	67.4	66.1	65.9	66.6	82.1
75–84	27.3	28.9	27.7	28.3	11.9
85 and over	5.3	5.1	6.4	5.1	6.0

(continued)

TABLE 4–7 *(continued)*

AGE, SEX, AND RACE	TOTAL	INPATIENT PSYCHIATRIC SERVICES			
		STATE AND COUNTY MENTAL HOSPITALS	PRIVATE PSYCHIATRIC HOSPITALS	NONFEDERAL GENERAL HOSPITALS	VA MEDICAL CENTERS
		Percent distribution			
Sex					
Male	45.4	54.4	35.2	39.1	97.0
Female	54.6	45.6	64.8	60.9	3.0
Race					
White	89.9	82.3	92.3	91.6	92.4
All other races	10.1	17.7	7.7	8.4	7.6
		Rate per 100,000 civilian population			
Total, 65 and over	387.8	78.0	54.1	230.4	25.2
Age					
65–74	429.2	84.6	58.6	252.0	34.0
75–84	349.2	74.3	49.5	215.5	9.9
85 and over	234.6	44.9	39.3	133.4	17.1
Sex					
Male	436.7	105.3	47.3	223.4	60.7
Female	354.8	59.6	58.8	235.2	1.3
Race					
White	384.4	70.8	55.1	232.8	25.7
All other races	420.6	147.5	44.7	207.8	20.6

Source: National Institute of Mental Health, *Mental Health, United States, 1987* (Washington, D.C.: U.S. Government Printing Office, 1987).

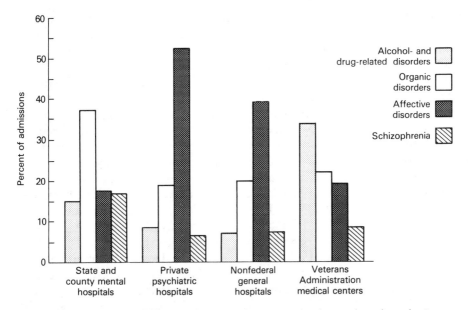

FIGURE 4–3   Percent distribution of admissions age 65 and over, by selected primary diagnosis and type of inpatient psychiatric service: United States, 1980

Source: National Institute of Mental Health, *Mental Health, United States, 1987* (Washington, D.C.: U.S. Government Printing Office, 1987).

(disturbance in perception). Figure 4–3 shows that the most common primary diagnosis for elderly patients in state and county mental hospitals (38 percent) was for organic disorders. Affective disorders were the leading diagnosis in private psychiatric hospitals (54 percent) and nonfederal general hospitals (40 percent), whereas alcohol and drug-related disorders were highest in Veterans Administration medical centers (36 percent). The second leading diagnosis in private, nonfederal general, and veterans hospitals was organic disorders.

True Prevalence

Mental hospital admissions rates, however, do not identify the true prevalence of mental disorder in a population, because they do not include untreated cases that fail to come to the attention of mental health reporting agencies. Admission rates may also be affected by the availability of facilities (thereby limiting the number of people who can be admitted) and by the amount of tolerance in a family or community for abnormal behavior. Admissions data are important because of their critical role in planning mental health services and securing government funding to support those services. But estimates of the true prevalence of mental disorder provide a more complete view of mental health problems in a community because they include both treated and untreated cases. Such data is obtained for treated cases from hospital and physician records and for untreated cases by community surveys that include measures of mental health and psychological well-being. Community surveys, however, are not precise measures of the prevalence of mental disorder, because they seldom involve a full psychiatric examination of the respondent and instead rely on psychological tests to estimate mental status. Nonetheless, it has been found that such surveys do produce consistent findings and provide a reasonable approximation of the types and extent of mental disorder to a population (Dohrenwend 1975).

When it comes to estimates of the true prevalence of mental disorder among the elderly, the best evidence suggests that about 15 percent of all aged people need mental health services (Butler 1985). Affective disorders, especially depression, are the most common mental disorder among the elderly in general. Other significant mental problems include organic mental disorders, alcohol and drug-related disorders, and suicide. However, the notion that older people are likely to show an increasing rate of mental disorders as they age overlooks the fact that many disorders can be treated successfully. Marie Haug, Linda Belgrave, and Brian Gratton (1984) studied the mental health of a random sample of noninstitutionalized elderly persons in Cleveland. They found, contrary to the expectation that mental health declines with age, that 32–40 percent of the respondents actually showed an improvement in psychiatric symptoms, especially depression, over a period of one year.

Of all of these problems, suicide, which is often associated with depression, is showing the greatest increase. Between 1981 and 1986, the suicide rate among elderly Americans increased 25 percent—reversing a decline that had lasted a half-century. In 1933, the first year in which the federal government collected data from all the states, the suicide rate among the elderly was 45.3 per 100,000 compared with an overall national average of 15.9. In 1981 it was 17.1 per 100,000 compared with a national average of 12.0. But from 1981 to 1986, as shown in Figure 4–4, the rate has steadily increased, with 1986 figures showing a rate for the elderly of 21.6 per 100,000 as against a national rate of 12.8. No other Western nation has witnessed a similar reversal in suicide rates among the elderly, and the reasons for this trend remain unclear. Some suggestions are that the quality of life available to people living physically longer lives may not be especially appealing for many of them. Longevity may produce greater concerns about becoming senile or contracting some other incurable health problem like cancer or heart disease in which the individual is relatively helpless and the financial cost is great. There is also a growing awareness among researchers of "rational suicide" by the elderly in which the person is not psychologically distressed but simply decides that his or her life is no longer worth living.

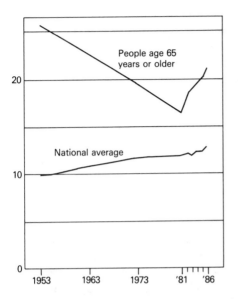

FIGURE 4–4 Suicides per 100,000 people age 65 and over and national average: United States, 1986

Source: Based on data from the National Center for Health Statistics.

Common Emotional Problems

In addition to full-blown mental disorders like the affective and organic mental disorders, the elderly, like everyone, experience day-to-day problems that have an impact upon their psychological well-being. Robert Butler (1985) points out that a sense of loss is particularly common for older people. He explains that losses in every aspect of late life can cause older persons to expend enormous amounts of emotional and physical energy in grieving and resolving grief. The aged frequently are confronted with multiple and simultaneous losses, such as the death of a spouse and friends, decline of physical health, and change in status and prestige. Other problems may be marital, such as divorce, or sexual, or there may be difficulty in dealing with retirement. And for some persons, Butler adds, there may be considerable stress over one's dying and inevitable death. Consequently, elderly persons appear to face some emotional problems that are clearly associated with old age.

Dementia (Alzheimer's Disease)

Another particular mental problem that is associated with aging is the onset of senility or dementia. Dementia is a major form of organic mental disorders, one example of which is Alzheimer's disease. According to the

Diagnostic and Statistical Manual of Mental Disorders, Third Edition (DSM-III), published by the American Psychiatric Association in 1980 and revised in 1987, dementia is the deterioration of previously acquired intellectual abilities to the extent that usual social behavior is severely affected. This disorder causes the brain cells to atrophy. The most prominent symptom is loss of memory, although there may be an impairment in judgment and control of impulses. Another symptom may be personality change in which an individual begins to act in ways markedly different from his or her typical behavior. The person may become unusually compulsive, cantankerous, uncooperative, paranoid, or perhaps withdrawn from others. For primary degenerative dementia of the Alzheimer's type, the age of senile onset is the late sixties or seventies, and for the presenile onset, before age 65. The latter condition is rare, but if it occurs, the average age is 58. These disorders appear more frequently in women than men.

Primary degenerative dementia is estimated to occur in about 4–5 percent of the United States population over age 65, with estimates that another 5–10 percent may be mildly or moderately impaired. The rate rises steeply with age. Among those over age 85—the fastest growing segment of the population—15 percent or more are severely afflicted. A less common form of dementia is multi-infarct dementia, which is brought on by a stroke. What makes dementia especially feared by the aged is that the disease involves a distinct loss of self and there is no medical cure at present (only 15 percent of dementia patients have treatable conditions). Thus, the majority of victims suffer a significant loss of their mental life. As one patient suffering from dementia of the Alzheimer type explained:

> Alzheimer's disease is worse than death. It leaves bone and flesh intact while it erases judgment and memory. I could live with death. Death is a part of the cycle of life. It's like spring, the end of winter. But this disease—it's unnatural. It's the end of hope.[2]

Although dementia is a particularly dreadful affliction of old age, it is not a normal feature of the aging process. The majority of aged individuals do not experience the disorder. The notion that if a person lives long enough he or she will become senile is clearly a myth (Butler 1985). Only a small percentage (4–5 percent), as noted, of all elderly become victims of Alzheimer's disease, and for those that do, the goal of treatment is to preserve whatever ability they have to function.

In summary, it should be kept in mind that most older people (about 85 percent) do not suffer from any mental disorder and lead lives that are not constrained by such afflictions. The vast majority of older persons also live in the community, not in institutions, so that they are able to pursue the social

2. Donna Cohen and Carl Eisdorfer, *The Loss of Self* (New York: W. W. Norton, 1986), 60.

activities common to their age-group. Old age, for most, means a time of memories and reflection, as one's mental abilities recall experiences and, it is hoped, satisfactions from the past; it means a time to look forward to enjoying the years that are left in a mentally and physically healthy condition. Although future trends in longevity point toward greater numbers of mentally disordered elderly, they also point toward significantly greater numbers of mentally healthy aged.

HEALTH POLICY AND THE AGED

Health policy for the elderly is growing in importance as the number of the aged increases, the prevalence of chronic health problems in old age persists, and the costs of providing health care continue to rise (Estes and Lee 1986). Prior to 1965, a financial barrier to health care existed on a nationwide basis for the aged. Unless they could pay for medical care themselves or had adequate private health insurance, older people, especially the poor, had to rely on welfare policies of the various state governments and the charity of institutions and individual physicians.

However, in 1965, despite strong opposition from the American Medical Association, Congress passed legislation authorizing federally funded public health insurance for the elderly known as Medicare. Opposition from the medical profession to this program had been based on the desire to (1) minimize the federal government's role in health care delivery and prevent the enactment of regulations reducing the prerogatives of physicians; (2) curtail any possible threat to the fee-for-service system in which physicians set the fees and patients or their insurance companies pay them; and (3) offset the possibility that a public health insurance program for the aged might be turned into a national health insurance scheme for the entire nation, thereby significantly reducing the autonomy and perhaps income of physicians. The elderly, on the other hand, had been almost priced out of the private health insurance market because they were hospitalized more often than the rest of the population and had to pay high premiums on reduced incomes. Clearly there was a need for protection of the aged against the high costs of health care, especially hospitalization.

As it turned out, Medicare, along with its companion program for the poor (Medicaid), did not place physicians under the supervision of the federal government or change the structure of health care delivery services. In fact, Medicare became a financial boom to organized medicine and to hospitals as billions of dollars have been channeled into health care over the years. Moreover, Medicare has made two significant contributions to health care delivery in the United States. First, although it may not have met all the needs of the elderly for health care, it has provided needed services for many of the aged where these services were not previously available. Overall, the financial barrier to health care has been significantly reduced for older people, and the benefits have improved the quality of life and longevity of many elderly Americans. Second, Medicare has helped establish the precedent of the federal government's involvement in the administration of health care. Such involvement is now an important and substantial reality, and whatever happens in the future organization and scope of health services in the United States is now dependent on federal government decisions.

Currently, Medicare provides hospital insurance (part A) and supplemental medical insurance (part B) for people 65 years of age or older, regardless of financial resources; disabled persons under age 65 who receive cash benefits from Social Security or railroad retirement programs; and certain victims of chronic kidney disease. Hospital insurance benefits in 1990 include (1) inpatient hospital services for up to 90 days for an episode of an illness, plus a lifetime reserve of 60 additional days of hospital care after the initial 90 days have been used; (2) care in a nursing home for up to 100 days, after hospitalization; and (3) up to 100 home health visits after hospitalization.

Supplementary Medicare insurance benefits include (1) physicians' and surgeons' services, certain nonroutine services of podiatrists, limited services of chiropractors, and the services of independently practicing physical therapists; (2) certain medical and health services, such as diagnostic services, diagnostic X-ray tests, laboratory tests, and other services, including ambulance services, some medical supplies, appliances, and equipment; (3) outpatient hospital services; (4) home health services (with no requirement of prior hospitalization) for up to 100 visits in one calendar year; and (5) outpatient physical and speech therapy services provided by approved therapists.

There are specified deductible and coinsurance amounts for which the beneficiary is responsible. The deductible in 1990 on the hospital insurance (part A) was $592 and on the medical insurance (part B) was $75, with a 20 percent coinsurance amount also required for most part B services. The hospital insurance was financed primarily through Social Security payroll deductions, whereas the medical insurance plan, whose participation is voluntary, was financed by premiums paid by the enrollees and from federal funds. The medical insurance premium in 1990 was $28.60 a month.

In 1988, Congress passed the Medicare Catastrophic Coverage Act, which significantly expanded Medicare benefits to the nation's elderly. The major changes authorized by this legislation were 365 days a year of hospitalization, an annual ceiling on hospital ($560) and doctor ($1,370) bills, payment of 50 percent (increasing to 80 percent) of prescription drugs, and 150 days of nursing home care per year without requiring previous hospitalization. Although these new benefits undoubtedly helped many elderly persons, the legislation was repealed in 1989 because of (1) widespread protests by older people, especially the more affluent aged, who resented having to pay a surcharge of $22.50 per every $150 paid in federal income tax (up to a maximum surcharge of $800 per person or $1,600 per couple) and (2) a failure to provide protection from bankruptcy for long-term nursing home care. A $4 monthly deduction from Social Security checks to help pay for the new program also ended with the repeal. As this book goes to press, action in Congress for a new Medicare benefit package has not taken place, although there has been considerable discussion, and the probabilities are high that some new changes (expansions) in benefits will take place.

One new measure that was subsequently approved in Congress, however, is the passage in late 1989 of the Physician Payment Reform Act. This legislation, scheduled to begin in 1992, will change the way in which medical doctors will be paid. The law stipulates the amounts to be paid for physician services, with increases over current allowances being given to physicians in family practice (38 percent) and in internal medicine (17 percent), whereas doctors in specialties like ophthalmology, radiology, pathology, general surgery, and others will be paid lower percentages than in the past. Ten percent bonuses will be paid to doctors who practice in rural and inner-city areas. The law also limits how much a physician can charge a Medicare patient above the scheduled amount. This measure is intended not only to reduce costs, but to provide greater emphasis on primary and preventive care by increasing the amounts paid to doctors working in those areas.

The Medicare program is under the overall direction of the Secretary of Health and Human Services and is supervised by the Bureau of Health Insurance of the Social Security Administration. Most of the day-to-day operations of Medicare are performed by commercial insurance companies and Blue Cross/Blue Shield plans that review claims and make payments. Requests for payment are usually submitted by the provider of services and signed by the beneficiary; reimbursement is made on the basis of reasonable charges as determined by the private insurance companies who issue the payments. In 1987, a total of $81.6 billion in Medicare benefits were paid under coverage that extends to about 31 million elderly and 3 million disabled people.

A continuing controversy about Medicare is how to pay for it. In 1967, the federal government spent $4.5 billion on Medicare; by 1980, the cost reached $35.7 billion and went over $81 billion in 1987. Congress has favored Medicare beneficiaries themselves paying for extra costs in the form of monthly deductions from Social Security checks and an annual surcharge based on income. Many of the elderly, in turn, feel that the cost of the additional benefits should be absorbed by the general population.

One far-reaching, cost-cutting measure passed by Congress in 1983 was the establishment of Diagnostic Related Groups (DRGs), which is a fixed schedule of fees for care rendered to Medicare patients by hospitals. Hospitals make money if they keep costs below what Medicare pays, and they can lose money if their costs exceed the rate. This situation requires hospitals to be both cost conscious and more efficient when it comes to treating patients covered by Medicare.

Besides the rising cost of the Medicare program, there is a gap in coverage for long-term treatment in nursing homes or in the home of the patient. Only some 29 percent of elderly requiring long-term care lived in institutions in 1988. The remainder lived at home and were assisted by family members and other informal sources, such as neighbors or friends, who provide the majority of care for the noninstitutionalized. In-home care for the aged from formal health care providers tends to be used primarily by those elderly who are better educated, have financial resources, and have the worse mental or physical health (McAuley and Arling 1984). In 1988, Medicare paid less than 2 percent of its budget for nursing home care. Nursing homes, in turn, received less than 5 percent of their overall income from Medicare. Therefore, Medicare provides little support for nursing home residents (about 50 percent of all costs for nursing home care is paid by the resident or his or her family). Some elderly persons receive public insurance benefits for nursing home care under Medicaid, the Federal government's health insurance program for the poor administered by the various states, but in order to qualify for this coverage a person's financial assets must be low. After exempting the value of one's house, automobile, and personal property, the person's assets usually cannot exceed $2,000. For elderly people with savings who are facing long-term care in a nursing home, this means they must eliminate nearly all of their savings before they can qualify for Medicaid. Once on Medicaid, all income except a small personal allowance must go to nursing home costs with Medicaid paying the remainder. Financing the costs of long-term care in institutions for the elderly is clearly going to be a major policy issue in the United States in coming years.

On balance, however, when it comes to provision of hospital and medical care on a national basis for the aged, Medicare, despite its problems, has been a success. Many elderly people have been able to overcome the financial barrier for health care that blocked both their access and ability to pay in the past. Future legislation is likely to expand benefits and address the problem of long-term care in either in-home or institutional settings.

SUMMARY

This chapter has focused on the health of the elderly in the United States and has found that the general level of health is good. Elderly people tend to rate their health very positively, especially when they compare themselves to their peers, because they have survived to old age and are able to function in their environment. Of course, elderly people are usually not in as good a physical condition as younger adults, and the health of some aged persons is poor. But overall, a majority of older people have been able to maintain a good state of health.

Older people are hospitalized more often than any other age-group in American society. However, a majority (95 percent) live outside of institutions like nursing and old-age homes, and most (67 percent) not only rate their health as good or better than average, but have not been confined to a bed for a single day in the past year (62 percent) or had any limitations on their activities (60 percent). A majority likewise claim that they do a good job in taking care of their health.

Health problems, nonetheless, exist because health seriously declines for all older people at some point. Heart disease is the most significant life-threatening illness for the aged with respect to physical health, and depression is the most common mental health problem. Some particular difficulties experienced by the aged are caused by stress associated with loss of a spouse or close friends through death. Of all the elderly, black Americans tend to have the poorest health, whereas Asian Americans, on balance, have the best. Compared with older non-Hispanic whites, the health of elderly blacks, Hispanics, and American Indians is clearly worse.

The principal policy measure for enhancing the health of the aged is the federally funded health insurance program Medicare. Medicare is expensive and surrounded by controversy with respect to increasing costs, and gaps do exist in the program—such as relatively few benefits for long-term care like that given in nursing homes. But in general, Medicare has been a success and has played a key role in improving the health of the aged in America.

The Aged Self

The focus of this chapter is on the perception of aging and its effects upon the self-concept of the older person. How do aged persons view themselves? Are they different because they are old? Or are they essentially the same person they always were—just older? This chapter will explore this aspect of the aging process by initially reviewing the literature in sociology on the concept of self and then extending the discussion to account for the self-images of the elderly in contemporary society.

THE SELF

The self is the image that the individual has of his or her self "as a physical, social, and spiritual or moral being" (Gecas 1982:3). The best-developed analysis of the concept of self in sociology is found in symbolic interaction theory, which is explicitly focused on the study of micro-level social relationships. The contributions of George Herbert Mead, Charles Horton Cooley, and Erving Goffman provide the foundation for this approach and are reviewed in this section. A discussion of the self-concept in old age follows.

Mead

Symbolic interaction theory, as introduced in Chapter 3, has its origin in the work of George Herbert Mead (1863–1931) in social psychology at the University of Chicago in the early twentieth century. Mead advocates, in *Mind, Self, and Society* (1934), that the concept of "self" refers to an individual's awareness of being a distinct entity in society. In other words, the self is the awareness that one is a particular individual, distinct and different from other people, but nonetheless part of the same society. Mead explains, however, that a sense of self is not present at birth; rather, it arises in the process of social experience as people relate to other individuals and the wider society. In this way individuals gain an understanding of themselves and their place as particular persons in the larger social order.

A child is born into a family of significant others who are significant because they provide that child with a specific social identity. This identity includes not only a name and an appraisal of physical and intellectual characteristics, but also knowledge concerning the social history of a particular family and group, with all that that means in terms of social status, worldview, and cultural background. People become social objects to themselves as they experience how they are viewed by other people and the social group, community, or society as a whole to which they belong. Thus, individuals gain a sense of who they are through interacting with other people and experiencing the manner in which others respond to them socially and they, in turn, respond to others. They may not necessarily be passive in this exchange when it comes to asserting their sense of who they are, but definitions by others are a central component in formulating one's own concept of self.

Yet Mead points out that in order for the self to develop in its fullest sense, it is necessary not only to take on the attitudes of other individuals directed toward the self as a social object, but also to acquire the attitudes of the group and society in which the person holds membership. To accomplish this, the individual has to learn to take the role of others; that is, to develop the capability to comprehend a situation from the standpoint of other people.

Mead illustrates the process by which this happens in his discussion of play, the game, and the generalized other. When children play at being mothers, fathers, astronauts, and the like, they are in essence acting out what they perceive to be the roles of those kinds of people. Thus, through play they learn that certain roles represent specific types of behavior. When children become older, they begin to play in organized games that have formal rules that apply to everyone. In order to play a game correctly, the child must understand his or her role in relation to the roles of the other players. When playing baseball, for example, a player must know how the other players are supposed to play their positions if he or she is going to play according to the rules and be part of the team. When members of a team come to know and understand each other's role, they can anticipate each other's play and capitalize upon this familiarity with one another's role to react collectively to situations that develop during the game.

Insofar as the child is able to understand the role of others and allow the actions and attitudes of these others to influence his or her role with reference to common goals, the child is well on the way to developing a distinct sense of self and becoming a socialized member of society. Realization about the existence of specific roles and attitudes is followed by recognition of the existence of roles and attitudes whose application is widespread. Peter Berger and Thomas Luckmann describe this development as follows:

> Primary socialization creates in the child's consciousness a progressive abstraction from the roles and attitudes of specific others to roles and attitudes in *general*. For example, in the internalization of norms there is a progression from "Mummy is angry with me *now*" to "Mummy is angry with me *whenever* I spill soup." As additional significant others (father, grandmother, older sister, and so on) support the mother's negative attitude toward soup-spilling, the generality of the norm is subjectively extended. The decisive step comes when the child recognizes that *everybody* is against soup-spilling, and the norm is generalized to "*One* does not spill soup"—"one" being himself as part of a generality that includes, in principle, *all* of society insofar as it is significant to the child.[1]

At this point, the child can identify not only with significant others (specific people), but also with a generalized other (defined as the attitudes of a society, community, or group as a whole). The generalized other is not a person at all; rather, it is a conscious awareness of the society that exists outside of the individual. Mead states that it is in the form of the generalized other that a group or society influences behavior by entering as a determining factor into the individual's thinking. Thus, Mead claims that the self reaches its fullest development by becoming a reflection of the general social system or group to which the person belongs.

Mead makes a further distinction about the self by describing what he surmises are the self's two basic components: (1) the "I" (the unsocialized self) and (2) the "me" (the socialized self). The "me" is that part of the self that is conscious of the norms, values, and traditions of society; it governs the "I" in such a manner that the self reflects the influence of the generalized other. At times, however, the "I," which is that part of the self that is selfish, impulsive, and oriented toward self-fulfillment, takes over and directs behavior toward purely individual ends. Consequently, the self may embrace behavior that conforms to social expectations and collective interests, or it may pursue its own self-interest even if it is at the expense of the group. Neverthe-

1. Peter L. Berger and Thomas Luckmann, *The Social Construction of Reality* (New York: Anchor, 1967), 132–133.

less, as Herbert Blumer (1969) explains, in asserting that the human being has a self, Mead is pointing out that people are able to perceive of themselves as social objects, to communicate with themselves, and to act toward themselves and others on the basis of their own self-direction.

Cooley

Charles Horton Cooley (1864–1929), Mead's contemporary at the University of Michigan, further illustrates the development of the self with his theory of the "looking-glass self." Cooley (1964) likewise maintained that our self-concepts are the result of social interaction in which we see ourselves reflected in the meanings and evaluations that other people attach to us as social objects. Cooley compares the reflection of our self that we see in others to a reflection in a mirror, or looking glass:

Each to each a looking glass
Reflects the other that doth pass.

What Cooley is describing is a form of self-consciousness in which the individual becomes aware of his or her self in relation to others by imagining what he or she looks like to others (Lindesmith, Strauss, and Denzin 1988). Cooley's looking-glass self-concept has three basic components: (1) we see ourselves in our imagination as we think we appear to the other person; (2) we see in our imagination the other person's judgment of our appearance; and (3) as a result of what we see in our imagination about how we are viewed by the other person, we experience some sort of self-feeling, such as pride, satisfaction, or humiliation. Consequently, an individual's perception of self as a social being is strongly related to the reactions of other people. The second element in the theory of the looking-glass self—the imagined judgment by others—is, in Cooley's view, quite essential to the formulation of an individual's concept of self. The way we *think* we appear to others is a major basis for our self-image.

Goffman

Erving Goffman (1922–1982), who was on the faculty of the University of California at Berkeley and the University of Pennsylvania, is noted for the dramaturgical, or "life as theater," approach in sociology. The symbolic interactionist orientation is obvious in Goffman's (1959, 1967) belief that in order for social interaction to be viable, people need information about other people in social situations. Such information is communicated through (1) a person's appearance, (2) a person's experience with other similar individuals, (3) the social setting, and (4) most important, the information a person communicates about himself or herself through words, gestures, and actions. This fourth category of information is decisive because it is subject to control by the individual and represents the impression the person is trying to project—the impression others may come to accept. This information is significant because it helps to define a situation by enabling others to know in advance what a person expects of them and what they may expect of him or her. Goffman calls this process "impression management."

Goffman says people live in worlds of social encounters in which they act out a line of behavior, a pattern of verbal and nonverbal acts by which individuals express their view of a situation and their evaluation of the participants, particularly themselves. The positive social value individuals claim for themselves by the line that others assume they have taken during a particular encounter is termed a "face." This face is an image of self projected to other people who may share that face. One's face is one's most personal possession and is the center of security and pleasure, but Goffman is quick to point out that a person's face is only on loan to him or her from society and can be withdrawn if the person conducts himself or herself in a manner others deem as being unworthy. A person may be in the "wrong face" when information about that person's social worth cannot be integrated into his or her line of behavior, or a person may be "out of face" when he or she participates in an encounter without the line of behavior of the type that participants in that particular situation would be expected to take.

Goffman further explains that the maintenance of face is a condition of interaction, not its objective. This is so because one's face is a constant factor taken for granted in interaction. When people engage in "face-work," they are taking action to make their activities consistent with the face they are projecting. This is important because every member of a social group is expected to have some knowledge of face-work and some experience in its use, such as the exercise of social skills like tact. Goffman sees almost all acts involving other people as being influenced by considerations of face; for example, a person is given a chance to quit a job rather than be fired. A person must be aware of the interpretations that others have placed upon his or her behavior and the interpretations that he or she should place upon their behavior. Therefore, Goffman's view of the self is that it has two distinct roles in social interactions: first, the self as an image of a person formed from the flow of events in an encounter; and second, the self as a kind of player in a ritual game who copes judgmentally with a situation.

Goffman claims that the self is a sacred object. This is because the self represents *who* we are. For someone to challenge the integrity of that self as a social object is an embarrassing situation. Each self is special; it is always with us; and in social relationships, that very special self we have tried to nourish and protect for a lifetime is put on display. Goffman has said that role-specific behavior is based not upon the functional requirements of a particular role, but upon the *appearance* of having discharged a role's requirements. Thus, stress could be induced when people perceive their chosen face or performance in a given situation to be inconsistent with the concept of self they try to maintain for themselves and others in that situation. Otherwise, people might not be so willing to take such great care that they act out lines of behavior considered appropriate to their situation.

What the work of Goffman, Cooley, and Mead signifies for our understanding of the concept of self is that people have an image in their mind about who they are in relation to other people in terms of their appearance, social standing, role relationships, personal qualities, and other attributes. They acquire this sense of self through interaction with others in which they display their self-image and test its validity. Their self-concept thus becomes the basis upon which they see themselves and present themselves to others. In a very real sense, people are social objects interacting with other people in social situations in which their behavior is guided by their sense of self. Self-concepts are extremely important to each person; they influence a person's course of action and are important in understanding and predicting behavior. We will now discuss what aging does to one's self-concept.

AWARENESS OF AGING

In analyzing how older age impacts upon the self-concept of adults, a brief review of the manner in which old age begins to present itself to the individual is in order. As Lynn White (1988) explains, although growing older may have positive and pleasurable aspects, it is unarguable that aging is associated with declines in physical condition and appearance. Old age is also associated with a loss of more youthful social roles. This situation will be reviewed in this section.

Physical Losses and Denial

People who are aging typically experience reduced energy, weight gain, higher fat-to-body-weight ratios, thinner hair, increasingly loose skin, and worsening teeth, hearing, and vision (Barash 1983; Kligman, Grove, and Balin 1985; Verbrugge 1982; White 1988). And, as White (1988) and others (Korthase and Trenholme 1982) point out, such changes are generally regarded as reductions in attractiveness. "The evidence," states White (1988:488), "seems to make it clear that aging is associated not simply with changes but with *declines* in performance and attractiveness." Aging is most apparent in one's appearance. The skin becomes dryer, wrinkles, and begins to sag; hair thins or falls out; and excess weight, beginning especially in middle age, may appear. All of these conditions go against prevailing standards of attractiveness in Western society, where pleasing, youthful looks and a physically fit body are the norm for beauty, and beauty, in turn, is a form of status.

Murray Webster and James Driskell (1983), for instance, found in their research that not only is it considered better to be beautiful than ugly, but people who possess a high state of attractiveness are considered more competent as well. Even though no direct relationship between doing things well and beauty may exist, more attractive people were simply *assumed* by the Webster and Driskell sample of college students to have more ability. In other words, because they looked good, they were thought to be able to cope better in most situations. Because normative standards of beauty may be equated with status, failure to measure up promotes lower status, although clothing, cosmetics, hairstyle, and a strong or interesting personality can help otherwise plain people become attractive. But when it comes to beauty per se, old people are able to sense that they are at a distinct disadvantage. As Malcolm Cowley (1980:7), in his book on what it is like to be 80 years old, comments, sometimes when old people look at themselves in the mirror, they ask themselves: Is this really me?

Declines in sensory acuity like hearing and vision, although perhaps not always as obvious as the loss of physical attractiveness, nevertheless may influence an older person's sense of self. Hearing changes in old age include a decreased ability to hear higher frequency sounds and pitches, discriminate between sounds, and determine from where sound emanates. There may also be a decreased sensitivity to touch, smell, and taste. Older people, for example, may have difficulty detecting sweet and salty tastes because of decreased numbers of taste buds; hence, they may use large amounts of sugar or salt to compensate for the loss. Visual changes include a decrease in pupil size (which decreases the amount of light entering the eye), reduced night vision, decreased sensitivity to subtle changes in colors (especially in greens and blues), increased sensitivity to glare, and a decrease in the ability to discriminate fine visual detail, perceive depth, and have good peripheral vision. Cowley describes the effects on an 80-year-old person as follows:

> We don't have to read books in order to learn that one's eighties are a time of gradually narrowing horizons. Partly the narrowing is literal and physical, being due to a loss of peripheral vision: "Incipient cataracts," the oculist says. Trees on a not-so-distant hillside are no longer oaks or maples, but merely a blur. It is harder to distinguish faces in a crowd—and voices, too, especially if several persons are speaking at once. Would you like to see or hear by drawing closer? Your steps are less assured, your sense of balance is faulty; soon you hesitate to venture beyond your own street or your home acres. Travel becomes more difficult and you think twice about taking out the car.[2]

Other changes in old age involve the central nervous system. These include a slowing of psychomotor responses, reaction times, and performance of complex tasks. Short-term and recent memory loss takes place in some older people; learning performance also tends to decline with age,

2. Malcolm Cowley, *The View From 80* (New York: Viking Press, 1980), 54.

although the decline is not significant until after age 70. As for intelligence, the elderly tend to do less well on one-time intelligence tests that put a premium on speed of response, but perform well when tested several times over a long period. However, to date it remains unclear as to the exact effects of aging on intelligence. It cannot be demonstrated that people generally become less intelligent just because they get old, but some older people do show a decline in mental functioning, particularly at the oldest ages. For the elderly in general, however, education appears more important than age in explaining individual differences in overall intellectual ability.

Another important area of change involves sexuality. Older men take longer to become sexually aroused and ejaculate; the latency period between intercourse takes longer, perhaps several days; and erections may be less firm. Older women, in turn, experience less vaginal lubrication and a reduction in breast and vaginal engorgement and nipple erection during sexual stimulation. However, the elderly do not lose the ability to have sexual intercourse. The best single predictor of an ongoing sex life when old is the pattern of one's sex life when young (Barash 1983). As Helen Singer Kaplan (1974) explains, elderly men remain potentially responsive to sexual stimulation, especially if active sexuality has been maintained over the years. Kaplan further points out:

> As far as the purely sexual functions are concerned, some men compensate for their age-related decline in sexuality by seeking out and creating intensely stimulating erotic situations, fantasies and partners. They may avail themselves of sexual techniques that rely heavily on intense physical stimulation of genitals and of erogenous areas. Other men, by contrast, cease having sexual intercourse in their fifties and sixties. This abstinence is, of course, not purely a function of the physical effects of age, but rather a psychological avoidance of the painful feelings of frustration, anxiety, or depression that may be elicited by confrontation with their declining performance. Impotence is a frequent complaint in this age group.[3]

As for older women, Kaplan indicates that following a peak period of sexual responsiveness in their late thirties and early forties, women move into the menopausal years of the fifties. At this point there is an abrupt cessation of ovarian functioning and drastic decline in the secretion of estrogen and progesterone. In some women, these endocrine changes produce irritability, depression, and emotional instability. Other women are not materially affected by menopause. Sexual responsiveness at this time, as in the earlier ages in women, varies among individuals. After menopause, Kaplan summarizes female sexuality for women in their sixties as follows:

> A woman who has regular sexual opportunity tends to maintain her sexual responsiveness; without such opportunity, sexuality declines markedly. Apart

---

3. Helen Singer Kaplan, *The New Sex Therapy* (New York: Quadrangle, 1974), 109.

from the effect of opportunity, a slow gradual physical decline in sexual drive seems to occur in women as in men. After 65, a women tends to be less preoccupied with sex than she was at 40, but still may seek out and certainly can respond to sexual opportunities.[4]

Thus, people can maintain and enjoy an active sex life in old age. Old age, nonetheless, means a change—a decline—in sexual responsiveness at some point for both men and women. Moreover, as David Barash (1983) points out, regardless of how the elderly feel about sex, the young seem to be uncomfortable about sexuality in the elderly. Sexually active aged men may be depicted as lewd and reprehensible ("a dirty old man") by younger adults, and sexuality in old women is traditionally regarded, according to Barash's analysis, as laughable. Negative stereotypes such as these, combined with evidence of a declining capacity for sex, might well contribute to a devaluation of self in a youth- and sex-oriented culture.

White (1988) studied awareness of physical aging among men and women ages 20–60 in a national sample of over 1,500 persons. These persons were initially interviewed in 1980 and were then asked in 1983 whether in the last three years either they or their spouse had experienced a change for the worse in eyesight, hearing, teeth, energy, hair, and skin. White found, as expected, that the perception of physical aging increases with age. However, women were generally not more sensitive than men to signs of physical aging. Rather, there were more similarities than differences in the ways that men and women perceived themselves as becoming old. This finding led White to conclude that both sexes become aware of aging in much the same way and to reject the notion that women are more sensitive toward aging than men.

White also found that people tend to maintain relatively youthful images of themselves for as long as they can; that is, they tend to deny the physical evidence of aging for as long as possible. White's (1988:500) findings supported earlier research by Zena Blau (1956) "that awareness of aging is a change in self-concept that is avoided as long as positive responses from our social environment make such avoidance possible." Although White's sample did not include persons over the age of 65, her findings regarding the tendency to deny signs of aging in one's appearance are consistent with the results of other studies that included samples of the elderly. This research depicts older Americans' tending to reject the idea for as long as possible that they are old (Rosow 1974; Drevenstedt 1976; Bultena and Powers 1978).

For example, Gordon Bultena and Edward Powers (1978) studied 611 people in Iowa in 1960 and returned in 1970 to restudy 235 of the original respondents. Most of the remainder had either died or moved away. The median age of people in the restudy group was 76, and more than one-fourth were over age 80. Bultena and Powers found that a majority rejected the idea

4. Ibid., 112.

that they were old. Instead, many defined themselves as middle-aged; a few said they were simply elderly. Irving Rosow (1974) likewise found that older people often refuse to acknowledge that they are old; the older they are, the later they claimed that "old age" begins. Or, as one senior citizen put it: "To me old age is always fifteen years older than I am" (Rosow 1974:11).

In sum, old age is a time of physical decline and loss of youthful body. Resistance to the idea of a less attractive physical self appears to underline, as suggested by White (1988), tendencies among the elderly to deny old age for as long as possible. Signs of physical aging present a clear threat to the self-image of many of the elderly.

Social Losses

Rosow (1974) explains that old age is also the only stage of life that has systematic social losses rather than gains. When one is elderly, the major tasks in life, such as having a career and starting a family, are finished. Thus, an older person's responsibilities decline, whereas dependency on others because of reduced income or physical and mental infirmities may increase. Roles for the elderly include those of being (1) retired, (2) widowed, (3) an aged dependent, or (4) chronically ill. As Harold Cox (1988) reminds us, these roles are not highly valued, nor do they bring high status. Moreover, there is not a specific role meant for the elderly in developed countries that confers enhanced status in the wider society as a result of age alone. Also, in American society people are not typically socialized to experience decline. Thus, Rosow argues that the elderly are not prepared by society for the inevitable social losses that old age brings, nor are they taught how to lead a dignified life within the limitations of advanced age. "With no incentives or compelling pressures from the culture to embrace their age," states Rosow (1974:148), "and no meaningful norms by which to live, they simply are not socialized to an aged role."

However, Robert Atchley (1988) observes that Rosow's argument about society not socializing the elderly for participation in a particular role of "old person" is not an entirely accurate description of role relationships among the aged. Atchley points out that elderly persons usually have few required contacts with the general community. Instead, they associate on a daily basis primarily with people they know and who know them. Typically, they continue to function in their usual roles in the family and in their networks of friends; they are just older. Therefore, Atchley (1988:119) makes the important point that "most roles older people play are roles they have been socialized to for a long time."

Furthermore, the role of retirement for the elderly may be enjoyable and provide greater freedom to pursue one's personal interests. In fact, the elderly have greater freedom of choice and a wider range of choices about how to spend their time than any other age-group in American society

(MacNeil and Teague 1987). Therefore, although the aged may not generally fill roles of great power and influence because of their age, old age does have its compensations, and the effect of role loss in the wider community can mean a greater preoccupation with one's self and private activities.

SOCIETY'S VIEW OF THE AGED

Many past studies, as will be discussed, suggest that society's general view of the aged, at least in the Western world, tends to be negative. According to Rosow (1974), the position of the elderly has several consequences; namely, that they are devalued, are negatively stereotyped, are excluded from social opportunities, lose roles, confront severe ambiguity in later life because they have no specific role, and struggle to preserve self-esteem through youthful self-images. The crux of the problem, indicates Rosow, is not that the elderly do not have role models, but that such models are primarily youthful. Rosow explains:

> The elderly judge themselves according to standards of youthfulness. This implies norms of minimal change, or preserving roles, activity, health, energy, beauty, vitality, and élan. The best life is presumably that which changes least from middle age. This minimal change increases their chances of retaining social position, participation, prestige, and other advantages of middle age.[5]

Because the aged generally do not perform vitally important functions for a society that emphasizes youth, aged persons typically reach the point in their lives where their importance wanes. As Rosow points out, the most youthful and well-preserved aged are the most admired among the general public. When older people look less well-preserved, their social worth is likely to decline. "Older people's youthful self-conceptions," states Rosow (1974:147), "contrast sharply with younger persons' treatment of them." That is, the elderly may regard themselves as middle-aged, but younger persons may see them as old. Eventually, flattering self-images of youthfulness by older people are challenged. Rosow asks that if the elderly view themselves as middle-aged, whereas others see them as old, what is the social reality of the situation? He answers this by claiming that the standards that govern are those of youth. Therefore, if older people are perceived and treated as elderly by younger people, their social position becomes established.

Cowley (1980) explains that although many older people like to think of themselves as still young, messages from the social environment are louder, in most cases, than from within the person. "We start growing old in other

5. Irving Rosow, *Socialization to Old Age* (Berkeley: University of California Press, 1974), 146.

people's eyes,'' states Cowley (1980:5), "then slowly we come to share their judgment.'' Cowley provides an example of this situation by relating his feelings when he almost had a collision with another automobile and the driver of the other car jumped out and started to yell at him until he got a good look at him. The angry motorist then said, "Why, you're an old man!" and got back in his car and drove away. Then a young woman offered him her seat on a bus. Although the offer was meant to be kind, Cowley found it devastating. Cowley states:

> "Can't I even stand up?" I thought as I thanked her and declined the seat. But the same thing happened twice the following year, and the second time I gratefully accepted the offer, though with a sense of having diminished myself. . . . All the same it was a relief to sit down and relax.[6]

Humor can also be an important indicator of social attitudes, because it often reflects widely held social stereotypes. Erdman Palmore (1971) studied attitudes toward aging as suggested by humor. Some 264 jokes were singled out and analyzed to indicate prevalent societal attitudes. Over half of the jokes reflected a negative view of aging, the most disparaging being those whose principal subject matter was physical ability, appearance, age concealment, mental abilities, and being an "old maid." The majority of jokes about being a male "old-timer" and still having sexual ability were either positive or ambivalent. Jokes dealing with old men generally tended to be much more positive than those dealing with old women; in fact, most of the age-concealment jokes referred to women. This study suggested that (1) the popular culture generally devalues old age, and (2) a double standard may exist in which aging women are viewed more negatively than aging men.

The so-called double standard in aging may be related to sex-role stereotypes in American society that equate female beauty and sexuality with youth. With very few exceptions, aged women are not generally depicted in the popular culture as "beautiful," but aged men can be considered "handsome" or "distinguished." Instances of older men marrying young women, for example, tend to be more common than older women marrying young men.

The groups in society that appear to hold the most negative views of old people are young and middle-aged adults. By contrast, studies involving children find little evidence of devaluation of old age. In a review of children's literature between 1870 and 1960, Mildred Seltzer and Robert Atchley (1971) found little evidence of negativity toward aging. Elizabeth Thomas and Kaoru Yamamoto (1975) found a rather positive attitude toward the aged in a study of children and adolescents. There was general agreement that older people were "good" and "wise," and the qualities of being "pleasant,"

6. Cowley, *The View From 80,* 5–6.

"happy," and "exciting" were seen to decrease with age but were nonetheless present in old age. Only on the qualities of being "active" and having "power" were the elderly rated negatively. Thomas and Yamamoto suggest that rather than developing negative attitudes toward aging in childhood, what apparently happens is that people acquire negative stereotypes of aging as they themselves begin to feel threatened by old age.

The above discussion, however, pertains to conditions in Western society. In Asia, the elderly typically occupy a position of respect and honor largely because of the lingering influence of Confucianism and the tradition of ancestor worship. In the Confucian system of social relations, a clearly defined order of superiority-subordination guided behavior. This system subordinated the young to the old, females to males, and subjects to rulers. Although the Confucian system was overturned in China and North Korea by communism, and in South Korea and Japan through rapid industrialization and capitalism, the cultural traditions it fostered still persist. In China today, the old are not left to live alone but are expected to remain in the family setting and serve in an honored role. To be old is to be accorded greater respect in Chinese society, for age is equated with wisdom (Fairbank 1989). Japan has a national holiday, Respect for the Elders Day, that honors the aged; the sixty-first birthday is also a time to be honored by the family. The young are taught to be respectful to the old, and seats are reserved on buses and trains for aged citizens. In many Asian countries, approximately three-fourths of the elderly population live with their children (Martin 1988). Although the reality of actual living conditions for many of the elderly in Asia may be less than ideal, their social role is equated with much higher status than in the West.

The stereotypes of old age in American society have, in the past, emphasized characteristics like economic insecurity, poor health, loneliness, rigid attitudes, and failing physical and mental powers. Despite the fact that the majority of the elderly have not been poor, lonely, in bad health, senile, or mentally ill (Neugarten 1970, 1971; Atchley 1988), negative stereotypes have tended to persist (Larson 1978; Ward 1979); that is, they have tended to persist until the 1980s. Keeping in mind that the current generation of the elderly in the United States is better educated and more economically affluent than past generations, there are signs that negative stereotypes are beginning to change. Robert Binstock (1983) has found that the stereotypical views of elderly people have changed from the 1970s' characterization of them as poor, frail, politically powerless, and victimized by mandatory retirement and a youth-oriented society. In the 1980s, Binstock observed that a view of the elderly emerged that depicted them as relatively affluent, politically powerful, and receiving more than their fair share of the federal budget.

Binstock's findings point toward a major change in social perceptions of older people. As America passes through the 1990s into the twenty-first century, the image of the aged may well be different from and exceedingly more positive than what most of the past literature suggests. This changing perspective is likely to be influenced by the significantly larger population of elderly persons, their more prominent role in influencing national politics, and their greater economic resources. An adjustment for the better thus appears to be coming in society's view of the aged.

This development is consistent with modernization theory. As discussed in Chapter 3 modernization theory holds that the status of the elderly will improve in mature modern states as these societies come to terms with their aged populations (Cowgill 1986). As noted, this is especially likely to be the case as the aged accumulate political power and economic influence by virtue of their large numbers and proportions in developed societies. Modernization theory is an important perspective on aging in relation to understanding the aged self, because it explains how and why developed societies have formulated negative norms and values concerning old people and their social roles. In societies oriented toward achievement, activity, and productivity, the aged typically do not fill important positions or contribute strongly to mainstream economic activities. Occupying not only a less desirable, but actually devalued, social position regulates the aged to a marginal position in such societies. Consequently, the view of self in old age is operationalized in a less than positive social environment. However, modernization theory suggests that this environment is going to change with a maturing of the process of modernity. This means that the general social context in which elderly people find themselves in the future is likely to be increasingly supportive of positive views of the aged.

The Aged's View of Themselves

A review of the research literature shows that a few older studies (Mason 1954; Rosow 1967) found low feeling of self-worth and well-being among the aged. However, the bulk of the research indicates that the elderly have a generally positive impression of themselves. For example, Caroline Preston (1967) compared the attitudes of retired and nonretired older people and found no significant differences between the two groups in terms of life satisfaction. She suggested that the aged felt more positive about themselves than had been previously assumed. Other research (Riley and Foner 1968) suggests that negative orientations toward the self tend to decrease with age.

Bernice Neugarten (1971), in turn, argued that a major problem with many past studies had been to try to generalize that most old are either unhappy or happy. These generalizations failed to take into account considerable variance among individuals in the manner in which they cope with the aging experience. Neugarten pointed out that the aged in American society are not a homogeneous group. She demonstrated this in a fifteen-year longitudinal study at the University of Chicago on the adaptational patterns of about 2,000 people aged 70–79. Three principal areas of life among the aged were examined: personality, life satisfaction, and extent of social-role activity. As a result of their data, they were able to construct four major types of personalities common to the aged: (1) integrated, (2) defended, (3) passive-dependent, and (4) disintegrated.

The majority of these respondents were classified as having an *integrated* personality, that is, they were characterized as being high in life satisfaction, mature, and open to new experiences, and as having good cognitive abilities and a view of themselves as competent. The integrated personality consisted of three subtypes, each of which was based upon the person's role activity. One subtype, termed the *reorganizers,* included those who engaged in a wide variety of activities, such as business and community affairs. The second subtype was classified as the *focused;* these were people who remained active, but only in a few select roles. The other subtype was the *disengaged,* people with well-integrated personalities who experienced satisfaction with their lives but demonstrated low activity. Members of this latter group had high self-esteem and appeared to be complex, self-directed individuals, yet they had voluntarily withdrawn from role commitments to be content with the "rocking chair" approach to old age.

The second major personality category was the *defended.* These were hard-driving, ambitious, achievement-oriented individuals who were very defensive about aging. The defended personality consisted of two major subtypes. First was the *holding-on* group, which continued to work hard and maintain relatively high levels of activity as a means of obtaining satisfaction from life. Next were those defended personalities described as *constricted.* Constricted individuals combated aging by trying very hard to maintain their health through diet and general activities, while also being oriented toward maintaining youthful physical appearance.

The third major personality was identified as *passive-dependent.* There were two subtypes common to this group. *Succorance-seeking* individuals had strong needs to be dependent and have other people respond to them. They were somewhat active and seemed to adjust to aging in a positive manner so long as they had some other person or persons to depend on for assistance and support. The second subtype, of whom only a small number were found, was the *apathetic.* The primary characteristic of this person was passivity. These people had little interaction with others, engaged in few activities, and seemed to have little interest in what went on around them.

The fourth major personality type was the *disintegrated.* Very few people qualified for this category. The disintegrated personality consisted of people who demonstrated gross psychological disorganization and who were generally able to maintain themselves outside an institution only because of family arrangements or the tolerance of other people in their social network.

Although recognizing that other personality types common to patterns of aging may exist, Neugarten has suggested two important conclusions about aging in American society. First, she pointed out that older people deal with aging in a number of ways. She was impressed by the fact that variation rather than similarity seems to be the rule among the aged, and she suggested that such variation may become even more pronounced in the future. This was so because, at the time of her study, most data on the aged were derived from people who tend to be poor, foreign born, and poorly educated. As Americans who have enjoyed the financial affluence and higher standards of education characteristic of the mid-twentieth century become old, she believed these people would have even greater freedom in selecting their lifestyles. And second, she suggested that people age in accordance with the behavior that is generally typical of lifelong patterns of responses. In other words, people don't change their basic personality just because they grow old.

Two variables, however, that have been found to have a significant impact upon the self-perceptions of older individuals are health and socioeconomic status. Regardless of one's personality, a particularly significant variable affecting an individual's adjustment to old age is his or her level of health. As discussed in the last chapter, one's health in old age is the single most important factor in determining the quality of life that is available. Aged persons in good health are invariably found to have a better quality of life and a more satisfying lifestyle, as well as a more optimistic outlook on life in general, than do those in poor health (Maddox 1962; Palmore 1981; Haug and Folmar 1986).

For example, Preston (1968) studied older people who were about to retire. She found that those who reported more chronic health disorders and more incapacity due to illness showed a greater tendency to think of themselves as being "old" than those who did not report such health problems. In another study, Arthur Schwartz and Robert Kleemeier (1965) examined two groups of elderly people and two groups of young people who were categorized by age and state of health (sick or well). They noted that among those who were sick, illness tended to have a greater effect on the self-perceptions of the aged than the young, but the relationship was due to the combined effects of illness and age, not just to age alone. Palmore (1981), in a series of longitudinal studies carried out at Duke University between 1955 and 1976 among a sample of aged persons living in North Carolina, found that high satisfaction with life contributed, in turn, to better health in that those who felt positive about life had a better mental outlook and were more prone to be physically and socially active.

The second variable that needs to be mentioned is socioeconomic status. As Arlie Russell Hochschild (1973) has observed, the assumption that old age is the great leveler because it affects the rich and poor alike is not necessarily true. It is much better to be old and rich than to be old and poor. The upper social classes tend to have a longer life expectancy than the lower classes. In effect, what Hochschild is saying is that the shorter a person's life expectancy, the poorer that person's health and morale. Therefore, lower-class people may begin to "feel" old at progressively earlier ages than upper-class people. For instance, Caroline Preston and Karen Gudiken (1966) found that indigent older people expressed significantly more negative than positive feelings about themselves when they compared themselves with "others my age." Negative self-reporting among the indigent aged appeared to be a manifestation of depression. George Maddox (1962) also noted that social class position is related to optimism and pessimism about health. Older people of high social status were much more likely than other people to be optimistic about their health. Older people of low social status tended to be pessimistic about their health, even when they were medically assessed to be in good health. In sum, as Palmore (1981) found, persons with higher socioeconomic status have, on the whole, better physical and mental health, higher intelligence, greater happiness, and more social activities in old age.

Besides the effect of poverty on the health status and general outlook of the aged, the aged poor are more likely to be socially isolated. Rosow (1967) found in Cleveland that middle-class older people tended to have more good friends in old age than working-class older people had. Hochschild summarizes this situation as follows:

> Removed from the economy, the old have been cast out of the social networks that revolve around work. Lacking work, they are pushed down the social ladder. Being poor, they have fewer social ties. Poverty reinforces isolation. To eliminate enforced isolation, we have to eliminate poverty, for the two go together.[7]

However, to summarize the literature on the self-image of the aged held by the elderly, the overall situation seems to be that older people feel quite good about themselves. But health and socioeconomic status influence such perceptions, either positively or negatively, depending upon one's level of health or income and lifestyle. On balance, most elderly people seem to define themselves in a positive manner and do so regardless of negative views of the aged prevalent in the wider society.

Personality Change in Old Age

As reported in the preceding section, Neugarten (1971) found that people do not change their basic personality as they age. This is an important finding and speaks directly to the issue of whether or not self-concepts differ in old age. According to continuity theory, discussed earlier in Chapter 3, the personality tends to remain stable over time. Continuity theorists, like Neugarten (1964), point out that if changes in personality do occur, they tend

---

7. Arlie Russell Hochschild, *The Unexpected Community* (Englewood Cliffs, NJ: Prentice-Hall, 1973), 140.

to be minor. That is, there may be some personality change in old age as people adapt to new situations, but the change is not likely to be great or out of character with the individual's past approach to life. As a person grows to maturity and passes on to the stages of later maturity and old age, he or she will have developed a stable set of values, attitudes, norms, and habits that have become an integral part of his or her personality. Therefore, if the personality undergoes change in old age, that change tends to be consistent with past traits and predispositions—unless the individual has never developed a stable personality.

Neugarten (1964) indicates that the *only* internal dimension of the personality that seems to change with age is introversion. That is, older people tend to turn their interests and attention more inward on themselves and less on external factors. This turning inward is not a withdrawal from the external world; rather, it appears to be just a greater emphasis upon an inner life aimed at gaining greater self-understanding and self-acceptance. In old age, perhaps the person focuses more on placing his or her life in personal perspective.

Atchley's (1988) position that there is a large amount of continuity in the central features of one's personality appears correct; that is, one's basic personality is not likely to change greatly in old age from what it was as a younger adult. If a person had a positive self-image when young, he or she is likely to have a positive self-image when old. Other people, in contrast, never develop a positive self-concept, and they are not likely to do so in old age because of more limited opportunities for success. Atchley explains:

> Those global aspects of identity that remain with the individual regardless of the social situation persist despite substantial changes in the details of everyday life. Once formed, the core or global identity tends to be resilient, and the components of identity can apparently contain a multitude of conflicting details without causing the individual to doubt the validity of the global concept.[8]

THE AGED SELF

The sociology literature reviewed at the beginning of this chapter on the concept of self discussed the work of Mead, Cooley, and Goffman. Mead (1934) described how the self is formed as a result of social experience and illustrated the evolution of the self with the example of play, the game, and the generalized other. Mead emphasizes the importance of being able to take the role of others and recognize the existence of external norms, values, and attitudes that function as a generalized other in the person's thinking. Cooley (1964), with his concept of the looking-glass self, like Mead, emphasizes the role of other people in influencing the individual's perception of self. People

8. Robert C. Atchley, *Social Forces and Aging,* 5th ed. (Belmont, CA: Wadsworth, 1988), 104.

tend to incorporate into their self-image the image of themselves that they see reflected in others. This process would suggest that the elderly might tend to have a negative self-concept because of a declining physical condition, the loss of valued roles, or the prevalence of youthful norms.

Yet it should be noted that Mead's focus is on the self that emerges during childhood and adolescence as part of primary socialization. Cooley's insight also has particular relevance to the time in life when one's sense of self is being formed. In old age, the self is mature and rests upon a lifetime of noting the responses of others. At this point, one's self-concept is likely to be entrenched, and feedback from significant others should be less important than when young.

The self that Goffman (1959, 1967) describes, however, is particularly relevant for the old as well as for the young. One of Goffman's central themes is that the self is a sacred object to individuals because it represents who and what we are. Thus, people take particular care to nurture and protect their self-image by employing "face-work" during social interaction and letting conditions of "face" (both theirs and others) guide their behavior. Although this situation promotes the idea that the self is not a possession of the person, but rather is a product of the interaction between the person as an actor and his or her audience, Goffman points out in his essay on role distance (1961) that there is a distinctly personal side to people. It is the personal or sacred aspect of human conduct, states Goffman (1961:152), that "has to do with 'personal' matters and 'personal' relationships—with what an individual is 'really' like underneath it all when he relaxes and breaks through to those in his presence." In the profane and worldly part of one's behavior, Goffman sees the self as a player in a ritual game of social interaction coping judgmentally with situations. People expose themselves to others, and, as Goffman (1967:31) puts it, sometimes "lead themselves into duels" in which they take their shots from other people as they place their self-concept at risk in the game of life.

It would seem that the elderly likewise participate in the game of "life as theater," because aging also usually requires the older individual to defend a positive self-image. As Atchley (1988:111) explains: "Using past successes, discounting messages that do not fit our existing self-concept, refusing to apply general beliefs about aging to ourselves, selectively perceiving what we are told are all ways to defend ourselves against ageism." Atchley's basic point is that most people maintain a sense of themselves that reflects a positive level of esteem, and this level of esteem, based on past life experience, is not likely simply to disappear by virtue of old age alone. People who lose self-esteem in later life, explains Atchley (1988:111), are those (1) whose physical condition has severely deteriorated, (2) who have become too dependent or whose life has become too restricted, or (3) who have lost control over their living situation so that they are essentially defenseless. As shown in numerous studies, most people, states Atchley, have the resources to maintain a positive self-concept in old age. In fact, self-esteem often increases with age.

Two excellent studies that aptly describe the aged self are those of Sharon Kaufman (1987) and Walter Gove, Suzanne Ortega, and Carolyn Briggs Style (1989). In her book *The Ageless Self,* Kaufman reports on the results of her two-year study of some sixty urban, white, middle-class Americans between the ages of 70 and 97 living in California. Although her data may not be representative of all elderly people—namely, the poor and racial minorities—her findings are nonetheless highly suggestive of how the self may generally cope with aging. Kaufman's central theme is that the self is indeed ageless. The old people in her study expressed a personal identity that had maintained continuity over the life span, regardless of the physical and social changes that came with old age. That is, they defined themselves as being essentially the same person they were when younger; they had only gotten older. For example, one woman, age 92, was asked whether she felt differently about herself than when she was younger. The woman replied:

> No, not too differently from the way I felt before. Except that I tire more readily. But the fact is, one isn't a different person, though perhaps some personality traits do become more pronounced.
>
> I always think of myself as younger, though not at any specific age, just at some time in the past. Whenever I'm walking downtown, and see my reflection in a store window, I'm shocked by how old it is. I never think of myself that way.[9]

Responses from other elderly persons reflected the same perspective:

From a man, age 78:

> Psychologically, I don't think I'm any different than I was when I was a young man. I haven't got the fire and ambition that I had in those days, but outside of that, I don't think I'm radically different.[10]

From another man, age 92:

> No. I have the same attitude now, toward life and living, as I did 30 years ago. That's why this idea of not being able to walk along with other people—I'm more slowed down—it hurts my ego. Because inside, that's not really me.[11]

9. Sharon R. Kaufman, *The Ageless Self* (Madison: University of Wisconsin Press, 1987), 9.
10. Ibid., 9.
11. Ibid., 11.

Another man, age 81:

> I can see that there are certain traits in me that have carried through from youth to now. A conservative attitude, a wish to conform to the law, to pressures. And, I've always been cheerful. I still am. I mean I don't wake up with a gloomy or grumpy attitude. And I do like to be busy; I have always been friendly. I still feel that way.[12]

A woman, age 84:

> I feel the same now as I did then, oh yes. The only way I know I'm getting old is to look in the mirror. But I've only *felt* old a few times—when I'm really sick.[13]

Consequently, Kaufman advances the notion that old people maintain a sense of continuity with their past lives that helps them cope with changes that occur with advanced age. They stay the same (in their mind), but their body becomes old. The factors that figured most prominently in influencing the lives of the elderly people in Kaufman's study over the life course included socioeconomic status in childhood (many had originally come from poor families; others began life in relatively affluent circumstances), family ties, level of education, geographic mobility (where they had lived), and work (their occupation or profession). These factors, along with their own personal values and goals, gave them a sense of who they are—regardless of the fact they were now old. Kaufman concluded:

> All research participants made it clear to me that *aging* per se is not a substantive issue in their own lives. They do not, now that they are over 70, conceive of themselves in a context of *aging* and act accordingly. Rather, they deal with specific problems, changes, and disabilities as they arise, just as they have been doing throughout their lives, and they interpret these changes and problems in light of already established themes. It appears that the concept of aging is too abstract, too impersonal to be an integral part of identity. This is not to say that my informants ignore or deny limitations which arise in that process. Nor does it mean that the changes experienced in old age have no psychological effects. But while dealing with the physical and mental manifestations of old age, old people also maintain an ageless sense of self that transcends change by providing continuity and meaning.[14]

Successful adaptation to old age, in Kaufman's view, involves older individuals' connecting meaningful past experiences with current circumstances. Thus, being old does not mean adopting a new self-concept; instead, older people take their sense of self and personality with them to the last stage of life and adapt to the situation as best they can. Kaufman's message is that

12. Ibid.
13. Ibid., 13.
14. Ibid., 161.

the elderly do not perceive meaning in aging itself; rather, they perceive meaning in being themselves in old age.

The Gove, Ortega, and Briggs Style (1989) study consisted of a national survey of nearly 2,250 adults, 18 years of age and older. Gove and his colleagues determined that as people age, their self-concepts are not qualitatively different from those of younger persons, except that they may feel somewhat more positive about themselves, have fewer negative attitudes, and be somewhat better integrated individuals. Moreover, both males and females appear to experience their sense of aging in similar ways. Like the Kaufman study, the general impression of Gove and his associates was that as people age they become increasingly comfortable with themselves and their situation. "There is no evidence," states Gove and colleagues (1989:1138), "that old age is associated with a poor evaluation of one's self and one's life."

A major contribution of Gove and colleagues' research was to reject a role theory of aging. Briefly stated, the role theory of aging maintains that the degree to which people have a meaningful existence over the life course is dependent upon their social roles. Young adulthood is a time of role acquisition; then in late middle age a person moves into a position of role transition, followed in old age by role loss. Because a person's self-esteem is associated with his or her roles, that person's sense of self would be more positive at younger adult ages and then decline with age because of role loss.

However, because Gove and his associates found that one's sense of self did not decline in old age, a role theory of aging did not provide an adequate explanation of the self-concepts of the aged. Instead, Gove and associates suggest that there is an adult psychological maturation process in old age in which the aged person moves from an absorption with self, characteristic of younger and middle-aged people, toward an acceptance of one's being. Gove and associates note that their findings are consistent with Erik Erikson's (1963) concept of the last stage of life known as ego integrity. In the stage of ego integrity, there is an acceptance of one's fate and a sense of continuity with earlier stages of one's life. The person looks inward and attempts to gain a sense of meaning and integrity at the end of life. Cowley, in the conclusion to his book *The View From 80*, captures this feeling very well:

> There are tangible aids to remembering, notably letters, old snapshots, daybooks, and mementos, if we have saved them. Old tunes ring through our heads and some of them bring back pictures; this one was "our" song, Doris said, and you see the look on her face when she hummed the words. What became of Doris after she married somebody else and moved to California? And Mr. Wagner, the boss who used to dance the gazotsky at office parties? Characters crowd in on us, each making a contribution, and gradually our world takes shape. We tell stories about it, perhaps only to ourselves, and then arrange the stories in sequence: this must have been our second act and this was the third. All these efforts, if continued, might lead to an absolutely candid book of memoirs; old persons have nothing to lose by telling the truth. For others it

might lead to nothing more than notebook jottings and advice to the young that might or might not be remembered. No matter: it is a fascinating pursuit in itself, and our efforts will not have been wasted if they help us to possess our own identities as an artist possesses his work. At least we can say to the world of the future, or to ourselves if nobody else will listen, "I really *was*"—or even, with greater self-confidence, "I was and am *this*."[15]

SUMMARY

At the beginning of this chapter the following was asked: How do aged persons view themselves? Are they different because they are old? Or are they essentially the same person they always were—just older? The answer would appear to be that the self is ageless; in other words, the elderly have essentially the same self-concept that they had when younger. Their physical bodies will have changed with age, and perhaps certain adjustments may have been made in their sense of self to accommodate the fact that they have become old; but overall it appears that they remain in their mind the same person they were when younger. In effect, the continuity of their lives from childhood into old age provides them with a full sense of who and what they are.

This chapter began with a review of the concept of self in sociology and social psychology as expressed by Mead, Cooley, and Goffman. Mead explains how the self is formed during childhood as a result of social interaction with significant others and develops through play and games to a realization of the generalized other. The generalized other refers not to a person but to the attitudes, norms, and values of an organized group, community, or society as a whole. Cooley is known for his theory of the looking-glass self, which helps us to understand that individuals see themselves reflected in other people, which plays an important role in the formation of their own self-concept. Goffman, through his notion of face-work, explains the manner in which people nourish, display, and protect their sense of self. Goffman, representing the "life as theater" approach, explains that people put their sense of self at risk as they confront social situations.

The problem that the elderly face in relation to their self-concept is that old age is a time of physical and social decline and perhaps loss. Moreover, younger people and society itself, in the past, have not generally held the aged in high regard. The elderly, in contrast, have tended to have a positive view of themselves, and the evidence generally suggests that personality does not change in old age, nor do old people change their self-concept to something that is radically different from what it was when they were young. In fact, older people, as they come to terms with their life and develop a feeling of continuity with their life experiences, appear to feel somewhat more positive about themselves than do younger people.

15. Cowley, *The View From 80*, 73–74.

From the standpoint of social theory, the symbolic interactionist perspective—as represented by Mead, Cooley, and Goffman—provides a particularly useful approach toward analyzing the self-concept in general, and in old age in particular. Symbolic interaction theory explains the origin of self in childhood in relation to significant others and its development through the life course through social experiences with other people. It allows us to see that when a person reaches old age, he or she has typically constructed a sense of self formulated over time and in response to the views of others and the wider society.

Two other theories focusing more directly on aging—continuity theory and modernization theory—further our understanding of the aged self. Continuity theory explains the manner in which the basic personality of the individual in old age is continued. That is, the elderly person's overall personality is generally consistent with what it was in younger adulthood (Neugarten 1964). Modernization theory, in turn, helps to explain why modern societies have generally devalued the aged, but notes that stereotypes of old people are becoming more positive in advanced stages of modernization (Cowgill 1986). The fact that people tend to maintain a positive self-concept in old age and the trend toward more positive images of old people in the most developed societies suggest that a social environment more supportive of the aged self is evolving.

Ageism, Gender, and Racial Minority Status

Thus far in this book we have reviewed the situation of the aged in American society and found a general improvement over conditions in the mid-twentieth century and earlier. This is not to say that the elderly do not have problems as a group or that life for many older people is not unpleasant. However, we see that, as the twenty-first century approaches, there is an increasingly larger population of people over the age of 65; and, especially in developed countries like the United States, overall living conditions for the aged are improving. The current generation of older people in the United States are more numerous, better educated, and more affluent than in the past, and this trend will continue. Furthermore, the overall health of the aged in the United States is relatively good, and their sense of self is typically not impaired just because they have become old. For that matter, studies cited in the last chapter indicate that there is a tendency in late life to feel even more positive about one's self.

However, the aged in society face some special problems that are caused not by themselves, but by society at large. A particular problem is that of ageism, or prejudice against the aged, in which old people may be discriminated against simply because they have become old. Gender and racial minority status can also produce differences in the aging experience in that older women and minorities have to cope with more negative situations than do aged men and members of the white majority. In this chapter, we will review these issues.

AGEISM

A negative influence in the daily lives of old people is that of ageism, which is a form of prejudice against people because they are old. Prejudice is a term describing an unfavorable attitude toward a category of people that is based on traits believed to be negative. Often prejudice exists in the form of a prejudgment, in that people have a negative attitude toward an individual or specific group in society before having any personal knowledge about them. If people are prejudiced and keep their prejudices to themselves, then little actual harm is likely to be done to the person or persons against whom the prejudice is directed. However, if those prejudices are operationalized in the form of discrimination, which means *acting* on one's prejudices, people will not be treated fairly or equally.

Discrimination can be either positive (providing special advantages) or negative (subjecting others to disadvantages). When it comes to being old, typically there have been more disadvantages than advantages. The elderly have been subject in American society to discrimination in employment and in treatment from public agencies with respect to job training, vocational rehabilitation, and preventive health care (Graebner 1980; Atchley 1988; Chudacoff 1989). Preferences for younger people are the basis for discrimination against the aged.

Ageism, or age prejudice, can therefore be described as a dislike of old people that is based upon the belief that old age causes the elderly to be unattractive, unintelligent, asexual, unemployable, and senile (Comfort 1976). Although one-fourth or less of the American population has been found to express negatively prejudicial attitudes against the aged (McTavish 1971), Robert Atchley (1988:268) estimates that most Americans have at least a mild degree of prejudice against aging and old people.

Ageism causes the elderly to be stigmatized. According to Erving Goffman (1963:3), stigma can be defined as "an attribute that is deeply discrediting." Goffman, a symbolic interaction theorist, explains that the term *stigma* apparently originated with the ancient Greeks, who used it to refer to marks on the body. These marks were intended to represent something unusual or morally bad about the persons having them. Usually, the marks were brands cut or burned into the body to identify the bearer as a criminal, slave, or traitor. Thus, any citizen encountering the stigmatized person was entitled to treat him or her badly, or, once aware of the mark, was expected to avoid contact altogether with that person. In contemporary society, Goffman explains, there are three main sources of stigma: (1) abominations of the body, such as various types of physical deformities; (2) blemishes of individual character—that is, perceived mental disorder or weakness, homosexuality, dishonesty, criminality, drug and alcohol addiction, political radicalism, and so forth; and (3) the stigma of race, religion, and nationality. The person with such attributes is therefore someone who is different from most other people, but different in a negative (supposedly less human) way. "On this assumption," stated Goffman (1963:5), "we exercise varieties of discrimination, through which we effectively, if often unthinkingly, reduce [a person's] life chances."

The old are stigmatized largely in regard to "an abomination of the body"; that is, they have lost their youthful looks and lack physical attractiveness. And they may also suffer "blemishes of individual character" in that they may be perceived as senile, slow, stupid, or some other personal trait that is associated with the fact that they are old. The question thus arises as to how old people became stigmatized in society, and the answer appears to lie in two general areas: (1) fear of aging and (2) social values in relation to aging.

Fear of Aging

Becoming old is something that most people probably wish to avoid because it signifies loss of physical attractiveness, a decline in health, and the nearness of death. Even some of the elderly themselves may be fearful of continued aging because of what it signifies (Klemmack and Roff 1984). This negative image of old age, as Bernice Neugarten (1971) pointed out, is responsible for the fear of aging and the rejection of the thought of becoming old. Young people do not wish to be old or reminded of the fact that old age is inevitable, so they avoid the elderly and devalue them. In effect, they are denying that they, too, will someday be old. In disliking aging, the tendency for some is also to dislike those persons in general who are experiencing it and to consider them inferior because of it.

Aging and Social Values

Russell Ward (1979) explains that any stigma attached to the elderly must also be seen in relation to what is valued in society and presumed lost by becoming old. What the aged principally lose are their former role as a productive and active contributor to society and their self-image as physically attractive. Developed societies tend to remove the aged from the mainstream of social activity through planned retirement. This event takes place at a time of life when the aged person is usually no longer responsible for child rearing, financial support for children, and other tasks central to family maintenance. Although there is a positive side to this situation, in that the aged person gains the freedom to pursue his or her own interests and pleasures without work and family responsibility, it nevertheless is true that the elderly enter a status—retirement—that is not particularly important in achievement-oriented societies. In essence, the elderly go to the sidelines, and younger people assume the active social roles that contribute to and are valued by the larger social system.

In the United States, the normative expectation is that people will be active, achievement oriented, productive, and able to plan for the future. Aged persons generally do not meet these expectations because these are norms for young adults. Americans are a youth-oriented society, a situation that can be easily verified by examining the range of consumer goods and advertising that emphasizes youthfulness—even for elderly people. For example, cosmetic companies in the 1990s are grappling with how to approach the increasingly larger population of older consumers. The trend has been to emphasize the youthful looks and beauty that an older woman can maintain if she fights against looking old by using cosmetics.

Regardless, to be old is to enter a stage of life that is socially devalued, because it indicates that the person no longer participates in adult roles on the same level as before. Looking at the situation from Goffman's (1959) perspective of "life as theater," the old would no longer be serious players in social interaction. They would be on the sidelines. This problem is compounded by the lessened physical appeal assigned to the old by a youth-oriented society.

In order to show how this situation came about in America, David Fischer (1978) examined the impact of modernization on the elderly. His thesis is consistent with the modernization theory of aging, which holds that the processes that cause societies to change from a rural and agrarian system to an urban and industrial society change the roles of the elderly and reduce the status and esteem they are accorded (Cowgill 1986). Fischer, a social historian, began his analysis with the colonial period. Less than 2 percent of the population in the American colonies was age 75 or over. Because mortality rates were high and old age relatively rare, the elderly were regarded by most people as special. Elders, especially among the Puritans in New England, were placed in charge of churches and held the most important positions in town councils. The old were not just esteemed out of affection or deference to age, but, Fischer found, they were almost venerated along religious lines. They were seen as good, wise, and experienced in a manner consistent with biblical norms. There was no concept of retirement because of age, so the elderly leaders of the church and the community usually continued in office until they died.

However, not all of the elderly were regarded with esteem. Upper-class old people were held in high esteem. But the aged among the lower class, in stark contrast, were scorned because they were old (but not considered wise) and particularly because they were poor. Nonetheless, the general view of the aged in colonial times was one of authority and respect. This position was reinforced among the affluent because the control of land was usually maintained by the oldest male in the family, thus ensuring that younger family members accorded him the respect due his position as manager of the family's economy. Thus, from about 1607 to 1770, the predominant attitude toward the aged was one of respect.

Fischer explains that this situation resulted in a cult of old age in which the aged person of affluence was revered. But this cult of old age was significantly weakened and eventually replaced by a cult of youth in the eighteenth and nineteenth centuries. Between 1770 and 1820, a transition in attitudes, influenced by revolutionary values, spread that was far more supportive of youth as the ideal. At this time, wealth replaced age as a qualification for leadership; fashions in clothing became more youth-oriented; and derogatory terms were coined, like "gaffer," "codger," "fuddy-duddy," and "geezer," that made fun of old people. After 1820 until the mid-twentieth century, youth became increasingly emphasized at the expense of age. With the establishment of mass education for the young—along with retirement programs, residential separation, and diminished income for the aged—older people were pushed into a lower status. The country turned to youthful heroes for inspiration: Daniel Boone, Andrew Jackson, the defenders of the Alamo, George Armstrong Custer, Teddy Roosevelt, Charles Lindbergh, and the like. In politics, youth was often considered an asset if political and social change was an important issue. Old people, in turn, were increasingly considered a social problem requiring welfare in order to establish adequate pension and health benefits.

Carole Haber (1983) notes that the rejection of the old was not the result of any sudden aversion to old age, but evolved over time as aging became associated with poverty. Dependence in old age, a lack of material goods, and poor earning power for old people in general resulted in the notion that poverty was the elderly's usual state. Even though there were powerful and responsible elderly men and women, they were clearly a minority, and being old came to mean also being poor and relatively useless. Howard Chudacoff (1989), in turn, identifies late nineteenth-century industrialization as the period when discrimination against the aged began in earnest in the United States. By the early twentieth century, the belief that old people could not keep up with modern manufacturing and business methods became especially strong. The result was the spread of ageism in the workplace and the wider society.

Thus, modernization and poverty, as well as decreased physical attractiveness, have undermined the position of the aged in a society emphasizing achievement and youth. Yet the story is not over. The elderly at the end of the twentieth century are in the best position they have been in as a group since the colonial period. Today they have large numbers, greater wealth, and more political power than they have ever had, and, as they occupy a more dominant role in national affairs and consumerism in the twenty-first century, attitudes may become exceedingly more positive. Signs of this trend are already appearing, as seen in the findings of Robert Binstock (1983), indicating that the stereotype of the elderly is changing in the United States from that of being poor and victimized by society to one of being relatively well off, being politically powerful, and taking up too much of the federal budget.

As the aged gain increasingly greater benefits as a result of their political influence (22 percent of all voters in the 1988 presidential election were age 60 or over), lead interesting and active lives, and become a major focus for the marketing of goods and services, ageism is likely to diminish in American society. Although modernization theory maintains that the elderly lose status and esteem when societies urbanize and industrialize, it also predicts, as previously noted, that—when modern societies come to terms with having large aged populations—more positive cultural and institutional adaptations for the elderly will take place (Cowgill 1986). Social historians in the twenty-first century are likely to see a marked improvement in both the status of the aged in Western societies and attitudes toward them.

GENDER

Whether or not ageism affects women more so than men is not known, although this may be the case. Certainly, men are devalued in old age, but the situation may be more acute for women. The major problem that women face in relation to society's reaction toward them as an old person is a loss of attractiveness. Society's standards of female beauty and physical appeal are more or less exclusively youthful. Therefore, women may be more aware of the aging process than are men because the physical signs of aging produce graver social consequences for them (Levy 1988). Denial of aging has therefore been considered more of a female trait, because older men have often been considered to be more physically attractive than older women (Drevenstedt 1976). When it comes to physical appearance, a double standard seems to exist in the popular culture in that elderly men may be thought of as "handsome" or "distinguished," but elderly women are not as likely to be considered "beautiful." As discussed in Chapter 5, this tendency toward a double standard rests in the fact that sexual stereotypes in American society equate female beauty with youth more so than it does male handsomeness. Marriages among couples of widely varying ages typically consist of older men marrying much younger women, rather than the other way around. As a result, women have been characterized as clinging to a youthful self-image longer than men. What is suggested by this situation is that aging is more threatening to women than men because it has more negative implications. But this situation may become less true of future elderly cohorts as more positive views about the aged in general become more prevalent in advanced societies.

Lynn White (1988) has suggested, however, that both men and women become aware of aging in much the same way. White found that men tend to report more decline in their hearing and greater hair loss than women, whereas women tend to report greater declines in eyesight and energy as well as in the quality of their skin and figure. But women do tend to have worse uncorrected vision than men and to be more obese, whereas hair loss is invariably a male rather than female condition, and men tend to have greater hearing loss (Verbrugge 1982). White (1988) suggests, accordingly, that male-female differences in awareness of aging are largely the result of real differences in the aging process and that when all signs of aging are considered, there is really not much difference between the sexes in recognizing the onset of old age.

When the effects of aging on people in society are considered on the basis of gender, it seems most likely that there is indeed little or no difference in awareness of the actual process among men and women. Gray hair, dry skin, wrinkles, and loss of energy—along with the fact of chronological age—provide indisputable evidence of aging. The impact of that process, however, may be somewhat greater on women when it comes to social consequences and connotations of beauty and sexuality. But the struggle against the inevitable change in one's looks most likely peaks in late middle age rather than old age. Once women are aged, there may be little or no difference about the effects of aging on their appearance in comparison with old men. It is only a minority of elderly men who retain physical attractiveness in late life; for the great majority of aged people, men and women, there are more important matters than looks. In fact, old age may be the time of life when looks matter the least.

Gender differences in the aging experience are most likely to occur in relation to changes in work and parental roles that take place in late middle age. Ken Smith and Phyllis Moen (1988) studied role changes in midlife among women and found that events at this time have particular significance for later life. Midlife is the period when the last child usually leaves home, thereby typically providing the woman with a sense of loss and mild depression, but also lessened responsibility and greater freedom to pursue personal interests. Generally, the departure of the last child from the home—the so-called empty nest transition—is anticipated and does not significantly disrupt the lives of women experiencing it (George 1989). Some women may join the labor force at this time or continue to be employed without child-care duties in the home. Employment outside the home for women ages 55–64 has, in fact, risen since the 1950s because of the expansion of employment opportunities in the post–World War II economy (DeViney and O'Rand 1988). Others may participate in enhanced social activities or travel. This time in late middle age can be a preretirement period in which one begins to prepare for older age.

A second major event identified by Smith and Moen (1988) that occurs frequently among women in midlife is marital dissolution through either divorce or death of their husbands. Smith and Moen note that divorce is increasingly less common as couples age together, but older wives are especially likely to lose their husbands through death. The average age at which people experience loss of a spouse through death is age 56 (Lopata 1973), and most widowed women spend approximately twenty years of their life in that status (Ferraro 1989). Becoming a widow in late middle age signifies the beginning of the transition into old age with reduced chances for financial well-being. Whereas the empty nest transition tends to increase financial well-being by ending the expenses for raising children, marital dissolution through death or divorce tends to decrease it. Therefore, to a large extent, a married woman's financial situation at the beginning of old age is strongly influenced by events during late middle age. Smith and Moen (1988) note that those women who remain married in the middle years have greater economic well-being in later life.

Another area of research concerning differences between older men and women pertains to retirement from a job. Women historically have had less access than men to pension plans, and they tend to receive smaller pensions than men when they are entitled to them. Jill Quadagno (1988b) suggests that the reasons for this include the fact that many women do not work long enough at a particular job to accumulate seniority and that often women have been employed in jobs that do not provide pensions, have few fringe benefits, and offer little job security. Typically, these are small businesses that rely on temporary labor, or firms whose policy is not to provide pensions to its employees because of the cost. Long-term workers in such businesses are thus disadvantaged, but they work at these places because they need the job. Other research suggests that the responsibilities of women for child care reduce the chances of many women at being competitive in obtaining and retaining better-paying jobs; this also leads to lower pensions (O'Neill 1985).

In a study of patterns of retirement in some 93 countries, including the United States, Fred Pampel and Sookja Park (1986) found that the majority of women worldwide withdraw from the labor force during old age. The rates of withdrawal are greater than they are for men and take place even in countries where formal retirement is rare and pension systems are weak. The level of a nation's industrial development (high or low) and the status of women (high or low) both contribute to the position of women in the labor force and their situation in old age. Highly industrialized societies had the better pension plans for both men and women, and the quality of these helped influence the time of retirement for both sexes. But the study also found that the positive effects of industrial development on female retirement were constrained by sexual inequality (which existed in all societies) and large family size (high fertility disrupted careers and labor force participation, leading to lower retirement benefits). Overall, pension benefits for women are less than those for men, and this appears to be the case in both developed and especially in developing countries.

Women also live longer than men, on the average, and some researchers have characterized very old age as primarily a female experience (Longino 1988). Longevity has mixed benefits, however, as women are more likely to be widowed and experience poverty in old age. Moreover, women tend to have smaller Social Security benefits and less retirement income from pension plans. As Judith Levy (1988) suggests, these lesser benefits likely reflect the long-term and cumulative effects of women's disadvantaged work histories, wage differentials, and segregation into lower prestige jobs at earlier ages. Consequently, elderly men and women, particularly at the oldest ages, tend to have different living arrangements and relationships. Levy states:

> Because men tend to marry younger women who eventually outlive them, men age 85 and older are far more likely to remain married in old age. They are also more likely, in view of women's longevity rates, to have a spouse to care for them should they become infirm or disabled. Should their spouses die, the comparatively larger proportion of single eligible females permits men more opportunities for remarriage. Perhaps for these reasons, men are more likely to experience old age while living in their own homes; women are far more likely to experience the last phase of the life course residing in an institution or with relatives.[1]

In sum, women are much more likely to be disadvantaged in old age than men.

MINORITY GROUPS

An unanswered question regarding racial minority groups in American society is whether they are placed in a situation of "double jeopardy" as a result of old age. That is, does being both old *and* a member of a minority group place a person in particularly adverse circumstances? Some have suggested that it does not, because aging is so powerful an experience that all old people face similar problems despite their race (Kent 1971). In other words, what distinguishes an elderly white, black, Hispanic, Asian, or Native American from other people is the fact that first and foremost he or she is old. If race is a negative factor in their lives, then it is due more to the association of race with poverty than to race per se. Aged persons living in poverty are among the most disadvantaged groups in society, regardless of their race.

It appears that old age has the attributes of a master status in that it overrides the significance of other statuses. The situation for elderly whites and racial minority persons, if poor, is much the same; the situation for elderly whites and minority persons, if affluent, is also much the same.

---

1. Judith A. Levy, "Intersections of Gender and Aging," *Sociological Quarterly* 29 (1988): 484.

Therefore, what determines quality of life the most in old age is socioeconomic status and health, not race. These conditions favor whites in the United States but are not exclusive to them alone.

Although some earlier studies (Dowd and Bengston 1978) support the double jeopardy hypothesis, there is not a great deal of current evidence showing that aged members of minority groups suffer more than their white counterparts at the same socioeconomic level. The damage to a person's life caused by racism most likely happens at earlier ages. Old age appears to bring on more similarities than differences for persons sharing the same socioeconomic status. The problem for minorities is that fewer of them are financially affluent, and life is thus harder for them in old age because of their greater poverty over the life course.

Black Americans

Blacks constitute 8 percent of all persons over the age of 65 in the United States. Elderly blacks do not have worse health generally than older whites (Ferraro 1988), nor do they lose more income when they retire (Pampel 1981). However, this does not mean the situation for older blacks is especially good. Proportionally fewer blacks than whites, as noted in Chapter 4, live long enough to reach old age. In general, blacks also have lower incomes than whites. Although levels of income decline more for whites than for blacks in old age, blacks have less income to begin with. Thus, the relative advantage remains with whites.

In addition, blacks are more likely than whites to retire because of poor health, be unemployed in old age, or find it necessary to continue working when old in order to support themselves (Markides and Mindel 1987). Blacks are also more likely than whites not to live with a spouse in old age (Gibson 1986). Furthermore, most elderly blacks living in poverty are women, and their financial situation tends to be worse than that of men because of a history of especially low incomes. All of this would suggest that many elderly blacks are disadvantaged because they are also poor. The 1987 median income for black families headed by persons age 65 and over was $14,107 compared with $21,474 for elderly white families. Thus, the median income of elderly black families is about one-third less than that of aged white families. Blacks are also more likely to have fewer financial resources from earlier periods of employment to use in old age than whites because of either unemployment or low-paying jobs.

According to William Julius Wilson (1987), the black population in America as a whole has been in a disadvantaged position initially as a result of slavery (until 1865) and later because of massive undereducation, which lasted well into the twentieth century. As the United States moved from an agricultural/early industrial stage in the nineteenth century to a late and postindustrial period in the mid-twentieth century, blacks were generally not as competitive in the labor market as whites for skilled positions. A majority of white immigrants to the United States were able to secure levels of education and income that provided them with a good standard of living; blacks, on the other hand, were handicapped by racial discrimination and lower levels of education and income. A majority lived outside the political, social, and economic mainstream of society.

Yet significant numbers of blacks were able to take advantage of increased opportunities following the civil rights gains of the 1960s. Many blacks have seen a great improvement in their life situation and have achieved social, economic, and political success. For the poorest blacks, however, life chances appear to be deteriorating further (Farley 1984; Pinkney 1984; Wilson 1987). For example, the gap between blacks and whites in underemployment and unemployment in the nation's large cities has widened substantially since the 1970s, with young, poorly educated blacks having the most difficulty securing jobs (Farley 1984; Lichter 1988; Pinkney 1984).

Wilson (1987) points out that the social conditions facing low-income urban blacks have worsened to the extent that rates of unemployment, out-of-wedlock births, households headed by females, dependency on welfare, and violent crime have increased to their highest levels ever. Wilson blames this development not so much on racism as on the increasing isolation of lower-class blacks in a changing economy. Wilson notes that both middle-class black professionals and working-class blacks have moved out of ghetto neighborhoods in the inner city in search of safer neighborhoods and better schools for their children. Left behind is a high concentration of the most disadvantaged segments of the black population—a black underclass—whose social and economic isolation has become more pronounced than ever before. At the same time, the American economy has been changing from a manufacturing to a service and information-oriented base. This situation has produced extraordinary rates of joblessness for those persons, many of them low-income blacks, who lack the education and job skills to adapt to these economic changes. The inner-city black poor, therefore, rank among the most disadvantaged groups in American society; they may, in fact, have the poorest life chances of anyone. Elderly blacks living in inner-city poverty obviously share the disadvantages common to the urban black underclass as a whole.

However, Rose Gibson (1986) suggests that for many blacks the retirement years are the happiest and most secure of their lives. Gibson provides two possible reasons for this situation. First, declining physical health in old age, combined with the more strenuous and distasteful jobs at the bottom of the occupational hierarchy, which many blacks hold, makes work more punishing. Second, many blacks in retirement can look forward to a steady and reliable income from Social Security. For those blacks living in poverty, a steady income may have been infrequent at earlier ages.

Gibson also refers to elderly blacks as "psychological survivors," pointing out that even though they lack adequate financial security, education, and often the company of a spouse, they seem to be able to sustain themselves psychologically as they age. She observes, for example, that suicide rates among the elderly are much lower for blacks than for whites and that older black women, who are the most likely to be poor, have lower suicide rates than either elderly black males or whites in general. Gibson suggests that religion is a particularly strong factor in the lives of the black elderly by providing strength through prayer and a sense of belonging. "I suspect," states Gibson (1986:368), "that it is the communal as well as the intrinsic aspects of prayer that are helpful to older blacks; 'getting together to get things done.' " Other research on the function of religion in the lives of older blacks supports Gibson's claim. Neal Krause and Thanh Van Tran (1989) found in a nationwide sample of elderly blacks that the effects of stressful life events and negative feelings of self-worth were offset or counterbalanced by religious involvement. Robert Taylor and Linda Chatters (1986) found that informal support from church members in time of need was second only to support from family members among elderly blacks. Church members were a greater source of informal help than friends and were the preeminent source of aid during illness.

Gibson (1986) also notes the use of informal support networks in dealing with problems. Gibson found that older blacks draw from a more varied pool of informal helpers—family, church members, friends, acquaintances—than whites and are more versatile in utilizing these helpers in old age. Whites, in contrast, were more likely to seek help just from their spouses in old age or from specific family members if spouses were not available. Other research finds that black elderly parents tend to both give and receive help from family members more so than do elderly white parents (Mutran 1985). Blacks thus appear to be involved with a larger informal support system in late life than whites.

In sum, Gibson concludes that not all aspects of old age have negative connotations for blacks. For elderly blacks in general, Gibson suggests that certain psychological factors may be very important in sustaining their longevity and life satisfaction. These factors include a positive outlook on life, effective ways of dealing with stress, and the use of informal networks of social support in obtaining help in time of need. Gibson is particularly impressed with the strengths in late life of black women who are experiencing the most rapid increase in population of any racial/ethnic group in American society 80 years of age and older. The increase in numbers of elderly black women, combined with the high proportion (about 45 percent) of black families with only a female head of household, may mean, in Gibson's view, that the adults in many black families in the future will consist of several generations of women. Consequently, an important role for the older black woman appears to be that of serving as a surrogate parent to her grandchildren in families without the father present, whose absence is due to unemployment, divorce, separation, or death.

Hispanic Americans

Most Hispanics living in America either are descendants of people residing in territory that was annexed by the United States following the war with Mexico in 1845, or they or their relatives entered as legal or illegal immigrants some time thereafter in a pattern of northward migration that continues today. Many of these persons were unskilled laborers who worked in agriculture in the American Southwest during a period of rapid industrialization and urbanization. As a result, the Hispanic population, the majority of whom are Mexican-Americans, have tended to have relatively low-paying and less prestigious jobs. Many Hispanics today, however, live and work in urban areas. For example, about 80 percent of all Mexican-Americans live in cities (Gelfand 1982). But as a group, they remain economically and socially disadvantaged relative to non-Hispanic whites (Markides and Mindel 1987).

An important fact about Hispanics is that they will become the largest minority group in American society in the twenty-first century. Approximately 400,000 Hispanics a year enter the United States, either legally or illegally, as immigrants—considerably more than any other ethnic group from elsewhere in the world. Current migration patterns, combined with a high fertility rate (the fertility rate of Hispanic Americans is about 50 percent higher than that of non-Hispanics) is resulting in a large population gain. From a population of 9.1 million in 1970, the number of Hispanics had increased to 14.6 million by 1980 and to 22 million in 1990. By 2010, Hispanic Americans will exceed over 35 million and, if this trend continues, which is likely, Hispanics will outnumber blacks as the nation's largest minority group. As Fernando Torres-Gil (1986) points out, the United States is already the fifth largest Spanish-speaking country in the world, after Mexico, Spain, Argentina, and Columbia. If Puerto Rico is included, the United States would rank ahead of Columbia. According to Torres-Gil (1986:326), the presence of rapidly increasing numbers of Spanish-speaking persons in the United States "forces us to acknowledge a reality that we have too long ignored: the Western hemisphere is composed primarily of Spanish-speaking persons with a Latino heritage." And people with this heritage are becoming an increasingly significant segment of the American population.

Hispanics are a highly diverse group in American society, and there are differences as well as similarities between them. In 1988, the Hispanic population in the United States was composed not only of Mexican-Americans (52.3 percent of all Hispanics), but also Puerto Ricans (12.7 percent), Cubans (5.3 percent), persons from Central and South America (11.5 percent), and persons from the Caribbean and elsewhere (8.1 percent). Within this population, Puerto Ricans generally have the highest unemployment rates and lowest incomes and levels of education. Cubans, in contrast, have the highest incomes and levels of education, along with the lowest unemployment rates. Mexican-Americans generally fall in between these two groups with respect to income, education, and jobs (Torres-Gil 1986).

When it comes to aging, however, Hispanics represent a young group within an aging society. Over one-third of all Hispanic Americans are age 15 or younger, compared with some 23 percent of the general population in 1985. The median age for Hispanics in that year was 23, compared with 25 for blacks, 29 for Asians, and over 32 for non-Hispanic whites. Hispanics constitute only about 3 percent of the population age 65 and over in the United States. However, Hispanics are aging too, and the number of Hispanics reaching old age each year is increasing. In time, Hispanics will constitute a much larger proportion of the elderly population than they do now. As a relatively young population group increasing rapidly in a society that is growing older, Hispanic Americans will face a unique situation. "No other American population group," states Torres-Gil (1986:328), "has had to evolve, assimilate, and attempt to achieve full participation in American social, economic, educational, and political life while the country was being increasingly affected and redirected by its aging population." There are more questions than answers about how the twin processes of Latinization and aging will affect the future of the United States.

This situation is further complicated by the lessened assimilation of Hispanic groups into an Anglo culture. Hispanic Americans live in closer proximity than do other immigrant groups to their original homelands and thus are better able to maintain cultural and family ties. Although many Hispanics have assimilated, others have maintained their language, culture, customs, and ethnic solidarity. Today, Hispanics appear to be the least assimilated minority group in American society. Another problem is poverty. Hispanics are twice as likely as non-Hispanics to be poor (Torres-Gil 1986), and some have claimed that this is true for the elderly as well (Locayo 1984). Figures for 1987 show that the median income for Hispanic families headed by persons age 65 or over was $14,377, compared with $21,474 for non-Hispanic white families with aged persons as the head. Consequently, when it comes to median income, elderly Hispanic families in general have about one-third less income than elderly non-Hispanic white families. Data on income for Hispanics, however, is somewhat skewed, because Cubans tend to receive relatively high incomes, whereas Mexican-Americans and Puerto Ricans receive considerably less. Moreover, many Hispanics are likely to have had significantly less earnings than non-Hispanic whites over their life span, so they, like blacks, have accumulated fewer financial resources to draw on in old age. Poverty, therefore, is a fact of life for a considerable portion of the Mexican-American and Puerto Rican population as a whole and for the elderly within that population.

Little is known about the retirement experience of Hispanic Americans. The existing research, however, suggests that retirement is not a distinct event (Markides and Mindel 1987). Rather, the aged Hispanic works at a job as long as he or she is able. Withdrawal from the labor force thus tends to be gradual. Many Hispanic workers are forced out of the labor market before retirement age because of deteriorating health (Becerra and Shaw 1984).

Furthermore, because of irregular employment, especially among Hispanic migrant workers, elderly Hispanics tend to draw lower Social Security benefits than Anglos and are less likely to receive retirement incomes from private pensions.

A positive factor for elderly Hispanics is the Hispanic family and neighborhood. Hispanic families tend to be large and feature an extended network of relatives who are available to provide social support. Although some sources suggest that the level of support rendered to its elderly by the Hispanic family has eroded, Hispanics are more likely than Anglos to live near large numbers of family members, and a sense of responsibility toward aged family members remains a tradition (Becerra and Shaw 1984; Locayo 1984). Neighbors and friends in predominantly Hispanic neighborhoods are also an important source of help, friendship, and social interaction for older Hispanics. In fact, older Hispanics tend to draw on friends for assistance and social interaction in old age more so than do elderly Anglos. As Rosina Becerra and David Shaw (1984) explain, despite the poor physical environment found in Hispanic enclaves or barrios, studies of life satisfaction among aged residents show a very high proportion satisfied with their lives in these communities. The reasons for this satisfaction appear to be found largely in the context of barrio life, which provides social and cultural familiarity and the presence of established networks of friends and relatives. In addition, older Hispanics are more likely than their Anglo counterparts to live in households with relatives. Despite adverse living conditions, such as poor housing and high crime rates, many elderly Hispanics prefer the barrio as a place to live because of its generally supportive nature.

Hispanic Americans represent an important ethnic group in American society whose increasing size and cultural distinctiveness only partially explain their potential impact on the larger social system. Particularly important is the fact that Hispanics constitute a young population group in an aging society. As the wider society will be faced with adjusting to increased Latinization when Hispanics become the nation's largest minority group in the twenty-first century, Hispanics will have to cope with being young in an aged social structure. This social structure will undoubtedly place great emphasis upon securing advantages for old people. Hispanics, on the other hand, will be interested in securing greater political and economic gains for Hispanics. Thus, there is a very real potential for conflict in which majority-minority group relations between Anglos and Hispanics will be affected by both ethnic and age differences. Yet, as Torres-Gil (1984:344) reminds us, Hispanics are aging too, and they have a stake in ensuring that *all* elderly are treated fairly.

Native Americans

As the original settlers of North America, Native Americans, or American Indians, suffered a series of military defeats and dislocations at the hands of whites from the seventeenth until the late nineteenth century. In the aftermath of the Indian wars, most American Indians lived on reservations in relatively isolated sections of the country and worked in predominantly agricultural occupations. In the mid-twentieth century, significant proportions of Indians began to migrate to cities, so that today about half of the Indian population live in urban areas. A majority, however, have relatively low-paying and less prestigious jobs.

American Indians and native Alaskans constitute less than 1 percent of all persons 65 years of age and older. The exact number of older people among Native American populations has been difficult to determine, but 1980 census data placed the number at that time at 75,000. This makes them the smallest major racial/ethnic group among the aged. About 30 percent of the aged Indian population live on reservations, and perhaps another 25 percent live in rural areas. Some social services are available to aged Indians on reservations, but Indians living elsewhere suffer disadvantages similar to those of poor blacks (Atchley 1988); that is, they are severely disadvantaged in terms of education, income, jobs, and housing.

In many traditional Indian tribal cultures, there was no concept of retirement. Older people remained active as long as they were able; once they were senile or no longer physically fit, they were abandoned, killed themselves by starvation or exposure to extremes of weather, had a member of their tribe or family kill them, or were allowed to die of old age. Yet despite the trend toward a quick death once productivity was impossible, elderly Indians generally enjoyed high esteem because of their age and experience. Very often they (especially males) served in tribal positions of leadership. Today, the prestige associated with old age has persisted among Indians, and old people are often highly regarded in Indian communities. The concept of retirement has also become more accepted; and because of high rates of unemployment among Indians generally, it is not uncommon for elderly Indians to help support younger family members with their old-age benefits (Edwards 1983). Overall, aged Indians join older blacks and Hispanics in being in a disadvantaged position relative to non-Hispanic whites.

Asian Americans

Most Asian Americans of Chinese and Japanese descent are relatives of persons who migrated to the United States during the nineteenth and (for the Japanese) early twentieth centuries primarily as agricultural workers. The majority settled in Hawaii and California. The Chinese came first, beginning in the 1840s and continuing until 1879 when Congress passed a Chinese Exclusion Act. With renewals, this act prohibited Chinese immigration until its repeal in 1943, when China was a World War II ally of the United States. Japanese immigration took place largely between 1870 and 1924 until their immigration was likewise halted. Intense competition with whites in the labor market on the West coast, reinforced by strong feelings of racism, led to the ban. Filipinos came in large numbers in the 1930s and had fewer immigration problems because the Philippines was a possession of the United States between 1899 and 1934; a second wave of Filipino immigration took place in the 1970s. The majority of migrants from China, Japan, and the Philippines came as unskilled laborers who were attracted to greater economic opportunities. Many eventually entered service occupations and started small businesses, whereas others remained in agriculture.

Immigration from other parts of Asia has been more recent. Some Koreans immigrated to the United States at the turn of the century, but this immigration was cut off in 1905 when the Japanese established military control over their country. Migration from South Korea has taken place largely since 1965, and Koreans are currently America's fastest-growing Asian minority group. The most recent migration has involved South Vietnamese and Cambodian refugees who entered the United States in the 1970s in the aftermath of the Vietnam War. In the 1980s, Chinese and Filipinos constituted the largest groups of Asians in the United States, followed by the Japanese. In total numbers (about 3 million), Asians are a distant third behind blacks and Hispanics as an American minority group.

The first Asians, as noted, who settled in North America in relatively large numbers were from China and Japan. Initially, almost all of the Chinese and Japanese migrants were men, but eventually families migrated as well or the men arranged for brides to be sent to them from their homeland. Despite severe prejudice and discrimination, both the Chinese and Japanese have shown remarkable economic and social mobility, especially in the period following World War II. They reached the point that a high proportion have now surpassed whites in levels of education and occupational prestige. The Japanese, however, became somewhat more integrated than the Chinese into the American social and economic system. Many Chinese retreated into "Chinatowns" in large cities and entered service occupations like the restaurant and laundry business. Of all the Asian minority groups, the Japanese have the highest incomes (Kitano 1985).

Asian Americans constitute 1 percent or less of all elderly persons in American society. Their situation has been described by Morrison Wong (1984). Wong points out that approximately half of all elderly Asian Americans live in California. Most of the remainder live in either Hawaii or New York. By ethnic group, about 50 percent of all aged Japanese live in California and another 40 percent live in Hawaii; Chinese and Filipinos are only slightly more dispersed, with significant proportions (about 15 percent) also living in New York. The great majority of elderly Asian Americans are thus concentrated in three states, and almost all of them also live in urban areas. In terms of education, income, and socioeconomic status generally, elderly Asians as a group rank below aged whites. The socioeconomic gains of Asian Americans is largely an achievement of younger and middle-aged persons, for older Asians tended to have low-paying and less prestigious jobs. As Wong (1984:205) explains, a majority of aged Asians "were involved in jobs in the periphery—jobs that are characterized as low in status and pay and offering little chance of advancement.'' This is especially true of elderly Chinese, because about one-third live below the poverty line. However, Japanese and Filipino elderly show a fairly low proportion, about 8 and 4 percent, respectively, living in poverty.

The fact that so many elderly Chinese (one-third) live below the poverty line suggests to Wong that the claim that Chinese families tend to take care of their own is a myth. However, large numbers of Chinese elderly are single men, and a majority tend to live in low-income housing in "Chinatowns" in major cities. In traditional Asian culture, old age is esteemed, and elderly parents often live with their children. To a certain extent, such traditions are eroding in modern Asia (Martin 1988) and have eroded to a greater degree among Asians in the United States. As Toshi Kii (1984) explains, the majority of Asian elderly are immigrants who broke away from the traditional work and family organization when they were young and entered a new environment. In addition, there is a considerable sexual imbalance, especially among Chinese elderly, with the greater proportion being males who never married or who left their wives in China because of immigration restrictions. The children of Asian Americans have also obtained greater economic freedom from their parents and have had greater opportunities for upward social mobility through education and careers in more prestigious occupations; consequently, the traditional Asian family structure featuring a close-knit extended family has tended to break down. Nevertheless, the proportion of elderly Asians living with their families is still somewhat higher (ranging from 23 percent for Filipinos to 16 percent for Japanese) than the national average of about 12 percent (Kii 1984). Like Hispanics, many Asian elderly, especially Chinese and also Japanese to a lesser extent, have settled in ethnic enclaves in large cities where they have found informal support systems among others who share their language and socioeconomic experiences. Kii summarizes the situation of aged Asian Americans by noting:

> Despite the general understanding that Asian Americans are more familistic in terms of caring for their elderly, the history of their immigration has forced many contemporary elderly to live outside of the normal family structure. Their occupational careers have not prepared them for comfortable retirement. Indeed, poverty is more rampant among them than among the elderly in the general population. Ethnic communities appear to be important lifelines for many of the Asian American elderly simply because of the language barriers they face and because of the discrimination and prejudice they have encountered in the wider society.[2]

---

2. Toshi Kii, ''Asians,'' in *Handbook on the Aged in the United States*, ed. Erdmore Palmore (Westport, CT: Greenwood Press, 1984), 206.

SUMMARY

This chapter has discussed various ways in which society influences the aged. A very negative influence from the wider society is ageism, which is a form of prejudice against the elderly simply because they are old. Ageism stigmatizes older people and causes them to be socially devalued by young adults in particular and the larger society in general. The reasons for these developments stem from a widespread fear of aging and from social values in contemporary society that are youth oriented. Such values may be changing, however, as larger numbers of elderly persons with higher levels of education and income influence the direction of society in the twenty-first century.

Old age is a more difficult period for older women than men because of the greater likelihood of experiencing poverty and the loss of one's spouse through divorce or—most likely—through death. Moreover, retirement benefits are generally not as much for women as for men because of a history of lower-paying jobs for women, lessened seniority on the job due to absences for childbearing, child care, and other family responsibilities, and jobs that do not provide pensions. Sexual inequality in work and retirement has been found to exist throughout the world (Pampel and Park 1986).

As for racial minority groups, the common denominator for elderly blacks, Hispanics, Native Americans, and Asians is that they are more likely than non-Hispanic whites also to be poor. Poverty, rather than race, is typically the greatest problem for minorities in old age. Aged minorities are not necessarily in double jeopardy (suffering from both race and age discrimination), because age tends to bring on more similarities than differences—regardless of race—for persons sharing the same socioeconomic status. The problem for minorities is that fewer of them are financially affluent, and life is thus harder for them in old age because of their greater poverty. The damage caused by racial discrimination to a person's life and economic well-being is something that usually happens at earlier ages rather than late life.

Hispanics represent the fastest-growing minority in American society and will overtake blacks as the largest minority in the twenty-first century. Yet Hispanics as a whole tend to be younger than the general population, which may present some special difficulties in an aging society. That is, in the next century, the United States will be experiencing both greater Latinization and aging at the same time. Obviously, this situation will require major social and cultural adjustments. But Hispanics are aging as well, and the quality of life of aged Hispanics, as well as aged blacks, American Indians, and Asians, will be important social issues in years to come as the aging of society forces adjustments to the nature of social life in the United States.

The aged in society currently have significant problems with respect to their position as old people and the manner in which old age shapes situations involving ageism, gender differences, and minority group experiences. The problems of the aged, however, appear to be ones caused largely by society, rather than by the aged themselves. As the age structure of society changes toward increased numbers of elderly, the direction of change featuring a decline in ageism is positive and appears to be happening. But inequities in the quality of life available to elderly women and racial minorities persist.

Chapter *7*

Work and Retirement

A person's occupation or profession represents one of the most important features of that person's social identity. One's job is clearly a major factor in determining self-esteem, satisfaction with life, and socioeconomic status. Yet old age represents the time of life in modern society when a person begins to end his or her working career and enter a phase of social existence— retirement—that is a role typically identified with old people. Although it is becoming increasingly common for persons to retire in late middle age, retirement remains *the* normative social expectation for the lifestyle typical of the aged in Western society. This situation is especially true for males, but is also becoming the case for employed females (Pampel and Park 1986). To make the transition from a valued work role to a role of secondary importance to society, that of retirement, marks one of the most important status passages in an individual's life course. Consequently, the situation of the aged in relation to work and retirement is central to understanding the social processes that influence the later stages of life.

WORK

Until the early twentieth century, older persons tended to remain in the American labor force because of the demand for workers to support the nation's industrialization (Morrison 1986). Retirement was not common. Employed persons worked as long as their health permitted. Labor unions emerged in the late nineteenth century and, in negotiation with management for improved worker benefits, began obtaining job security and old-age pensions for older workers. However, in some cases, increased security was gained along with mandatory retirement rules. That is, senior workers were not to be the first to be laid off or fired in an economic recession and were to be given a pension at retirement, but they were also required to retire at a certain age (usually age 65) whether they wanted to or not. Job security and mandatory retirement were initially considered to be a form of protection for older workers; yet during the surge of industrial development in the twentieth century, mandatory retirement also became a means to get rid of aged employees and bring in younger people.

According to William Graebner (1980), discrimination against older workers became particularly acute in the late nineteenth and early twentieth centuries, despite efforts by labor unions to protect them. A capitalist economy that was highly competitive and committed to high productivity in the pursuit of short-term profit preferred youth. Many employers felt that aged workers could not maintain productivity in enterprises requiring speed and the ability to keep up with machines. For example, in the printing business, Graebner (1980:22) found that "between 1895 and 1915, older workers were phased out for younger men with better eyesight, more speed, and more endurance." Age limits on hiring became commonplace in American industry, and some companies simply fired workers when they became old. Graebner comments on the situation for machinists:

> Aging machinists faced the same problems as their counterparts in printing and arrived at similar conclusions. Faced with the competition of younger men and liable to dismissal at the first sign of age, machinists who had not yet reached middle age felt compelled to deceive their employers by dyeing their hair. As employers demanded more from their workers and increased the speed of their tools, older machinists who could not keep pace were replaced by boys.[1]

A few businesses favored older workers because of their dependability and experience; but most, faced with constantly improving technology, felt that in a rapidly changing business world, adaptability was an essential quality that was not characteristic of most older workers. This situation was compounded by workers' demands for shorter working hours, so a way had to be found to combine shorter hours with high productivity. Younger workers had the energy to turn out more goods in shorter time than older workers. Hence, young workers were in demand, although a certain number

1. William Graebner, *A History of Retirement* (New Haven: Yale University Press, 1980), 24.

of older workers were usually maintained because of their experience, dependability, and loyalty to the company.

Retirement thus became a means to restructure the age components of the work force, and it had the advantage of being impersonal and egalitarian. Retirement "allowed," states Graebner (1980:53), "the powerful turn-of-the century impulse toward efficiency to coexist with a system of labor-management relations that was still permeated with personal and human relationships." Just firing older workers outright was a policy that most public and private employers would have found difficult to carry out (although some did) because of the opposition of labor unions, politicians, and the general public. It was not good for business to have a reputation for age discrimination and disloyalty to long-time employees. Retirement was an acceptable method to replace older workers with younger ones and thereby reduce unemployment and fuel the national economy. The effect on the aged worker, however, was nonetheless negative, because it devalued his or her potential and forced retirement regardless of the individual's ability, talents, experience, or desires.

Malcolm Morrison (1986) explains that many of the negative stereotypes about older workers actually developed during 1920–1940—before retirement became fully institutionalized in American society. At this time, prevailing management techniques, cloaked in the aura of "scientific methods," mandated increases in the speed of work regardless of the consequences for the workers. Morrison describes the outcome as follows:

> Management's concentration on speed was based on the theory that a worker's lifetime individual capacity was relatively fixed, and that it declined over time until it was exhausted. The intense speed required for industrial work was thought to increase stress, which, it was assumed, would result in an absolute decline of productive capacity with age. With an increasing immigrant labor supply, union demands for reduced weekly hours, and the advent of automation, this "wear-and-tear" theory gained wide credence and was used to justify both the dismissal of older workers as well as the imposition of age limitations in hiring.[2]

Although there was never much objective support for beliefs about the relationship between age and declining capacities, these views have persisted over time and have hardened with the addition of negative assumptions about skills obsolescence, reduced learning capacity, resistance to change, and slower decision making with aging. Despite considerable scientific evidence that, for most tasks, age is not related to reduced performance and that individual variations preclude any valid generalizations about age and perfor-

---

2. Malcolm H. Morrison, "Work and Retirement in the Aging Society," *Daedalus* 115 (1986): 276.

mance, the belief persists that age results in declining productive capacities. This belief has proven extraordinarily difficult to change.

During the economic depression of the 1930s, the aged possibly suffered more than any other group, for older workers had the highest unemployment rates; also, many elderly people lost their life savings when the stock market crashed and the economy slumped (Achenbaum 1983). As the plight of the elderly became increasingly clear, Congress passed the Social Security Act of 1935, which provided monthly payments to persons age 65 and over. This landmark decision was a major step in establishing a welfare system in the United States and marked a fundamental change in government policy toward the aged. The federal government, for the first time, assumed a broad responsibility for a group of people—the elderly—whose well-being had historically been left to individuals, families, employers, and private groups. In accomplishing this shift, the federal government mediated between various interest groups, including large business corporations, labor unions, and various agencies within the government itself (Quadagno 1984, 1988a).

Thus, the federal government assumed a major responsibility for the welfare of aged persons, and the aged, conversely, became legally entitled to benefits from the state; that is, older persons were given the *right* of financial support from the government. Although there is evidence to suggest that the Social Security Act was chiefly designed to get older workers out of the marketplace in order to improve job opportunities for younger workers who could be hired at lower wages (Graebner 1980; Quadagno 1984), the intent of the legislation was also to provide income security in old age in the form of a basic subsistence payment (Achenbaum 1983; Morrison 1986). Elderly workers were left to decide for themselves if they wanted to be employed, but a limit on their job earnings was imposed if they wanted to draw full Social Security benefits. The reason for this measure was to ensure that such benefits were not simply a supplement to income from employment, but were compensation for job earnings lost because of retirement.

Successive amendments to the Social Security Act since 1935 have extended coverage to disabled persons and widows and their dependent children, while generally liberalizing eligibility requirements. For those elderly who desired to keep working, the Age Discrimination in Employment Act of 1967 provided protection from denial of employment on the basis of age for all workers age 40 and over. The act was amended in 1978 to abolish mandatory retirement in the federal civil service and raise the mandatory retirement age from 65 to 70 in most other occupational groups. A subsequent amendment in 1986 eliminated mandatory retirement altogether in almost all jobs. This law thus ended forced retirement at age 70 and allows Americans to retire at older ages than previously. It is now legally possible for most elderly people to remain employed, regardless of their age, for as long as they have the ability and desire to work.

Because of this legislation, many experts expected an increase in the number of workers remaining in the labor force past age 65, but this has not happened. The decline in aged workers is shown in Table 7-1, which presents the sex and age distribution of persons in the United States labor force from 1960 to 1986. For the age-group 65 and over, Table 7-1 shows that the percentage declined from 4.6 percent of all workers in 1960 to 2.6 percent in 1986. For men age 65 and over, the percentage dropped from 4.9 in 1960 to 2.8 in 1986; the figures for women over the same period show a drop from 3.9 percent to 2.3. Therefore, even though the elderly have the right to continue to work if they so desire, there has been a decline since 1960 in the proportion of the labor force made up of older persons. The reasons for this trend, as Robert Atchley (1988) suggests, are threefold: (1) labor market problems for older workers (i.e., not having skills that are in demand, plant closings and mass layoffs, relocations of businesses, difficulty in finding work after becoming unemployed); (2) declining health; and (3) opportunities for retirement.

The U.S. Department of Labor also projects that the number of employed older workers is going to continue to decline between 1986 and 2000. For males, age 65 years and older, the 2.8 million workers in 1986 will shrink to 1.4 million in 2000; for females, the 2.3 million figure for 1986 will become 1 million in 2000. On the whole, it appears that fewer aged workers will be represented in the labor force at the beginning of the twenty-first century if current trends continue.

For those older persons remaining to be employed outside the home, the largest proportion work in a white collar job consisting of management/ professional and technical/administrative support positions. This is seen in the distribution of occupations for older workers shown in Figure 7-1 for 1986. Figure 7-1 shows that 56 percent of all workers were employed in a white collar position at ages 55–59, and this percentage decreases only slightly to 55 percent at ages 60–64 and 54 percent at ages 65 and over. Blue collar jobs decline from 28 percent at ages 55–59 to 17 percent at ages 65 plus. Service occupations, consisting of sales, information management, hotel and travel-related jobs, and the like, are shown in Figure 7-1 to increase from 13 percent to 18 percent, as does farming, with an increase from 4 percent to 11 percent. The latter increase most likely occurs because many older farmers stay active as others retire, rather than because of an increase in aged persons changing jobs to become farmers. The rise in the percentage of older workers in service occupations, on the other hand, may occur because of the postponement of retirement and the adoption of second careers by older people.

The great majority of persons who leave the labor force after age 62 do so because of retirement, but health also, over time, makes it more difficult to work. The National Center for Health Statistics (1987c), for example, conducted a nationwide survey in 1984 of persons ages 55–74, asking them about their ability to perform some ten work-related activities. Some 28 percent of the 9,800 people interviewed who had worked since age 45 had difficulty

TABLE 7–1 U.S. Civilian Labor Force—Percent Distribution, by Sex and Age: 1960 to 1986

YEAR AND SEX	CIVILIAN LABOR FORCE (1,000)	PERCENT DISTRIBUTION						
		16–19 YEARS	20–24 YEARS	25–34 YEARS	35–44 YEARS	45–54 YEARS	55–64 YEARS	65 YEARS AND OVER
Total: 1960	69,628	7.0	9.6	20.7	23.4	21.3	13.5	4.6
1965	74,455	7.9	11.1	19.1	22.6	21.2	13.9	4.2
1970	82,771	8.8	12.8	20.6	19.9	20.5	13.6	3.9
1975	93,775	9.5	14.7	24.4	18.0	18.2	12.1	3.2
1980	106,940	8.8	14.9	27.3	19.1	15.8	11.2	2.9
1983	111,550	7.3	14.4	28.5	21.2	15.1	10.8	2.7
1984	113,544	7.0	14.1	28.8	22.0	15.0	10.5	2.6
1985	115,461	6.8	13.6	29.1	22.6	15.0	10.4	2.5
1986	117,834	6.7	13.1	29.4	23.1	15.1	10.1	2.6
Male: 1960	46,388	6.0	8.9	22.1	23.6	20.6	13.8	4.9
1965	48,255	7.0	10.1	20.5	23.0	20.8	14.0	4.4
1970	51,228	7.8	11.2	22.1	20.4	20.3	13.9	4.2
1975	56,299	8.5	13.4	25.2	18.5	18.5	12.5	3.4
1980	61,453	8.1	14.0	27.6	19.3	16.1	11.8	3.1
1983	63,047	6.8	13.6	28.6	21.3	15.5	11.3	2.9
1984	63,835	6.5	13.5	29.0	22.0	15.3	11.0	2.7
1985	64,411	6.4	12.9	29.2	22.5	15.3	11.0	2.7
1986	65,422	6.3	12.5	29.6	23.0	15.3	10.6	2.8

(continued)

TABLE 7–1 (continued)

YEAR AND SEX	CIVILIAN LABOR FORCE (1,000)	PERCENT DISTRIBUTION						
		16–19 YEARS	20–24 YEARS	25–34 YEARS	35–44 YEARS	45–54 YEARS	55–64 YEARS	65 YEARS AND OVER
Female: 1960	23,240	8.8	11.1	17.8	22.8	22.7	12.8	3.9
1965	26,200	9.6	12.8	16.5	21.8	21.8	13.7	3.7
1970	31,543	10.3	15.5	18.1	18.9	20.7	13.2	3.3
1975	37,475	10.8	16.5	23.1	17.4	17.8	11.5	2.8
1980	45,487	9.6	16.1	26.9	19.0	15.4	10.4	2.6
1983	48,503	8.0	15.4	28.4	21.1	14.6	10.0	2.5
1984	49,709	7.7	15.0	28.6	21.9	14.5	9.9	2.4
1985	51,050	7.4	14.6	28.9	22.7	14.6	9.7	2.3
1986	52,413	7.3	13.9	29.0	23.3	14.8	9.4	2.3

Source: U.S. Department of Labor.

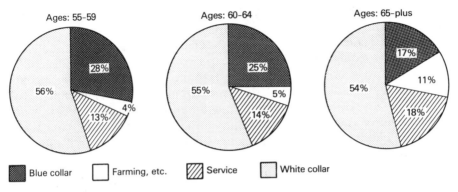

FIGURE 7–1 Occupation of older workers by age

Source: U.S. Department of Labor.
Note: 1986 data; white collar includes managerial/professional and technical/administrative support; blue collar occupations include precision production, craft, repair, and operators, fabricators, laborers. Totals may not equal 100 due to rounding.

stooping, crouching, or kneeling; 23 percent had experienced difficulty lifting or carrying 25 pounds; 22 percent had difficulty standing on their feet for two hours; 18 percent had problems walking one-quarter of a mile; and 15 percent reported they could not walk up ten steps without resting. On a more positive side, nearly 60 percent of the entire sample had no difficulty with any of the work-related activities, and this was especially true of those who were still employed (73 percent) or had retired for reasons other than health (60 percent). Of those who had retired because of health, only 14 percent had no difficulty with the work-related activities. The study concluded that the majority of persons who were retired for reasons other than health could have remained in the labor force. However, very few of these potential workers stated that they wanted to be employed. Rather, they had reached the time of life when, for them, retirement was the preferred option.

Unlike past periods of American history, the twentieth century has seen elderly workers gain the right to remain in the workplace. The Social Security Act and its various amendments provide them and their dependents with financial support as a basic right. In 1965, during the administration of President Lyndon Johnson, two other important measures were passed by Congress in behalf of the elderly. One measure, Medicare, provides financial support for medical treatment in old age, and the other, the Older Americans Act, authorized funds for a number of programs (e.g., area agencies on aging and senior citizens' centers) to improve the qualify of life of elderly Americans. Consequently, by the late twentieth century, the aged had emerged in American society as a bona fide interest group who had a role in establishing national priorities. Their impact on the government since the 1930s, states W. Andrew Achenbaum (1985:47), "depended not on whether they were given a chance to present their case, but on how well they competed against others in claiming an ever-growing share of the federal budget."

When it comes to participation in the labor force, older workers not only can decide for themselves when they will retire, but now have legal safeguards against discrimination on the basis of age. The trend currently appears to be one of encouraging the elderly to remain employed for a longer period of time. The cost of retirement benefits can be as high as 20 percent of the budgets of government agencies and private business corporations, and these costs are likely to increase as the proportion of older people in the general population increases. The cost benefit of retiring older workers on a pension and hiring younger workers at lower wages to take their place is disappearing. Furthermore, many companies are finding advantages to keeping older employees. "Prejudices against the elderly worker," states Achenbaum (1985:155–156), "are becoming harder to justify in the face of mounting evidence that older workers' skill, loyalty, and reliability typically outweigh the decrements of age."

The aging of the population also means that there will be a smaller pool of younger persons in the labor force, so older workers may find themselves in greater demand. The number of males ages 20–24 in the labor force is expected to decline from 12.5 million in 1986 to 7 million in 2000, and the number of males ages 25–34 will decline from 29.6 million to 16.6 million during the same period. For females ages 20–24, the decline will be from 13.9 million to 6.7 million. For ages 25–34, there were 29 million women in the labor force in 1986, which will drop to 15.1 million in 2000. Losses in numbers of younger workers will be greater for males than females, but the overall pattern is toward fewer younger workers. There may be greater need for older workers in the twenty-first century, not only because of their experience and reliability, but also because they are needed to fill the thinning ranks of younger employees. This situation forecasts greater participation by the elderly in job training (or retraining) programs and second careers.

RETIREMENT

Retirement constitutes a major status passage in an individual's life course brought on by the aging process. According to Barney Glaser and Anselm Strauss (1971:2), a status passage entails movement through a social structure in which people either gain or lose status, privileges, power, and prestige. There may be changed identity and sense of self, as well as a possible change in behavior. Although a person has a certain status associated with his or her socioeconomic position, there comes a time when that person must vacate the position. As Glaser and Strauss pointed out, a temporal dimension is implicit in all kinds of status; no one is able to assume a position or status forever. In any status passage, a person begins with a certain status and ends with a different one. Becoming married (or unmarried), being promoted (or demoted) at work, initiation into a fraternity or sorority, graduating from school, or completing specialized training are all forms of status passage.

The transition from work to retirement is such a status passage in that the person moves from being employed and an active member of a particular organization to being retired and no longer active in the organization. At the end, one's status has changed and become markedly lower than previously, because the individual is no longer a day-to-day participant, nor can he or she exercise his or her former status, authority, and influence. The status passages associated with aging (i.e., childhood to adulthood, adulthood to old age, work to retirement) are inevitable and irreversible; everyone goes through them, and no one has any choice in the matter because becoming old is universal.

Until the twentieth century, the United States did not have an explicit social policy regarding quality of life available to the aged after they retired. Old people were expected to get by as best they could and look to their families, religious organizations, labor unions, benevolent societies and charities, or local community if they needed support. Some private companies, especially railroads, began pensions in the late 1800s; later, a few states started pension funds for teachers, and, in large cities, retirement plans were initiated for policemen and firemen (Achenbaum 1985). Veterans of military service also received a pension from the federal government. Other programs providing old-age support came under the jurisdiction of various states and counties and were subject to considerable variation in administration and financing (Quadagno 1984). In these programs, the aged were placed in the same category as the poor and were subjected to similar administrative requirements. In a very real sense, being old came to mean being poor.

By the early 1930s, only 15 percent of all nonfarm workers and 20 percent of all labor union members had some type of pension plan (Achenbaum 1985). The federal government also had a retirement system for its employees, which went into effect in 1920. Few states provided any type of old-age pension, although some eighteen states had plans for old-age relief. By 1935, only Wisconsin had unemployment benefits. Thus, the majority of Americans simply had nothing in old age other than their own resources or what they could draw on from their family and whatever help was available in the community. There was no national pension plan, even though the majority of Western European countries had established government-sponsored retirement plans and national health insurance programs between 1883 and 1914.

The Social Security Act brought the United States into the ranks of the welfare states with respect to old-age benefits, but not in regard to health care. The United States remains the only major industrialized country in the world without some form of national health insurance for the majority of its citizens. But, with the passage of the Social Security Act in 1935, a national policy for aging emerged in which the provision of assistance to old people has become a major priority. The passage of Medicare, thirty years later in 1965, provided funds to help pay for the majority of costs for medical care for the aged. Thus, the elderly are prime beneficiaries of the American welfare state.

The Social Security Act is the most important event leading toward the establishment of a nationwide retirement system for the elderly in the United States. This act set the age for entitlement to old-age benefits at age 65. An amendment to the act passed in 1983 raised the minimum age of retirement for the receipt of full Social Security benefits from age 65 to age 67 for persons born in 1960 or thereafter. The latter measure was intended to encourage older people to continue working and to hold down the amount of federal funds spent on Social Security payments as the proportion of younger workers making contributions declines in the twenty-first century. By 2035, there will be only 1.9 workers per retiree (compared with 3.3 workers in 1990).

Table 7-2 shows that the number of beneficiaries, the amount of payments, and the average monthly benefits of the Social Security program increased significantly between 1970 and 1986. In 1970, Table 7-2 indicates, over 26 million retired workers, survivors of retired workers, and disabled workers received Social Security benefits; by 1986, the number of beneficiaries had reached well over 37 million. Benefit payments, as shown in Table 7-2, rose from almost $32 billion in 1970 to over $196 billion in 1986. For the same period, average monthly payments to retired workers rose from $118 to $488, to disabled workers from $131 to $488, and for widows and widowers from $102 to $444. Now shown in Table 7-2 are preliminary figures for 1987, which indicate that the average payment to retired workers rose to $513. Social Security benefits are financed by taxes. In 1937, employees paid only 1 percent in Social Security taxes on only their first $1,000 in earnings; in 1990, employees paid 7.65 percent on their first $42,000 of earnings.

The Social Security program has had a major impact on establishing the social expectation that retirement is normal in old age. A majority (over 75 percent) of retired persons have income in addition to Social Security—from savings, investments, and government or private pension plans—but establishment of Social Security has done the most to link the onset of old-age benefits with a retired status in the public mind. In other words, people expect that elderly persons are retired and that retired persons, in turn, are elderly. Thus, old age and retirement operate in tandem to produce a role in society—that of being retired—which is more or less exclusively that of the aged. Some people retire relatively young, in their midfifties, for example. But early retirement has not reached such large proportions that it has changed the normative expectation that retirement is associated with old age. This situation is borne out by the fact that some 89 percent of all persons in the United States age 65 and over are retired. People are considered retired when they do

TABLE 7-2   Number of Social Security Beneficiaries in Current-Payment Status and Average Monthly Benefit: 1986

YEAR	NUMBER OF BENEFICIARIES (1,000)				BENEFIT PAYMENTS (millions of dollars)				AVERAGE MONTHLY BENEFITS (dollars)		
	TOTAL	RETIRED WORKERS	SURVIVORS	DISABLED WORKERS	TOTAL	RETIRED WORKERS	SURVIVORS	DISABLED WORKERS	RETIRED WORKERS	DISABLED WORKERS	WIDOWS AND WIDOWERS
1970	26,229	17,093	6,470	2,665	31,863	21,076	7,721	3,067	118	131	102
1975	32,086	20,323	7,411	4,353	66,923	42,645	15,864	8,414	207	226	194
1980	35,585	23,309	7,598	4,678	120,472	78,025	27,010	15,437	341	371	311
1981	36,006	23,935	7,615	4,456	140,995	92,588	31,206	17,200	386	413	349
1982	35,839	24,425	7,442	3,973	156,137	104,985	33,815	17,338	419	441	379
1983	36,085	25,021	7,251	3,813	167,033	114,133	35,369	17,530	441	456	396
1984	36,479	25,474	7,182	3,822	175,762	121,023	36,839	17,900	461	471	415
1985	37,058	25,989	7,162	3,907	186,195	128,536	38,824	18,836	479	484	433
1986, total	37,622	26,490	7,155	3,977	196,692	135,949	40,896	19,847	488	488	444

Source: Social Security Administration.

not work full-time on a year-round basis and when they draw most of their income from a retirement pension (Palmore, George, and Fillenbaum 1982; Atchley 1988).

Currently, there is a "push-pull" effect with respect to retirement in the United States and other developed countries. The "push" toward retirement comes primarily from economic growth and the need for a young and recently trained labor force; the "pull" comes from government policies and private pension plans developed to make retirement more attractive financially and induce older workers voluntarily to leave the labor force (Pampel and Weiss 1983).

The growth in the number of retired workers over age 65, particularly males, has also produced a need and demand for better private and public (government and military) pension benefits (Pampel and Williamson 1985). These enhanced benefits, in turn, made it attractive for males under the age of 65 to retire as well. As Stanley DeViney and Angela O'Rand (1988:536) explain, "Policies that were earlier a response to the retirement of one age group (over 65) later became a factor in the retirement of another, younger age group." For men, this expectation is being realized in the United States at increasingly earlier ages (55 to 64).

The retirement role is of particular interest to social scientists because it tends to be age specific (a role for the elderly) and represents a major status passage from previous adult roles (namely, loss of one's former work role or career). Consequently, retirement represents a major change in an individual's life and requires an adjustment to new circumstances. The fact that retirement means the person leaves his or her former professional or occupational role—through which that person obtained a considerable degree of self-identity and status—and assumes a role of lesser importance to the wider society has suggested that this may be a time of stress and sensed personal loss. At the very least, it means a turning point in an individual's life experiences and the necessity to modify one's past lifestyle. In the next three sections we will review the problem of stress, the manner in which people typically experience retirement, and differences among people who retire.

Is Retirement Stressful?

On retiring, the individual departs from his or her usual environment of employment in which the roles, functions, and personal relationships associated with work typically are well-established. If the person has an important position or at least a position that is meaningful or even habitual for that individual, there can be discomfort and a distinct sense of loss at giving up one's occupational role. In fact, for some people, that role is their central role in life; that is, it is the role that provides them with their master status, which is the principal source of their social identity and position in the social system. Yet, although some may be reluctant to retire from their job because of the cost in terms of lost income, status, and self-identity, others may look forward to the experience as a time to relax and pursue their own schedule and interests. Achenbaum (1983) points out that on the basis of his review of relevant studies, many older workers do not consider it a "privilege" to continue working past retirement age. Achenbaum (1983:157) states: "Except for a minority of cases, older people wish to be occupied and enjoy a satisfying personal life, but they do not want to continue working."

Consequently, retirement may not have intense negative ramifications for the individual, because, as research shows, people typically have time to anticipate the experience and plan for it prior to its actual beginning (Mutran and Reitzes 1981). Other research shows that retirement does not affect one's health adversely and is not a direct cause of premature death (Ekerdt et al. 1983; McGoldrick 1989; Palmore 1981; Streib and Schneider 1971). People sometimes do die shortly after they retire, but it usually appears to be the result of a preexisting health condition rather than the effect of retirement per se (Parker 1982; McGoldrick 1989). Some studies, including those of a sample of retired men from an oil refinery in Texas (Owen and Belzung 1967) and a group of men in Great Britain from several different occupations who retired early (McGoldrick and Cooper 1989), report improved physical health to be a benefit of retirement. Among persons who retired because of ill health, retirement resulted in a reduction in the level of demands placed on them, which, in turn, was perceived by the respondents as a positive health measure (Ekerdt, Bossé, and LoCastro 1983). In sum, there does not seem to be a negative relationship between health and retirement.

In an extensive review of the literature on stress and retirement, with a focus on early retirement, Anne McGoldrick (1989) determined that retirement cannot be assumed to be a stressful life event for most people. Apparently only a minority view retirement negatively, and this seems especially so if it results in a significant loss of income. Otherwise, it appears that most people reach the point in their lives when retirement is desired. Research investigating retirement planning among males, for example, shows that most accurately predict their time of retirement and therefore are able to plan for it (Ekerdt, Vinick, and Bossé 1989). Thus, retirement was not an event that was not anticipated. Other studies have found no serious adverse consequences resulting from retirement for men (Fillenbaum, George, and Palmore 1985) or for both men and women (George, Fillenbaum, and Palmore 1984). Erdman Palmore (1981) found, in research conducted at Duke University between 1950 and 1976, that the elderly cohort under study (a sample of Durham County, North Carolina, residents) did not become completely inactive, isolated, or very lonely, nor did very many of them suffer from poverty or depression because of retirement. "Most appear," stated Palmore (1981:46), "to adapt to the 'crisis' of retirement with little or no negative effects."

Overall, it therefore appears that retirement in itself is not generally stressful. McGoldrick (1989) found that a growing body of evidence suggests that this situation is due to changes in attitudes toward work. Many people view their job primarily as a source of income and do not find the source of meaning of their lives from work alone. Family, friends, and personal pursuits providing pleasure, interest, and satisfaction are very important, and perhaps more important than work, in providing self-fulfullment. McGoldrick (1989:105) suggests that "as the concept of retirement becomes incorporated into a culture, the tendency to look on work as a temporary part of life increases, causing people to look elsewhere." As people enter late middle age and begin thinking about retirement, the possibility of satisfaction outside of their work situation may begin to take on greater importance. Problems associated with retirement appear due more to health, finances, and opportunities for enjoyment than to the act itself of retiring.

The Retirement Experience

Atchley (1988) identifies eight possible phases of retirement. First is the "preretirement" phase in which, as retirement approaches and becomes near, the individual begins to prepare for the experience. Preparation consists of adjusting to the separation from one's job and the work environment and making plans about retirement activities. When retirement occurs, states Atchley, the person takes one of three paths toward either (1) the "honeymoon," (2) the immediate retirement routine, or (3) rest and relaxation. The "honeymoon" is a retirement phase marked by euphoria in which retired people are busy doing all the things that they "never had time for before." Extended periods of travel are very common in the honeymoon phase, for example. This phase requires money and good health, and some people skip it altogether. But for those who go through it, they eventually leave this phase and settle into a less hectic routine that will characterize the remainder of their retirement days. Other people will move instantly into an "immediate retirement routine" that will most likely stabilize over time. In this phase they will adopt a schedule of activities at a regulated pace that will likely turn into a more or less permanent lifestyle. Still other individuals, after retirement, will enter the "rest and relaxation" phase, which consists of a very low level of activity. Many people just "take it easy" for a while, but eventually, Atchley notes, they get restless and become more active.

After experiencing one of the three phases in the initial postretirement period, movement into other phases takes place. Some people go into a "disenchantment" phase as they find that retirement is not enjoyable and does not live up to their expectations. Disenchantment, however, may be rare, for few people were found in Atchley's earlier studies (Atchley 1976, 1982) to be unhappy with retirement. Another possibility is a "reorientation" phase in which retired persons change their approach to retirement. Perhaps they become more involved in activities with friends and family, after initially pursuing their interests more or less on their own. But eventually, the great majority of retired persons enter into the phase of "routine" in which they know what they want to do and what they are able to do; thus, they develop a set of stable activities that becomes their own particular retired lifestyle. Finally, some may even adopt a "termination" phase and go back to their old job or find a new one. They do this because they prefer working or find that they have to work in order to support themselves in old age. Eventually, however, essentially all older people adopt the phase of routine as they settle into a particular pattern of living out their remaining years.

Who Retires?

Practically every American employed outside the home retires at some point when they reach old age. There are, however, some differences among people in the retirement process. According to Palmore (1981), the majority of people have retired in the past because of mandatory policies and health. With mandatory age limits on employment being eliminated, people still appear to view the sixties as the age in which retirement is appropriate. Women are more likely to retire than men, and married women, in contrast to single, widowed, or divorced women, tend to retire earlier. Married men, on the other hand, tend to retire later than their nonmarried counterparts. Palmore suggests that the reason for the greater likelihood of female than male retirement is that in the current generation of workers, the work role is more important for men than for women. Yet he notes that with greater sexual equality in the labor market, retirement rates of men and women are beginning to converge.

Education is also an important factor in retirement, in that the highly educated tend to retire later than the less educated. The reasons for this, states Palmore, are these: (1) the better educated are more likely to have jobs not affected by the physical decline that accompanies old age; (2) the work of the better educated tends to be more interesting and more rewarding; (3) the skills of the educated are likely to be in greater demand; and (4) better educated persons are more likely to be self-employed, so they can decide for themselves how long they wish to continue to work.

For persons under the age of 65, Palmore explains that it is either poor health, or disability, or the attractiveness of a pension plan that draws them toward retirement. The greater the physical strain and demands of the job, coupled with lesser rewards, as is the case for blue collar or manual labor workers, the more likely retirement is the preferred option for the older employee. Persons in lower skilled jobs are also more likely to retire earlier than persons in higher skill positions. However, regardless of a person's physical abilities or demographic characteristics, such as gender, level of education, type of occupation, or even a particular age, Palmore concludes that there is something about aging itself that markedly increases the desire for retirement. In other words, most people in advanced societies reach a point in life when they feel—for whatever reason (declining energy, pressure from others, eligibility for a pension, age discrimination, desire to pursue personal interests)—that it is time to retire.

The Future of Retirement

The Social Security Act firmly established the concept of retirement on a national scale. But, as Morrison (1986) explains, despite the general consensus about the value of retirement and its apparently positive consequences, there are serious social and economic questions about whether it can continue in its present form in an aging society. The social uncertainties, notes Morrison, revolve around the fact that retirement has both positive and negative consequences for the older person. The positive aspects of retirement are—providing one has sufficient income—the capability to pursue one's interests and to not have to work. The negative consequences are that the retired person loses his or her work status and moves into a less socially important role.

The economic questions have to do with the ability and willingness of society to continue providing Social Security benefits and health insurance (Medicare) through contributions of the active labor force. In the 1980s, it was necessary for the U.S. Congress to reallocate funds to prevent both the Social Security program and Medicare from becoming bankrupt. As Morrison (1986:270) points out, "It has taken national legislation to forestall the insolvency of the Social Security retirement program and the Medicare program in the United States, and although the measures enacted or proposed appear to remedy fiscal problems for the time being, few informed observers believe today's benefit levels can be maintained in the future without further program modifications that would involve additional taxation of workers and the retired themselves, and/or substantial reductions of benefits."

What is likely to happen, given the political influence of older voters and the national commitment to provide for the needs of the aged, is additional taxation with little or no reduction in benefits. In fact, pressure is likely to mount, as the age structure of society becomes older, to increase benefits for the elderly. In the future the aged will likely take up an increasingly greater share of the federal budget. The projected increase in the elderly population is virtually certain to require increased government spending for health and social services for the aged, because the alternative, holding expenditures constant or decreasing them, could seriously erode levels of health and quality of life available to old people (Lusky 1986).

One trend that counterbalances this situation is the likelihood of older workers remaining in the labor force for a longer period of time. With an increase in older persons and a decline in the proportion of younger adults, employers may begin to offer incentives to older workers to delay retirement or return to work after retirement. Morrison (1986) observes that with increasing numbers of people entering retirement and living longer in a retired status, retirement takes on the attributes of a separate life stage in which people are not generally productive. He suggests that it might not be good social policy to limit the overall productivity of as much as 20 percent of the total population. Therefore, changes may come about in both policy and practice that encourage the aged to continue their contributions to social, cultural, and economic life. This will mean allowing older persons the flexibility to remain productive, the elimination of ageism in the workplace and the larger society, and public promotion of the skills, talent, and experience the elderly can provide to the economy and the cultural life of the country. In short, notes Morrison, a new social conception of productive roles for older persons is needed. No longer can old people be cast in the public eye as a social and economic burden, or excluded from major participation in the ongoing activities of the wider society.

Retirement is a stage of the life cycle in developed societies that appears to have evolved into a basic right and normative outcome in the lives of employed persons. Although current trends point to tendencies toward earlier retirement in Western nations, this situation may be modified. Increased numbers of people may opt for early retirement if they are financially secure, but inducements are likely to be forthcoming in the twenty-first century to promote later retirements or to have phased retirements in which the older worker bows out of the workplace slowly. Phased retirement would consist of reduced work schedules, prorated salaries, and health and retirement benefits that are either continued or prorated as well. Partial pension payments may also be allowed at this time. Or retirees may be rehired as part-time workers or become independent contractors who provide their services to their former employer in return for a negotiated fee. Therefore, the retirement pattern in the future is likely to be one that is highly variable, as aged persons adopt different approaches to dealing with the period of life in which retirement has been common. All of this suggests that the aged will be closer to the social, cultural, and economic mainstream of society than ever before in modern history.

SUMMARY

Negative attitudes toward the aged extended to the workplace, especially as elderly workers were discriminated against during the industrialization of the United States. But this situation has improved, for older workers now have legal protection from discrimination and guaranteed benefits from Social Security and other retirement plans. Retirement is now a normative expectation in the lives of most working people. Older workers are pushed by retirement policies to retire from the labor force to make room for younger workers, and they are also pulled toward retirement by pension benefits.

Because retirement is typically an expected event, it is not especially stress-ful or negative. Other people, primarily males, are retiring from the labor force in greater numbers and at earlier ages. Attitudes are such now that most older people do not consider it a privilege to work past retirement age; instead, retirement is perceived as a desirable phase of old age that provides the opportunity to seek self-fulfillment in late life.

However, with a decline in the proportion of younger workers and an increase in the number of elderly in the twenty-first century, older people are likely to be in greater demand for employment. Thus, there is likely to be greater variation in the retirement years as older people opt for either retire-ment or full-time or part-time employment.

The Aged as a Social Force

A major theme of this book is that the elderly population in the United States, as well as in other developed countries, is in an advantaged position compared with past generations of old people. In the twenty-first century, the elderly will be a more important and powerful segment of society than ever before because of their large numbers, longevity, experience with the political system, and enhanced levels of health, education, and income. In this chapter, we will explore the manner in which the elderly are emerging into a major political force. Initially, we will discuss why the aged are more of a political interest group than a minority group in American society. Then we will review the development of the welfare state in Western society in relation to old-age politics.

THE AGED: A MINORITY GROUP?

Do the aged constitute an emerging minority group in American society, and, if so, is it in a minority group context that they will play a political role? According to Louis Wirth (1945:67), "We may define a minority as a group of people who, because of their physical or cultural characteristics, are singled out from the others in the society in which they live for differential and unequal treatment and who therefore regard themselves as objects of discrimination." It has been pointed out that many older people have experienced negative stereotyping, relegation to an inferior social status, discrimination, and segregation from younger people (Rosow 1974; Levin and Levin 1980). A common reaction of people exposed to these social and psychological stresses is the formation of a group identity with a specific belief and value system reflecting the needs and goals of group members. It has therefore been proposed that such a group identity may have developed among the aged in the form of a subculture, and the emergence of this subculture among old people marks them as a distinctive minority group (Rose 1965).

But is there really a subculture of the aged? The norms of older people tend to be middle-aged. That is, most old people judge themselves on the basis of how closely they reflect middle-age norms (Fontana 1977). They also like to think of themselves more or less as they always have—except that they are just older (Kaufman 1987; Gove, Ortega, and Style 1989). All of this would suggest that elderly people do not necessarily focus on age as the basis of their distinctiveness. This tendency undermines claims that old people are a subculture in their own right.

This becomes especially clear when one considers the definition of a subculture. A subculture is a system of values, attitudes, modes of behavior, and lifestyles of a social group that is distinct from, but related to, the dominant culture of society (Abercrombie, Hill, and Turner 1984:312). Aged persons, accordingly, do not appear to qualify as a subculture, because the values, attitudes, behaviors, and lifestyles they pursue are not especially different from those of middle-aged adults. Old age may cause a modification in an individual's behavior and lifestyle (because of reduced finances and energy and increased leisure time), but usually there is not a drastic change from the past unless the aged person's health fails. And, if the personality has continuity, as indicated by continuity theory (Neugarten 1964), the older person's lifelong values and attitudes are not likely to change a great deal either.

Thus, to describe elderly people as a minority group on the basis of a subculture of old age does not appear to be accurate, nor do the aged appear to be a minority in the same sense that blacks, Hispanics, American Indians, or Asians constitute minority groups in the United States. For instance, Gordon Streib (1965, 1976) points out that membership in a minority group is usually permanent and exclusive. Most people who are part of a minority group begin life in a minority status because of their race, ethnicity, or religion—and remain there. Yet *everyone* becomes old; no one starts out life that way. True, some people may choose to be a member of a minority group by changing their situation, such as changing from a majority to a minority religion. But most minority group characteristics cannot be changed, such as race or ethnicity, because people are born with these traits and the biological or cultural imprint is permanent. The only way to change such minority status is to move geographically to where the particular traits are those of the majority. Being elderly, on the other hand, is something that happens to people for only part of their lives if they live long enough, and it takes place regardless of where they reside. Thus, to become old is not something that is exclusive only to some people, because anyone may reach old age.

Furthermore, the extent of prejudice and discrimination against the aged as a group falls far short of the manner in which prejudice and discrimination have historically affected racial, ethnic, and religious minority groups. Such groups have been persecuted throughout much of human history because of their minority traits, but old people have not been singled out for persecution—killed, imprisoned, tortured, enslaved, or denied participation in the political process—simply because they became older. In fact, elderly people still enjoy relatively high status in Japan and developing countries of the Third World, and there is evidence that their status is improving in the developed nations of the West (Binstock 1983). Streib (1965) notes that, in the United States, elderly persons have never been denied (because of their age) the right to vote, own property, or hold political office, as has happened to blacks and women. It is therefore difficult to make a case demonstrating that elderly people suffer from prejudice and discrimination to the same degree experienced by blacks, Hispanics, and other racial/ethnic minorities.

Thus, it does not seem appropriate to depict old people as either a subculture or a minority group. The most apt description of the elderly is that they are a segment of society composed of people from varying backgrounds who have old age in common. Whatever sense of collective identity the elderly have most likely derives from being old, and this circumstance promotes age-specific similarities, feelings, and consciousness, but does not eliminate racial, social, and economic differences among them. The collective nature of the elderly seems best expressed within the context of being an *interest* group. An interest group is a voluntary association of citizens who attempt to influence public policy. Senior citizens' groups have become one of the most important political lobbies in the nation and have been highly successful in obtaining benefits for all older persons. What provides a sense of social solidarity and cohesion in such groups is an awareness of common problems and interests and the desire to work together to achieve a better life for themselves and the elderly who follow them. Thus, it is in the context of an interest group, rather than a minority group, that the elderly in American society influence the political process.

THE AGED AS AN INTEREST GROUP

Senior citizens' groups are organized throughout the country and are set up to provide various services, such as social activities, recreational opportunities, and assistance in the form of delivering hot meals, helping with household duties, and securing the delivery of health services. Many of these groups also are involved in politics at all levels of government, as they work to elect politicians who will support their interests and goals. Because these groups tend to keep abreast of public affairs and vote, they are a potent force in elections. Therefore, politicians usually pay attention to them and do not openly oppose them. In the presidential elections of 1988, for instance, some 22 percent of all voters were age 60 or over; this percentage is large enough to be a decisive margin in most elections. In 1982, the power of older voters was demonstrated when the Republicans lost twenty-six seats in the House of Representatives to the Democrats, who maintained they would oppose cuts in Social Security benefits suggested by the Reagan administration.

The most influential organization speaking for older persons on the national level is the American Association of Retired Persons (AARP). In 1978, the AARP had 10 million members, but ten years later, in 1988, there were 28 million members. Thus, the influence of the AARP rests in the fact that it can claim it represents one-fifth of all voters in the United States. The cost of membership is modest. Dues, only $5 annually, provide a third of the association's income; other money is obtained from selling products to assist aged persons, health insurance, home and automobile insurance, a pharmacy service, and advertising in their magazine *Modern Maturity*. In 1988, AARP had a budget of $235 million, an eight-story office building in Washington, D.C., ten regional offices, and a staff of 1,200 persons. Membership is open to anyone 50 years of age and older, and nearly 50 percent of all Americans in this age bracket belong to AARP.

AARP was organized in 1958 under the leadership of Ethel Percy Andrus as a nonprofit association intended to enhance the quality of life of older persons. Initially, its primary function was to provide inexpensive health insurance for the aged, rather than become politically powerful. But in working with members of Congress to support the well-being of the aged and in representing their views to lawmakers, AARP has become one of the most effective lobbies in Washington. Moreover, AARP has its own Public Policy Institute for analyzing policy issues and its own legislative division to support its lobbyists, whose job is to influence lawmakers. The AARP conducts its own research, works with its membership in contacting their government representatives about important legislation, and produces a large volume of publications discussing the needs of old people. The AARP does not donate money to politicians or political groups; rather, its influence comes from its size (in voting power) and the nature of its constituents (the aged). To oppose the needs of the elderly is not only a generally unpopular position for a politician to take, but also one that is likely to present serious problems about remaining in office. With an organization like the AARP, older people exert an important influence in the nation's politics; and with increasing numbers, this influence is likely to become even greater. Consequently, elderly people have evolved in the late twentieth century into one of the most influential segments of American society, and it is organizations like the AARP that have helped them do it.

Although the AARP is the most powerful of today's lobbies for the elderly, this organization is only one of several groups that have worked for the benefit of the aged and influenced legislation. There are, for example, some thirty organizations based in Washington, D.C., who directly represent the interests of the elderly (Achenbaum 1985). Besides the AARP, the most important organizations are the National Council on Aging (NCA), which represents nearly two thousand separate health care, social work, and social service agencies, and sponsors a national center for aging policy; and the National Council of Senior Citizens (NCSC), with strong ties to labor unions. The AARP, NCA, and NCSC are the so-called Big Three organizations for the elderly (Achenbaum 1983). Other important organizations include the American Association of Homes for the Aged (AAHA), the American Nursing Home Association (ANHA), and the National Association of State Units on Aging (NASUA), which support the interests of the aged and manage the delivery of specialized services. There are other groups, such as the Gray Panthers (a politically militant organization), the National Caucus on the Black Aged, the Asociacion Nacional Por Personas Mayores, which helps older Hispanics, and the National Association of Retired Employees, which helps protect the interests of federal workers.

The first major organization of importance for older people was the Townsend Movement, which began in the 1930s in California with physician Frances E. Townsend as its founder. The Townsend Movement claimed over 5 million members at its peak in 1935 and was important in influencing the enactment of the Social Security Act. Another group in the 1930s was the American Association for Old Age Security, which espoused not only pensions for the elderly but also a redistribution of the nation's wealth. The American Federation of Labor likewise supported old-age benefits as a means to protect workers after retirement, and another labor group—the American Association for Labor Legislation—worked to have old-age benefits included in the collective bargaining process between labor and management (Achenbaum 1983).

The Townsend Movement, labor unions and councils, business associations, and various state organizations and interest groups all vied for influence on Congress and President Franklin D. Roosevelt in relation to a federal program of old-age benefits in the 1930s. With the nation undergoing the Great Depression, the plight of the elderly was particularly acute because they had the highest rates of unemployment and private pension plans were not widespread (Graebner 1980; Achenbaum 1983). Considerable disagreement existed among many of the interested parties, as organized labor sought to tie old-age benefits to labor force participation, agricultural and political interests in the South wanted to minimize or avoid regulation of a national pension plan by the federal government, and various business interests demanded that taxes to support any form of social security be kept low (Quadagno 1984, 1988). State managers of pension plans in private industry were under pressure to respond to the economic hardships of the Great Depression and deal with labor discontent. Also, various members of Congress had their ideas about welfare for the aged.

In the meantime, the Townsend Movement advanced its own plan, which caused a political furor by demanding that every person over the age of 60 be given $200 a month and be required to spend the entire amount within that month in order to stimulate the depressed economy. The Roosevelt administration claimed that the plan was simply unworkable, and President Roosevelt created a Committee on Economic Security, which functioned to mediate between the various interest groups. Eventually, compromises were reached, and the Social Security Act marked the beginning of the welfare state in the United States. Labor received what it wanted in linking Social Security eligibility and benefits to participation in the work force, the states acquired administration of the program's public assistance services, and all persons 65 years of age and older received entitlement to a pension from the federal government.

According to Jill Quadagno:

> What was at stake in the debate surrounding the Social Security Act was the nature of the state itself. Organized labor, nonmonopoly capital, and Southern agricultural interests were struggling to keep social-welfare measures outside the jurisdiction of the state, whereas a core group of influential monopoly capitalists, national state managers and various citizens coalitions argued for increased centralization. The outcome of this battle was a reorganization of the state in a manner that expanded its role and incorporated interest groups more fully in its jurisdiction.[1]

With the passage of the Social Security Act, the federal government assumed the role and the duty of guaranteeing a minimum level of income to all elderly citizens. However, Quadagno (1984, 1988) points out that the Social Security Act did not happen by itself, and she notes that it was the Townsend Movement of elderly persons who provided the pressure for reform. Since the Social Security Act, and continuing until the present, the driving force in obtaining old-age benefits has been organizations representing the aged (Pampel and Williamson 1985). Before 1920, the elderly in the United States were unable to engage in collective action to solve the social problems of growing old; now, the aged have all the earmarks of a "modern" force in society, and a potent lobby exists to support their cause at the national level (Achenbaum 1983:169).

---

1. Jill Quadagno, "Welfare Capitalism and the Social Security Act of 1935," *American Sociological Review* 49 (1984): 646

THE AGED AND THE WELFARE STATE

With the Social Security Act of 1935, the elderly played a major role in influencing the federal government in the United States to adopt a welfare state approach to assisting old people. Since then, the aged have been able not only to influence the continuation of the program, but also subsequently to enhance it. However, in both the United States and Western Europe, public demand for social security programs for the aged was initially centered in labor movements, because the elderly themselves lacked political power. It was principally in the United States, not Western Europe, that the elderly pressured the national government as a major interest group to begin providing old-age benefits. Social welfare programs had begun in the late nineteenth and early twentieth centuries in most countries of Western Europe, but they were brought about through maneuvering for political influence over the working class between conservative governments, liberal and socialist political parties, trade unions, and wealthy capitalists. Thus, the *origins* of the welfare state in Western society are generally located in problems of the labor force in a capitalist economy, not the problems of the aged.

Evolution of the Welfare State in the West

Behind the development of the welfare state in Western Europe was the desire of many European governments and industrialists for a healthy population whose productivity could be translated into economic power. Greater economic power, in turn, meant an enhanced capability of projecting greater political and military power, as well as securing a higher standard of living for the nation and increased profits from trade and manufacturing. In some countries, providing state-sponsored welfare was also a means to reduce political discontent and the threat of revolution from the working class. Social insurance programs were essentially devised to protect the income of workers when sick, disabled, unemployed, or old. Private pension plans from business corporations had been unable to provide adequate coverage in the scope and quality necessary for all of a country's labor force, and it therefore fell to national governments to take greater responsibilities for the welfare of the governed (Myles 1984).

Initially, social insurance was provided by many of the Western European governments only to wage earners below a certain income level, but gradually benefits were extended to all or most of the population. In most of these countries, social insurance was provided first in the form of national health insurance and the protection of income lost to workers through sickness or disability. Old-age pensions tended to follow shortly thereafter. Germany established the first system of social insurance in 1883 and added old-age benefits in 1889. Austria initiated social insurance in 1888 and began providing old-age pensions in 1906. Denmark, in 1891, and Great Britain, in

1908, both initiated social welfare programs that included old-age pensions at the beginning. Some form of national pensions eventually became available for the elderly in the Netherlands in 1913, Italy in 1919, Belgium in 1924, and Switzerland, which had a national health insurance program in 1911 but waited until 1946 for a national pension system. France waited until 1930 to lay the legal foundation for a national-level social insurance program that included old-age benefits, although various nonprofit organizations were allowed to provide social security insurance as early as 1901. Elsewhere, old-age pensions for the general population began in Canada in 1927 and, as previously noted, in the United States in 1935.

The advent of the welfare state in the West, as British sociologist T.H. Marshall (1964) explained, is actually a culmination of processes that began in the eighteenth century. Marshall pointed out that the establishment of the welfare state is the latest phase in an evolution of citizens' rights in Western society. To *civil* rights (gained in the eighteenth century), like freedom of speech and equality before the law, and *political* rights (acquired in the late eighteenth and the nineteenth centuries), such as the right to vote and participate in the exercise of government, were added the *social* rights (achieved in the late nineteenth and the twentieth centuries) of protection from economic insecurity and the provision of at least a marginal level of economic welfare. The emergence of these various rights of citizenship, all promoting equality, states Marshall, is a paradox, because they came during the same historical period as the rise of capitalism, which essentially is a system of inequality. Inequality in the capitalist system stems from the fact that it is based on private ownership of property and the gearing of economic activity to profit in the marketplace. Individuals are not equal in the amount of property they own or acquire, their position in relation to the production of goods and services in the marketplace, and the amount of profits (or losses) they derive from their work. As John Myles (1984:30) comments: "This marriage between a protective state and a capitalist economy was a union of opposites, for it required an accommodation between two opposing logics of distribution—one that attached rights to the possession of *property* and another that attached rights to *persons* in their capacity as citizens."

Essentially, what had taken place, in Marshall's (1964) view, was a "war" between the rights of citizenship considered inherent in a democratic society by the general populace and the capitalist social class system. In the modern welfare state, individual rights of citizenship, not ownership of property, emerged as the basis for political representation and entitlement to public programs.

Old Age Pensions: Labor and the Aged

In this war between citizens' rights and the capitalist economic system, what role did workers play as potential retirees? In the United States, large corporations, rather than workers, were initially the most influential in establishing the principle of retirement. This was done in order to reduce unemployment during the Great Depression, maintain high worker productivity with a young labor force, and lessen production costs by hiring younger workers at lower salaries and placing older workers on pensions (Graebner 1980; Haber 1978). Consequently, it was in the vested interest of management in the United States to have a social security system (Graebner 1980; Brents 1986). Other studies show American, British, and French workers and their labor unions resisting proposals to create government-sponsored pension plans for older workers as a method to bind workers' loyalties to the state and reduce the influence of the unions; yet, some labor unions worked to establish national pension plans (Myles 1984). Marxists often opposed such measures because they increased the power of capital over labor.

However, since the 1940s, labor organizations have generally supported public pensions for the elderly. This development was aided significantly by the economic boom that followed World War II and influenced the current orientation of modern welfare states. Western governments during the postwar era began assuming increasing responsibility for distributing the national income, and the elderly were the major beneficiary of this development. Myles (1984) shows in his analysis that the traditional concept of providing public support for the elderly changed during the postwar era from that of providing social *assistance* to one of providing social *security*. That is, the intent of government was no longer to provide a safety net for old people unable to meet their financial needs; instead, the goal became that of providing a retirement income sufficient to replace wages from work. Old-age benefits thus turned into a method to support a standard of living for elderly persons that was not significantly lessened because of retirement. Private pensions were negotiated at the bargaining table between labor and management, but public pensions tended to be a consideration in this wage-setting process as well, because they were an important source of income after retirement. Old-age pensions, especially in Western Europe, became, in Myles's (1984:77) view, part of the "social contract" between government, employers' associations, and labor organizations to exchange wage demands for improved benefits. Myles found in his research on the politics of public pensions that a cohesive labor movement that is able to elect its candidates to public office and sustain political control for an extended period was the means by which adequate pensions for retired workers were achieved in many Western European countries after World War II.

Although the influence of labor unions on the provision of old-age pensions has been significant in the modern welfare state, the dominant influence today is the political power of the aged population. This is aptly demonstrated in research such as that by Fred Pampel and John Williamson (1985). Pampel and Williamson investigated, in some forty-eight nations, whether class politics (the power of the working class) or old-age politics (the power of the elderly population) was more important in influencing state expenditures for public pensions at different levels of political and economic development. They found that the more democratic a nation and the larger its aged population, the greater the political power of the aged in increasing pension expenditures. Social class variables, in contrast, had little or no effect on pension increases, thereby indicating the greater importance of age politics over class politics in national expenditures for old-age benefits.

Pampel and Williamson noted that, over time, age variables tend to become more important than class variables. The reason is that rises in public pensions can be correlated with changes in the age structure: state-funded pensions rise the most when the proportion of the aged increases in the general population. Countries like Sweden, Norway, and Austria are among those with the highest percentage of aged persons and highest pension expenditures. In countries like the United States, Canada, and Switzerland, labor unions have not been strongly centralized or exceptionally powerful, and socialist and liberal politics have also tended to be weak, yet expenditures for public pensions have nonetheless increased dramatically, as has the size of the aged population.

Key variables in old-age pension expenditures, other than the size of the aged population, include the extent of democracy in a country and its level of economic resources. Affluent nations, of course, can spend a higher proportion of their income on old-age pensions than can less affluent countries. Pampel and Williamson also found that age has no influence in nations with low levels of democracy. But in both developing and developed industrialized democracies, increases in the size of the aged population are correlated with increases in pension expenditures, with the highest increases coming in those countries having the highest levels of income and political democracy. In sum, the highest old-age pensions are found in those nations with the greatest (1) aged population, (2) levels of democracy, and (3) economic resources.

The strength of old-age politics and the difficulty of legislators in opposing plans to limit spending on the aged is based on the special nature of public pension expenditures. "Unlike nearly all other social welfare programs," state Pampel and Williamson (1985:782), "pensions benefit a large and easily identifiable population with ascribed characteristics and a high rate of voting." Pampel and Williamson point out that both the aged and the nonaged view pension benefits as a legitimate entitlement after decades of work and financial contributions. The large numbers of elderly persons who vote and feel deserving of pensions make them a strong interest group that can influence public policy in ways that mothers on welfare, the unemployed, children, and the poor cannot. Pampel and Williamson thus draw the appropriate conclusion that, whereas other social welfare programs may be influenced by the power of the working class in highly democratic societies, pensions appear to be more strongly influenced by the political power of the elderly population.

Differing Welfare Ideologies

Tension between the competing ideologies of the capitalist economic system and the rights of citizenship continue in the welfare states of the West, particularly in the United States. As Myles (1984) reminds us, a basic tenet of capitalist social relations was that whatever social benefits were to be provided outside of the marketplace should be a mirror image of the relative prices (wages) assigned by the market to the worth of an individual's labor. In other words, welfare benefits should not be out of line with the earning power of individual workers. Also, the amount of entitlements for measures like old-age pensions should, under a capitalist-oriented system, be determined by the individual's work history instead of through a system that provides everyone with the same level of support. Nor should welfare become so attractive that it motivates people not to work, or increases tax burdens on employers or the public to the extent that it undermines the economy. Hence, social insurance in a capitalist system needs to be based on labor force participation, and this is exactly what happened in the United States with respect to Social Security benefits (Quadagno 1984, 1988).

Entitlements based on citizenship, however, have a different orientation. They are aimed toward providing people with a normal standard of living, regardless of their position in the labor market. The welfare system of Western Europe is more advanced in this direction than in the United States. Many Western Europeans receive allowances for the maintenance of children, comprehensive health insurance, and protection for lost income due to sickness or injury. These benefits accrue to *all* qualified citizens, regardless of their income or position in the labor market. For example, in Sweden, West Germany, and elsewhere in Western Europe, all families with children receive an allowance intended to supplement family expenses for children's clothing, school lunches, and the like. The amount of the allowance paid by the state is based upon the number of children in the family. Income is not a criterion, and both affluent and nonaffluent families receive the same amount for the same number of children.

Welfare programs in the United States, in contrast, are not so extensive, and benefits are generally based on income. When most Western European governments were introducing social welfare programs around the turn of the century, the U.S. government was not deeply involved in regulating the economy, nor was there a significant threat of social revolution from discontented workers. Moreover, Americans have traditionally been less committed to government welfare programs and more in favor of private enterprise in dealing with economic and social problems. Except for the elderly, participation in the welfare system is not considered normative at all in the United States, and nonretired Americans who receive welfare tend to be especially stigmatized and socially devalued (Mead 1985). But in Western Europe, providing welfare and social security for the general population, not just the elderly and the poor, has evolved into a normal feature of the state's role. This situation implies a fundamental difference in the social values of Americans and Western Europeans, with Americans stressing individualism and Western Europeans viewing government in a more paternalistic fashion.

For example, Erwin Scheuch (1989), in discussing the results of a 1985 International Social Survey Programme (ISSP) question that asked whether it is the responsibility of the government to reduce differences in income between people with high incomes and those with low incomes, found that the results could be correlated by welfare state indicators. The more extensive the development of the welfare state, the more persons living in those countries believed the government should reduce differences in income. In Italy, some 67 percent of the respondents stated agreement with the government's responsibility in reducing income inequalities; in other Western European countries, those agreeing were 66.3 percent in Austria, 56.4 percent in West Germany, and 52.2 percent in Great Britain. In the United States, however, only 29.5 percent of the population sampled were in agreement. Other research, by Bernice Pescosolido, Carol Boyer, and Wai Tsui (1985), investigated public evaluations of government performance in providing medical care in eight Western welfare states, including the United States. Great Britain and the Netherlands had the highest public evaluations, followed by West Germany and Austria. The United States ranked seventh, just ahead of Italy, where the populace was particularly dissatisfied with government planning in health care. Those governments who had the most positive evaluations overall were those whose system of health benefits was considered by the population as the most innovative in *guaranteeing* health care.

Consequently, there are differences in orientations between welfare states, with Western European nations generally ahead of the United States in providing social welfare as a right of citizenship. This difference is important, because greater proportions of the gross national product (GNP) are spent on old-age benefits in Western Europe than in the United States. For instance, in 1984, the United States spent less than 9 percent of its GNP on old-age pensions, compared with 12.9 pecent in West Germany, 14.4 percent in Great Britain, and 16.4 percent in Italy. In 1982, Sweden already was spending 33.1 percent of its GNP on old-age benefits, and increases are expected in the future. By the year 2030, Italy's pension system is likely to reach 30 percent of its GNP, and Germany will not be far behind at 28 percent; in the United States, some 14 percent of the GNP will go for old-age pensions in 2030.

The Coming Crisis in Paying for Social Security

On the negative side, Western society's social security system is going to be in great difficulty in financing its old-age assistance programs in the twenty-first century, and this is especially the case in Western Europe.

Western Europe has a more generous welfare state tradition, and there is strong resistance to cutting benefits, as Italy, France, and West Germany found in the late 1980s. Unemployment is about twice as high in Western Europe than in the United States. Because it is politically difficult to encourage people to retire later, younger people are prevented from taking their place in the labor force. Additionally, Western Europeans are more dependent, on the average, on their state-supplied old-age pensions than are Americans. In many Western European countries, such pensions represent almost 90 percent of an individual's income, compared with an average of about 50 percent in the United States. The welfare states of Western Europe not only typically provide greater financial support to their older citizens than does the United States, but also collect a greater proportion of income from workers and employers to finance their system. For instance, in 1987 the social security contributions of West German workers and matching funds paid by employers amounted to 18.7 percent of a worker's monthly wages or salary, compared with less than 11 percent in the United States. Greater benefits mean greater taxes—something many Americans do not desire.

Western Europe appears headed for a major fiscal crisis earlier than the United States largely because its population is aging more rapidly and the number of workers paying into the system is decreasing faster. What is likely to come is either an increase in the age for entitlement to social security (which happened in 1983 in the United States, when it was mandated by Congress that persons born in 1960 and later will wait to age 67 instead of age 65 for Social Security benefits), a reduction in the amount of paid benefits, or allocations of even larger proportions of expenditures to support the elderly.

For the time being, Western Europe's old-age pensions and services for the elderly remain more generous than those of the United States. But there are signs of adjustments, as West Germany, for instance, which has the lowest birthrate in the world, began a restructuring of pension plans in 1983 and continues to do so today in anticipation of having significantly fewer people paying into the system in the twenty-first century. This situation will be altered somewhat with the unification of West and East Germany, but the financing of old-age pensions gives every indication of remaining a major issue of public concern among Germans in general. The guiding principle behind the German pension system is that persons who have retired from working will be able to maintain an adequate standard of living; therefore, old-age benefits are likely to remain high. In 1987, the average retired West German received a monthly pension from the government of approximately $710 (compared with $513 in the United States).

In the United States, the commitment from the federal government is also well-established, and the increasingly important problems of how to pay for public old-age pensions remain. Such benefits are taking up larger proportions of the budgets of private companies and federal agencies (for example, over 6 percent of military spending in 1985 went just for retirement pay).

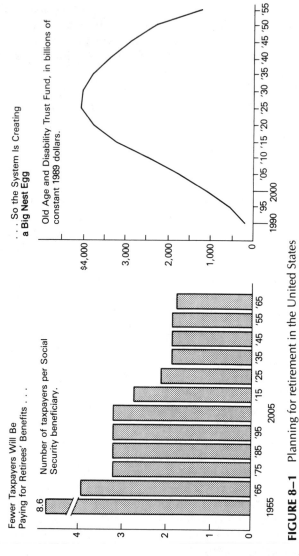

Fewer Taxpayers Will Be Paying for Retirees' Benefits . . .

Number of taxpayers per Social Security beneficiary.

8.6

4

3

2

1

0

1955 '65 '75 '85 '95 2005 '15 '25 '35 '45 '55 '65

. . . So the System Is Creating a Big Nest Egg

Old Age and Disability Trust Fund, in billions of constant 1989 dollars.

$4,000

3,000

2,000

1,000

0

1990 '95 2000 '05 '10 '15 '20 '25 '30 '35 '40 '45 '50 '55

FIGURE 8–1 Planning for retirement in the United States

Source: Social Security Board of Trustees Report 1989.

Nearly 21 percent of the federal government's entire budget in 1983 was allocated to Social Security. A particular problem with Social Security is that it pays out more money than it takes in, which resulted in increases in payroll deductions for Social Security during the 1980s to the current level of 7.65 percent on the first $42,000 earned. Taxes paid by the Baby Boom generation will keep the Social Security system adequately financed until the early twenty-first century, when the Baby Boomers start retiring. With a smaller population of workers following them, fewer workers will be available to support the largest number of retirees ever, and a crisis is likely to loom.

This situation is depicted in Figure 8–1, which shows the declining number of taxpayers per Social Security beneficiary for the years 1955–2065. In 1955, Figure 8–1 shows 8.6 taxpayers (workers paying into the fund through payroll deductions) for one Social Security beneficiary; between 1975 and 2005, the number of contributors to Social Security will drop to 3.3 per beneficiary. By 2015, the number of taxpayers per beneficiary will decline to 2.8, followed by further decline, beginning in 2035, to about 1.9 taxpayers per beneficiary in 2055; in 2065, Figure 8-1 projects another drop to 1.8 workers per retiree. Figure 8–1 also shows that the Social Security Trust Fund is expected to rise to $4 trillion (in 1990 dollars) by 2030. But at that time, the surplus will begin to decrease rapidly because of the large number of beneficiaries resulting from the Baby Boom generation and the much smaller ratio (about 2 to 1 of workers to retirees). Between 2035 and 2055, a period of only twenty years, the amount of the trust fund will drop from $4 trillion to $1 trillion—clearly indicating a future crisis in the funding of the nation's Social Security program as the low ratio of workers to retirees continues.

At present, the commitment of the welfare states of Western Europe to the well-being of its older citizens is somewhat more advanced than that of the United States, where the responsibility of the individual for his or her own welfare, including old age, remains an important social value. Yet the general trend in the welfare states of the West, including the United States, is that the rights of citizenship—civil, political, and social—have evolved into basic entitlements for the general population. Although crises in the funding of old-age benefits appear forthcoming, entitlement to those benefits on the basis of citizenship has been firmly established. The principal issue in the future will not be whether to continue such benefits, but what is the best method to finance them.

SUMMARY

This chapter has examined the role of the aged as a social and political force in society. The elderly do not appear to be a minority group in the political process along the same lines as blacks, Hispanics, and others. Rather, the aged constitute a political interest group and are supported by several influential organizations like the American Association of Retired Persons. The AARP and other senior citizens' groups are highly effective in lobbying for benefits for old people at all levels of government.

Through the enactment of the Social Security program in 1935, the United States became a welfare state. The welfare state in Western society evolved out of the struggle for the civil, political, and social rights of citizenship in which equality based on these rights surpassed the ownership of property and capital as the basis for political representation and entitlement to public programs. Much of the struggle in Western society to secure an adequate level of subsistence for the elderly was fought by labor organizations in the past, but the dominant influence in the present is the political power of the aged population. The more democratic a nation and the larger its aged population, the greater the political power of the elderly. Despite the tendency of Americans to have more individualistic attitudes about the responsibility for security in old age and Western Europeans to invest more responsibility in their government for providing such security, the clear tendency in Western society is toward guaranteeing an adequate level of well-being for old people. Although Western nations will face a financial crisis in paying for old-age benefits in the future, the right of entitlement to such benefits on the basis of citizenship has been established and is highly likely to continue.

Aging and Social Policy in Selected Countries

This chapter examines social policy toward the aged in selected countries. The purpose of most social security programs worldwide is identical in that they are intended to protect people from loss of income in old age, or as a result of disability, illness, widowhood, or other problems. Abram de Swaan (1988) points out that what distinguishes modern social security arrangements is their nationwide, collective, and compulsory character. They are nationwide in that they apply to everyone; collective in that resources are accumulated and paid out of a common fund; and compulsory in that benefits are defined, funds collected, and eligibility determined whether the individual wishes to join and contribute or not.

However, hardly any two social security systems in the world are alike. They vary from country to country in the manner in which they are organized, staffed, and financed, as well as in the amount of benefits they provide, the coverage they offer, and the historical, social, economic, and ideological factors that influenced their development (Øyen 1986). Yet, comparing social policies toward the aged in various countries is an excellent way to determine general trends, assess differences, better understand the situation in any one particular country, and obtain ideas about the advantages or disadvantages in the various approaches. In this chapter we will review social policy toward the aged in the United States, Canada, Great Britain, Germany, France, Japan, and China.

UNITED STATES

Some 28.6 million persons, or 12 percent of the total population of the United States in 1985, was age 65 or over. In 2025, the number of aged should be about 58.7 million, or 19.5 percent of the total population. Thus, the United States, like most other Western nations, will have about one aged person out of every five people in the general population in the early twenty-first century.

As noted in previous chapters, the United States is fully committed to supporting the elderly. The key legislation was the Social Security Act of 1935, in which the federal government assumed the responsibility for helping ease the financial burden of old age by providing monthly payments to qualified persons at age 65, the disabled, and widows and their dependent children. Other important legislation includes: (1) the Older Americans Act of 1965, which underscores the nation's commitment to older persons by providing a legal basis for coordinating and monitoring social services for the elderly through Area Agencies on Aging, and authorizing funding for various old-age assistance programs such as multipurpose senior citizen centers in local communities; (2) the passage of Medicare in 1965, which authorizes payment for most health care expenses for old people; and (3) the Age Discrimination in Employment Act of 1967 and its subsequent amendments, which end forced retirement for most Americans and prohibits denial of employment on the basis of age.

Eligibility and the amount of benefits provided to old people under the nation's Social Security program is based on prior participation in the labor force. Persons without such participation, or who are not disabled or surviving dependents of deceased workers, are not included. Nevertheless, it is extremely rare for an elderly person not to have some type of government-sponsored financial support in old age. The average monthly Social Security check in 1987 was $513, with a $25 increase authorized in 1990. Funds to support Social Security are collected through contributions, beginning in 1990, of 15.3 percent of a worker's earnings. Half (7.65 percent) is paid by the employee on the first $42,000 of annual salary, and employers pay the other half.

But in comparison with most other Western nations, the United States was relatively late in embarking on a national welfare program. And, although the elderly are the prime beneficiaries in modern welfare states, including the United States, the American system of social welfare is not as comprehensive as those found elsewhere. As shown in Table 9-1, which lists the dates of the introduction of various social welfare programs on a national level in Germany, Great Britain, France, Canada, and the United States, not only was the United States slow (1935) to provide old-age pensions, but it is the only nation not currently providing sickness benefits (coverage for wages lost because of illness), family allowances (allowances for child care and housing

TABLE 9–1   Dates of Introduction of National Social Welfare Programs in Selected Western Countries

	OLD-AGE PENSIONS	HEALTH INSURANCE	SICKNESS BENEFITS	FAMILY ALLOWANCES	UNEMPLOYMENT INSURANCE
Germany	1889	1883	1883	1954	1927
Great Britain	1908	1948	1911	1945	1911
France	1930	1945	1930	1932	1914
Canada	1927	1972	1971	1944	1940
United States	1935	—	—	—	1935

for the poor), and health insurance for the entire population. What this signifies is that there are gaps in coverage for the social welfare of all citizens, including younger persons. As Robert Hudson (1988:67) points out, "Many Americans will continue to arrive in old age with histories of low wages, poor health, limited education, and marginal family and social supports."

As also discussed in the last chapter, social welfare is not considered normative in the United States for anyone but the elderly. Therefore, if one is economically dependent on government assistance prior to old age, that person tends to be socially devalued and arrives at old age with a lifetime history of disadvantages. Programs to intervene in that person's life course at a younger age are limited to unemployment benefits and some educational and job-training opportunities. Health care coverage is available only for the most economically disadvantaged younger persons through Medicaid. Therefore, although the United States is a welfare state, its welfare system is clearly not as extensive as those found in Western Europe or Canada.

This is seen in the fact that when we speak of a welfare state in the United States, we are referring primarily to programs for the disadvantaged. There are government programs for the welfare of the general population, of course, such as public health, environmental protection, education, highway construction, and the like. But the term *welfare*, as used in the United States, generally refers to assistance for those living in poverty. To a somewhat lesser extent it applies to those who are old; but many elderly are not poor, and the notion of being "on welfare" would not accurately represent their social situation. Rather, Social Security payments supplement their income and represent partial replacement of lost wages or salaries due to retirement. However, regardless of the popular meaning of the term *welfare* in the United States. the American welfare state evolved to a large extent as a response to the needs of the elderly.

The development of the nation's Social Security system for the aged was reviewed in the last two chapters and will not be repeated here. Essentially, this system arose out of compromises between government, private industry, organized labor, and the lobbying of the aged themselves during the Great Depression of the late 1920s and early 1930s (Quadagno 1984). Prior to this time, there was no particular social policy regarding the elderly. Old people were generally on their own. Financial support (which was uncommon in the early twentieth century) came from savings and pensions, from families, or from whatever resources were available in the local community, such as churches or charities. For many elderly (perhaps a majority), to be old also meant to be poor. However, passage of the Social Security Act in 1935 signified the assumption of responsibility on the part of the federal government to provide at least a basic level of subsistence to the elderly. Subsequent revisions in the Social Security program, including an expansion of coverage and cost of living increases—along with the provision of Medicare to pay for most medical expenses and the spread of pension programs for full-time, permanent employees—have significantly assisted older people.

As the nation moves into the twenty-first century, the most pressing social policy issue for the aged will be the financing of the Social Security system and Medicare. Medicaid will also be affected because it pays a large share of the costs of nursing home care for the aged poor. The more affluent among the elderly have been required to pay income taxes on their Social Security allotments, and payroll deductions from the wages and salaries of active workers have been increased to the current 7.65 percent level. Individual out-of-pocket costs for participating in Medicare have risen, and cost containment measures for Medicare have been instituted by congressional legislation. A fixed schedule of fees (known as Diagnostic Related Groups, or DRGs) establishing limits on the amounts paid to hospitals for Medicare patients was passed in 1983. A major overhaul of Medicare fees (the Physicians Payment Reform Act), which was passed in 1989, set fixed fees for physicans as well. This legislation lowered the amounts (by 20 percent) usually paid to physicians providing specialized services, such as those provided by surgeons and radiologists, while increasing amounts paid (by 40 percent) for family practitioners and internists for preventive care. Thus, the focus of Medicare was to be oriented more toward prevention and health maintenance than treatment per se, especially treatment involving very expensive medical procedures. The amount physicians can charge patients in excess of payments they receive from the government was also limited to 25 percent in 1992, 20 percent in 1993, and 15 percent thereafter.

Thus, the pattern of social policy for the aged in the near future is likely to be one that preserves support for old people in the area of heatlh and social security, but does so within a context of cost containment. Payroll deductions to maintain Social Security appear to be adequate until the early twenty-first century because of the large Baby Boom generation in the active labor force. By 2030, when the Baby Boomers have retired, however, ther will be a major decline, as previously noted in other chapters, in the funding of Social Security due to the smaller population of active workers. This will likely mean changes in policy for the aged, such as financial incentives for older workers to remain in the labor force. Increased payroll deductions for Social Security are also likely to take place.

Whatever measures are taken by the federal government with respect to old-age benefits are likely to be done in conjunction with lobbying by the elderly, who form a powerful political constituency. In late 1989, for example, political pressure by the elderly resulted in the repeal of the 1988 Medicare Catastrophic Coverage Act, which funded long-term hospital care for old people. This act was repealed because of objections to a $4 monthly premium and a surtax (as high as $800 annually for some individuals) affecting about 40 percent of Medicare beneficiaries. The act also was opposed because it failed to cover the costs of long-term nursing home care. This development helps demonstrate that a unique policy situation in the United States—in comparison with other nations—is the immense political influence of the elderly. Social policy toward the aged is influenced more strongly in the United States by older citizens and the organizations representing them than elsewhere in the world. To a large extent, social policy toward the aged is shaped, within the context of fiscal restraints, by the influence of the elderly on Congress. The elderly are able to do this because they are well-organized, vote in large numbers, keep in contact with their legislators, and have effective organizations lobbying on their behalf. With a large and relatively healthy population of aged persons in the twenty-first century, the central task of policy-makers will be to find the financial resources to meet the social and health needs of the elderly without compromising opportunities for the young.

CANADA

In 1985, some 10.4 percent, or 2.6 million, of Canada's total population of approximately 25.5 million people were age 65 or over; by 2025, Canada's population is expected to reach 33.2 million, and the proportion of elderly will increase to 6.2 million, or 18.8 percent, of all Canadians. In comparison with other countries, especially those of Western Europe, Canada is still relatively youthful in demographic terms; but this will change by 2025, for the number of older people will have increased some 76 percent over the figure for 1985. In monetary terms, this will mean, according to John Myles (1988), a *graying* of the nation's budget, because in Canada, as in other modern welfare states, public programs for the elderly comprise the largest single category of expenditures. With significantly larger numbers of older people, the aging of Canadian society will be an increasingly important aspect of public policy. As Susan McDaniel (1986:117) points out, "There is no doubt that aging of the Canadian population will create new challenges for policy-makers."

Canada's initial step in the direction of social welfare for the aged was the passage of the Old Age Pensions Act of 1927. As Myles explains, this act was neither universal nor generous. It provided a pension of just $20 a month only to persons over the age of 70 with very low incomes; by 1951, this pension had been increased just marginally to $40 monthly, and one had to be very poor to get it. The first major change came in 1951 with the Old Age Security Act, which affirmed the benefit level of $40 per month, but extended the pension to include everyone, regardless of income, at age 70. By 1970, eligibility for the basic pension had been reduced to age 65, where it remains today, and the amount of the benefit has been raised significantly. Funds to support this basic pension are primarily derived from general taxation.

As of 1986, an elderly Canadian received a flat rate, in Canadian dollars (which is about 85 percent of an American dollar), of a maximum of $291.51 monthly as a basic pension. This amount is generally not enough to support an adequate standard of living for most retired persons, so it has been necessary to adopt a second tier of pension benefits—as has been the case in Great Britain—based on contributions from earnings. This additional earnings-related plan, known as the Canadian Pension Plan (which covers all of Canada but Quebec province) and the Quebec Pension Plan (which covers Quebec), both of which were passed in 1965, provides employees with a pension in addition to the basic plan. The Canada and Quebec Pension Plans pay the retired worker a maximum of 25 percent of his or her contributory average lifetime adjusted pensionable earnings. Both the employee and the employer each contribute to the plan 1.8 percent of the worker's wages or salary that falls between $2,500 to $25,800 annually; self-employed persons contribute the full 3.6 percent by themselves. In 1986, the maximum amount paid to a retiree entitled to full benefits under these plans was $486.11 monthly. When a worker dies and the pension is ended, the surviving spouse will be entitled to between $273.35 and $291.65 monthly under the Canada plan; a higher sum was available under the Quebec plan.

For those persons who retired soon after 1965 and were therefore not eligible for full benefits, an income supplement was provided in 1967 and remains in force today for elderly persons with low incomes. This supplement, the Guaranteed Income Supplement (GIS), paid $346 monthly to eligible single pensioners or $225 to each spouse if both are over age 65. This plan also provides a pension of $517 monthly to persons between the ages of 60 and 64 if their spouse has little or no income, or $570 monthly to widows and widowers ages 60 to 64 with low incomes. Over 50 percent of all elderly Canadians receive the GIS.

In addition to these public pensions, employed persons have access to pension plans established by their employers and personal savings plans. Canada thus offers a safety net for all its citizens by providing all the aged a flat rate of monetary support regardless of the level of their participation in the labor force, and they receive some supplemental pension of varying amounts as well.

Therefore, although the eligibility for social security benefits and the level of payments is determined in the United States by the length and amount of a person's contributions to the system from wages and salary, all Canadians receive a basic pension. Supplements to this basic pension are then determined by the person's history of contributions from employment. Persons lacking sufficient past contributions because of low incomes are still provided for, however, in Canada's approach. Myles explains that low-income persons actually fare slightly better than more affluent persons in the Canadian system of state pensions, leaving those persons with relatively greater financial resources to depend more on private pensions and savings, instead of the state, to maintain their standard of living.

Also, the Canadian government provides family allowances (1944), sickness benefits (1971), and national health insurance (1972) to all citizens. Canadian physicians, like those in the United States, are generally private, self-employed, fee-for-service practitioners; but unlike in the United States, doctors' fees in Canada are paid by government-sponsored national health insurance according to rates negotiated with the provincial government. Most hospitals also operate on a budget negotiated with government officials at the provincial level. Private health insurance is generally prohibited except for covering some supplemental benefits, such as semiprivate room accommodations. Thus, Canada essentially has a private system of health care delivery paid for almost entirely by public funds. The money to pay for this system is obtained from public tax revenues. The Canadian government is able to exercise greater control over the costs of care than can the United States government, because the former buys basically all the care provided and is in a strong position to determine how much it is willing to pay for it (Evans 1986).

With a relatively rapid increase in the proportion of its elderly population in the future, Canada will be faced with increased financial requirements to continue the health and social welfare of its aged citizens. Canada's approach to dealing with the needs of the elderly is not likely to change from the current system of providing a basic level of support to the general population as a right of citizenship. No longer is it the situation that old-age benefits provided by the state go only to the poor, for all elderly receive a pension and free medical care.

GREAT BRITAIN

The total population of Great Britain is expected to stabilize around 56 million in the years between 1985 and 2025, but the number of elderly is going to increase from 8.5 million to about 10.5 million during this same period. The proportion of aged persons in the general population will thus grow from 15.1 percent in 1985 to 18.7 percent in 2025, although the overall number of people in Britain will remain about the same. While the growth of the elderly population in Britain is relatively modest compared with many other countries, the increase is nonetheless significant because it will mean a substantial demand for health and social services as the nation moves into the twenty-first century.

Even though Britain is one of the world's most highly developed countries, it is not exceptionally wealthy and has a high rate of unemployment in comparison with some more affluent nations. In fact, during the late 1900s, various surveys found that old people in Britain not only had much less disposable income after retirement than active workers in their own country (Wells and Freer 1988), but also had less than the aged in West Germany, Sweden, Norway, Canada, and the United States (King's Fund Centre 1988). Nevertheless, there are some positive aspects to aging in Britain in that over 75 percent of the elderly are in good or fairly good health (Wells and Freer 1988). The vast majority of British elderly also are able to live in the community; only 5 percent reside in old-age homes. Furthermore, state pensions were increased somewhat in 1987, and in 1988 older workers with part-time jobs were authorized a weekly allowance of about $45 (as counted in U.S. dollars) from the government to supplement their salary for six months of the year.

State-sponsored old-age pensions were instituted by the Pensions Act of 1908, but the pensions provided only a minimum level of subsistence, for they were primarily intended to support only those aged who were quite poor. However, with the victory of the British Labour Party in 1945, Britain became the leading welfare state among English-speaking nations. This was accomplished with the passage of legislation beginning in the late 1940s that provided family allowances and rent or property tax supplements for housing for the poor, old-age pensions, sickness benefits, unemployment benefits, national health insurance, and the provision of a national health service—all intended to guarantee freedom from want as a right of citizenship. Thus, the provision of social welfare in Britain was transformed from providing benefits just for the poor or for the working class, to that of helping all citizens in need. As Myles (1984:40) explains, "The state, acting on behalf of all its citizens, would provide a safety net below which no member of the community would be allowed to fall."

When it came to health care, the National Service Act of 1948 allowed the British government to become the owner of hospitals and the employer of physicians, nurses, and other health care workers. Medical services, in turn, are provided free of charge to patients. About 10 percent of the funds to support the National Health Service is derived from payroll deductions and employers' contributions; most of the remaining revenue comes from general taxation.

General practitioners, or family practice physicians, are paid a set fee by the government for each patient on their patient list (up to 3,500 patients for a solo practice or 4,500 patients in a partnership, as long as the average number of patients per doctor does not exceed 3,500). A higher fee is paid for patients who are 65 years of age or older. General practitioners are the first line of medical care for all patients. If care by a specialist (known as a "consultant" in the British system) or hospitalization is warranted, the patient must be referred by a general practitioner. Generally, specialists are the only physicians who treat patients in hospitals, and they are paid a salary by the government. Other legislation includes a supplement to income for employed persons when they become sick or injured and death benefits for survivors.

As of 1988, men at age 65 and women at age 60 without dependents have a right to a basic state retirement pension of approximately $275 monthly, a $16 Christmas bonus, free medical care, free health service drug prescriptions, and free dental and eye checkups. A retired person with a spouse or other adult dependent receives a basic monthly pension of about $430. Qualification for the pension depends on the number and level of contributions over a specified period. In addition to the basic pension, there is an additional earnings-related pension based on the amount of earnings paid into the state retirement system; there is also a supplementary pension for persons whose basic and earnings-related pensions do not give them sufficient resources to live on. Although the state remains responsible for the basic pension, which all qualified persons are entitled to and which generally pays the same amount to everyone, employers are allowed to remove their employees from the state's additional earnings-related pension plan if their program equals or betters the state's plan. Moreover, the Social Security Act of 1986 gives the individual the right to choose between participation in either the state's earnings-related plan, the employer's plan, or a retirement plan sponsored by a bank or other financial institution.

In general, the elderly in Britain are more financially secure than ever before and are supported by an extensive system of supplementary benefits and free medical care. Nevertheless, important problems remain. The elderly in Britain, for example, have less spending power in relation to the cost of living in comparison with many other Western nations. As Nicholas Abercrombie and Alan Warde and their associates (1988) note:

> It has been estimated that three-quarters of the elderly, compared with one-fifth of the non-elderly, live on or below the poverty line. Part of this, clearly, is due to the loss of earned income. In fact, the proportion of elderly men over 65 who are still working has declined from over half in 1931 to some 15 percent in 1979. The result is that a large proportion of the elderly are solely dependent on the basic state pension, with supplementary benefit.[1]

Greater poverty among the elderly has meant worsening health. The aged in Britain tend to have lower life expectancies than older people in most

---

1. Nicholas Abercrombie and Alan Warde, with Keith Soothill, John Urry, and Sylvia Walby, *Contemporary British Society* (Cambridge, UK: Polity Press, 1988), 282–283.

Western European countries (King's Fund Centre 1988). In 1985, for example, life expectancy at birth in Britain was 74.1 years, matching West Germany, but behind Greece (74.4 years), Italy, France, and Denmark (74.8 years), Norway (76.2 years), and Sweden (76.6 years). Poverty among the aged remains a particular problem in Britain and affects both the length and quality of life available to them to a greater degree than found in some other Western European countries. The British government, although continuing to emphasize the right of social security in old age, is faced with coping with the rising costs of the aging of its population in much the same manner as other developed countries. However, they must do so with less financial resources than some of their more affluent neighbors like Germany. Consequently, in Great Britain the relatively rapid increase in the elderly population is a major social problem, for the aged consume an increasingly larger share of the nation's limited budget for health and social welfare.

GERMANY

The Federal Republic of Germany is growing older like other Western nations; however, when it comes to the age structure of German society, the country represents a special case because West Germany had the lowest birthrate in the world. The result was that the West German population was actually declining since births were not keeping up with deaths. For example, in 1985, West Germany had a birthrate of 9.6 births per 1,000 people, but the death rate was 11.5 per 1,000. For 1986, the West German birthrate rose slightly to 10.3 per 1,000, but births remained exceeded by deaths as mortality rates remained constant at 11.5 per 1,000. Consequently, the West German population was shrinking each year. The addition of East Germany to the Federal Republic does little to reverse this trend because the rate of East German births in 1986 was the same as the death rate (13.4 births and 13.4 deaths per 1,000 people). Therefore, in Germany as a whole, the western part of the country (with a population of 61 million in 1986) was declining while the eastern section (with a much smaller population of 17 million) was staying about the same. Overall, the German population remains in a state of decline.

Not only is the German population projected to become smaller; it is also becoming older. In 1985 there were 9 million persons over the age of 65, constituting 14.5 percent of the population in West Germany; by 2025, it is predicted that the number of elderly will reach 12 million, or about 19 percent of all West Germans. The addition of East Germans to the Federal Republic does not significantly change Germany's general pattern of aging and by 2025 almost one out of every five Germans will be age 65 or over.

This situation signals a major problem for Germany's social security system, because it means considerably fewer persons are available in the working-age population to provide income to fund welfare benefits and old-age pensions. Yet Erwin Scheuch (1987) suggests that the problem facing the German welfare system is not just the declining percentage of workers, because the effect of this development can be partially offset by later retirement, increases in the number of women in the labor force, and a young population of foreign workers. Scheuch therefore concludes that it is not the inability to collect money from workers at present levels to pay for health insurance and old-age pensions that will be the major problem in the next century. Rather, the primary problem will be one of rising costs, because an increasingly older population will mean a different mix of illnesses (more diseases associated with aging) and greater demand for health services to cope with these diseases.

The costs associated with the aging of its population are likely to be particularly high in Germany because of a tradition of paternalism on the part of the government, which dates back to the 1880s and the social policies of old Imperial Germany. Unlike the United States, Germany has a comprehensive system of social welfare services, including the provision of free health care for the vast majority of its citizens. What this means is that all Germans, as members of one of the most affluent societies in the world, can demand and receive an extensive array of social benefits from their government.

As Myles (1984) explains, Germany and the United States differ in attitudes toward welfare entitlements in general and old-age benefits in particular. Germany was the first country to introduce a system of universal health insurance and old-age pensions in the late nineteenth century, whereas the United States was one of the last to provide old-age benefits and, as noted, still lacks coverage for health care on a national basis. Except for the aged, participation in a government welfare system is not considered a normative practice in the United States. Those Americans who receive welfare tend to be stigmatized and devalued socially (Mead 1985). In Germany, in distinct contrast, providing welfare and social security for the general public, not only the poor and the aged, is a normal feature of the state's role. This contrast implies a fundamental difference between the value systems of the two countries: Americans emphasize individualism, whereas Germans manifest a high regard for the state.

The study by Bernice Pescosolido, Carol Boyer, and Wai Tsui (1985) on public evaluation of health care in eight countries, including West Germany and the United States, illustrated this difference. West Germans rated government performance lower if they believed that the government was taking less responsibility for providing medical services, but the Americans were not as prone to do so. A distinctive psychological orientation on the part of Germans, in comparison with Americans, helps us understand the different approaches to welfare. The German word *anspruchsdenken* cannot be translated literally into English, but essentially means a "mentality of entitlement." It signifies a readiness on the part of the individual to claim and use the welfare benefits to which he or she is entitled by law. As Scheuch (1987) explains, the current welfare system in Germany makes it possible for its citizens to demand the most in all welfare programs. Thus, Germans, on the average, appear to have a different mentality about the welfare state. They can use its services whenever and as long as it is necessary; therefore, Germans can approach the social welfare system for health care, pensions, and other benefits with an exceptionally strong sense of personal entitlement. The fact that *anspruchsdenken* has no equivalent in English underscores the lack of a corresponding mentality in American society (Cockerham, Kunz, and Lueschen 1988).

The historical basis for this orientation began in 1883, when Germany's Chancellor Otto von Bismarck introduced a series of social reforms. These reforms were intended to thwart the influence of socialist politicians, secure the loyalty of the working class, and espouse the paternalistic view that the state has the duty to provide for the welfare of its subjects. There is little doubt that Bismarck was aware of the advantage that might be gained from a social insurance program in his struggle against socialism (Craig 1982). Bismarck was a Prussian by birth, and Prussia—the leading state of Imperial Germany, which Bismarck had helped establish in 1871—had a tradition of state responsibility for the welfare of its citizens in return for their obedience and allegiance. Not only was a program of social insurance for all of Germany consistent with this tradition, but it offered Bismarck the opportunity to promote the national government at the expense of socialist politicians and workers' trade unions. Socialist members of the German Reichstag, or Parliament, were caught in a dilemma and were forced by political and public pressure to support Bismarck's plan in order to avoid being accused of disregarding the needs of the working class.

As Myles (1984) observes, Bismarck's measures were both a response to democratization and an attempt to suppress it. That is, Bismarck wanted to defuse the demands for political rights from an increasingly well-organized and leftist-oriented working class by providing them with social rights that linked workers to the state rather than to trade unions or socialist politicians. Included in Bismarck's reforms (national health insurance was provided in 1883) was a national compulsory old-age insurance program initiated in 1889. As David Childs and Jeffrey Johnson (1981:99) aptly summarize the outcome: "Whatever view we might now take of Bismarck's motives in introducing these schemes, there can be no doubt that they were excellent for their time and they became a model both for subsequent German governments and for foreign governments."

Following Germany's defeat in World War II and incorporation of its eastern lands into a separate Communist state, West Germany became a multiparty republic in 1949. The West German constitution, the Basic Law, guarantees the social welfare of its citizens, continues the comprehensive social security system developed by Bismarck, and now includes East Germans. The program that was established included health insurance, old-age pensions, sickness benefits for income lost to illness or injury, unemployment insurance, and family assistance in the form of child benefits, rent allowances (especially for the elderly), and public funds for the construction of low-income housing.

Participation in the state-sponsored health insurance program is compulsory for most Germans. Employees, the unemployed, foreign workers, students, farmers, household workers, and old-age pensioners are all required to be insured by one of several hundred health insurance organizations that are supervised by the federal government. About 12.6 percent of a worker's monthly gross earnings goes to pay for health insurance, with half the contribution made by the employee and half by the employer. Approximately 7 percent of the German population is excluded from coverage—namely, civil servants, employees with high salaries, and the self-employed—but they can take out private insurance or voluntarily join the state program. Health care is free to the individual and covers medical and dental treatment, drugs and medicines, and hospital care for an indefinite period of time. In the event of illness, the employer must continue to pay the employee's full wages for six weeks, and then the health insurance fund provides the individual with his or her approximate take-home pay for up to seventy-eight weeks. If the illness is more protracted, benefits are continued under a welfare plan unless the person is permanently incapacitated and is entitled to a disability pension. Since 1983, retired persons have been required to pay part (about one-sixth) of the cost of their health insurance from their pensions, with the remainder financed from contributions paid into the government's compulsory health insurance program by members of the labor force.

Participation in the statutory old-age pension plan is also mandatory for all wage and salary earners and farmers; self-employed persons and housewives may voluntarily join the program. Additionally, widows and orphaned children of insured persons are entitled to a portion of the insured's pension. Retirement normally takes place at the age of 65, but anyone who has contributed to the statutory pension fund for thirty-five years may retire at age 63; women may opt to retire at age 60 if they have made contributions for fifteen of the last twenty years prior to their application. The amount of the pension depends on the size of the individual's contributions and the number of years he or she was a member of the active work force. The pension contribution in 1988 stood at 18.7 percent of a person's gross monthly earnings—again, half paid by the employee and half by the employer. In 1988, the average monthly pension from the government-sponsored program was about $760. In addition to the "normal" old-age pension—that is, the one based on the state's statutory pension plan—many employees also receive a pension from a plan set up by their employer. The amount of this additional pension generally depends on how long the pensioner worked for the employer involved and the amount contributed to it.

Overall, German society has developed an effective "safety net" to provide for the welfare of its citizens, and this is especially true for the aged. The underlying principle of social security in West Germany is that the gainfully employed will support those who are unable to work for reasons of old age, sickness or disability, or unemployment. The employed, in turn, can expect similar support when they need it. The general social welfare of its population is guaranteed by the nation's Basic Law enacted in 1949; thus, the basis of government is clearly that of a welfare state. Nevertheless, in the future, Germany, like other welfare states, will face serious problems in funding its social welfare system as costs rise and the labor force shrinks.

FRANCE

Nearly 7 million people in France, representing some 12.4 percent of the nation's total population of 55 million, were age 65 and over in 1985. By 2025, the number of elderly in France will have increased to 11 million people, comprising 14.8 percent of the overall population. Thus, France's aged population will increase 36 percent between 1985 and 2025, which will be the largest gain in percentage of elderly in a Western European country for this time period. However, the projected growth in the percentage of old people in France will be considerably below the increases of 200–300 percent in developing countries in Asia and Latin America and the increases of over 100 percent in developed nations like Japan, Canada, the United States, and Australia.

Unlike Germany, which began its social security system in the late nineteenth century, France did not have similar developments until 1930. As a result of a law passed in 1901, there were numerous private organizations offering health and pension plans on a nonprofit basis to specific occupational groups. But the 1930 legislation laid the legal foundation for a truly national insurance program, which provided assistance for children and subsidized housing, health care, and old age benefits for low-income families. The system was reorganized in 1945 after the Second World War and expanded to include practically the entire population.

However, there is no single organization providing insurance coverage nationwide, nor do all individuals belong to the same organization. Rather, the French social insurance system remained divided among occupational groups. For old-age benefits, wage and salary earners in commerce and industry have their own organization, as do farmers and agricultural workers. Businessmen, craftsmen, professionals, and employees in the public sector are represented by several different organizations. As Anne-Marie Guillemard (1986:1321) notes, "The universal right to retirement was split up into as many pieces as there were funds." For health and family benefits, a similar system exists. Thus, there is only a minimum level of centralization in France's social welfare system. All of the various insurance organizations are nonprofit, supervised by the government, and responsible to their members. As Isidor Wallimann (1986) points out:

> Germany, Switzerland, the U.S.A. (and as a rule all or most modern welfare states) tend towards having one insurance system covering all citizens irrespective of their occupational or class location. This is also true for health insurance where states—such as Sweden, Great Britain, Germany, however not the U.S.A. or Switzerland—intend to provide coverage against illness for the entire population. It must be concluded, therefore, that the French welfare state is very unique in that it covers the entire population against such things as old age and illness by means of an insurance system which is not only more decentralized but also organized around the occupational or class location of individuals.[2]

With so many different insurance organizations involved in the French system of social welfare, how can uniformity and equality in covering the entire population be achieved? The answer is that the welfare system, including state-sponsored pensions, is not uniform or equal (Guillemard 1986; Wallimann 1986). Everyone is required to belong to an insurance organization, and all such organizations are controlled by various government agencies. The Department of Agriculture, for example, supervises the insurance organization for farmers and agricultural workers, and the Department of Social Affairs and National Security controls the salary and wage earners' insurance organization. These agencies all follow national policy, which provides some uniformity and coordination; otherwise, there are many differences and inequalities in coverage. Different organizations have different rates of contributions and levels of benefits. This situation tends to violate the principle of equity upon which welfare states are based. In contemporary France, as Wallimann (1986:1308) notes, "Those better off (such as the self-employed) maintain some of their privileges also in the social insurance system by virtue of the fact that they are permitted to quite autonomously form and shape their own insurance organization and its policy." Farmers and agricultural workers, on the other hand, are at a relative disadvantage with respect to the amount of premiums they can afford to pay to their own organization and the level of benefits they receive. Consequently, France's social welfare system is divided along socioeconomic lines and is subject to greater class conflict than similar systems in other Western welfare states. Nevertheless, as Wallimann observes, there is no evidence at present that the basic structure of France's social insurance system is going to be changed.

France also differs from other Western states in its method of financing social insurance. The French depend less on taxes on personal income to

2. Isidor Wallimann, "Social Insurance and the Delivery of Social Services in France," *Social Science and Medicine* 23 (1986): 1307.

meet their social needs than any other developed country (Wallimann 1986). Instead, about 42 percent of the funds come from contributions made by employers and employees, and 39 percent from property tax and taxes on goods and services. Income taxes provide only 19 percent of welfare spending in France, compared with about 45 percent in the United States and Canada, 40 percent in Great Britain, and 36 percent in West Germany. Employer contributions to health and retirement benefits are 14.25 percent of their payrolls, whereas employees contribute about 6 percent of their wages and salaries. Thus, "France is unique in that employers pay an unusually high share of all contributions into the social insurance system" (Wallimann 1986:1310). In 1980, over 60 percent of all social expenditures was paid by funds provided by employers. Other countries, like the United States, Canada, Great Britain, and Germany, tend to have equal percentages of contributions from employers and employees. But in France, employers are required to contribute heavily to social welfare because of the political success of socialists and labor unions in attempting to reduce or eliminate altogether the contributions of workers.

Another important difference between France and other Western nations was its increased spending on social insurance in the late 1970s and early 1980s, which only recently lessened because of a slowdown in the economy. Until the 1970s, old-age pensions, as John Ardagh (1987) observes, were so low that many elderly lived in poverty unless they were able to obtain assistance from their families or religious charities. However, following the victory of the Socialist party in France under François Mitterrand in 1981, the minimum pension for retirees that legally must be paid (no one can receive less) was increased by 25 percent. By 1986, the retirement minimum guaranteed by the government was about $430, and the official age of retirement had been lowered from age 65 to age 60. Higher pensions, earlier retirements, and longer life expectancy have meant a considerable strain on France's current budget for social welfare. Like other developed nations, France is confronted with serious problems in financing its welfare state. According to Ardagh (1988:423), "Old people are at last quite well protected by the State: but officialdom has not worked out how best to pay for this new largesse."

JAPAN

Defeated by the United States and its allies in World War II, Japan has recovered to become a giant in the world economy. With a 1986 population of over 121 million people, Japan has advanced to the first rank of world trading nations. In fact, Japan emerged in the late twentieth century as the world's leading creditor nation, exporting billions of dollars each year in loans and overseas investments. The Japanese government, however, does not engage in massive welfare expenditures, including generous pensions, for its own population, nor does it require high income taxes from them. The Japanese people are encouraged to save money for use in old age, and over 20 percent of all personal income goes to savings accounts. Private companies, in turn, are encouraged to establish their own welfare programs for their employees, which includes providing retirement plans, helping retired employees find postretirement work, and providing health insurance. "Businessmen oppose the government's assuming heavy welfare burdens," states Ezra Vogel (1979:191), "for they want to pay less in taxes and to avoid the large governmental administrative overhead required for a large public welfare system."

The problems facing Japan in relation to the aging of its population are not fundamentally different from those in other developed nations, with the notable exception that the Japanese are growing older at a faster rate than any other country. Some 10 percent of the Japanese population was age 65 or over in 1985. But by 2025, the proportion of elderly will reach 20.3 percent, which represents a pace of aging unexceeded elsewhere in the world at present. In the twenty-first century, China will replace Japan as the most rapidly aging society, but until then Japan will hold that position.

However, despite the rapid increase in Japan's elderly population, the Japanese government has responded not by expanding programs for the aged, but by limiting spending in order to conserve funds. In 1986, the government froze current pensions at 68 percent of average monthly incomes and delayed the age of receipt of full payment from age 60 to age 65. There was concern that Japan's social security system would go bankrupt, because the number of younger workers paying taxes to support the system was shrinking. In 1970, there were 8.5 workers paying taxes into social security for every person over age 65; by 1986, there were six workers per elderly person; and in 2020 it is expected that there will be only three workers.

Unlike the situation in the United States, the aged in Japan do not have effective organizations to lobby on their behalf with the national government. Thus, government measures with respect to social security usually do not become political issues to the extent found in the United States. With the exception of national health insurance, elderly Japanese have traditionally not relied on their government for extensive old-age benefits. Although there were various pension plans for government employees and workers in private businesses prior to World War II, it was not until 1960 that Japan created a national pension and health insurance system for all of its citizens, including the self-employed. Initially, benefits were lower than those available in most public and private pension plans already existing both in Japan and in the welfare states of Western Europe. But with the economic growth beginning during the 1960s, Japan increased its spending on social security from 5 percent of the national income in 1960 to 15 percent in the middle 1980s. Allowances for children (beginning with the third child), completely free medical care for older persons at age 70, and greater equality in the level of old-age pensions, especially for employees in the private sector, became part of the overall welfare system in the early 1970s. Prior to age 70, those persons without health insurance from private employers are generally covered by public insurance, but they must pay 30 percent of the cost out of their own pockets.

However, publically funded old-age benefits in Japan have never equaled the entitlements available in many Western European nations, even in the 1980s. For example, when Japanese social security spending in the mid-1980s was 15 percent, several Western nations, including the United States, had expenditures of over 20 percent. As Joji Watanuki (1986) explains, a Japanese welfare state has never been fully realized. Rather, public pensions were intended to supplement pensions from private employers, and old persons were also expected to be taken care of to a large degree by their family. Thus, the Japanese system of old-age security consists largely of three institutions: the government, private business, and the family—with the government making the least contribution.

In 1986, an employee of a large corporation in Japan with thirty years on the job received a lump sum payment at retirement of approximately $155,000 on the average. The retired employee also received a monthly pension of about $1,350, with the government paying some 20 percent of this amount. This may seem like a lot of money, but Japan is one of the most expensive countries in the world to live in, and the cost of housing is particularly high. Consequently, nearly 80 percent of all Japanese continue to work after the customary retirement age, which, in most large corporations, is between the ages of 55 and 60. Of those that continue to work, half are self-employed as farmers and shopkeepers; the remainder usually work full- or part-time in lesser jobs for the same company or for some other firm. Some 40 percent of retired Japanese who continue to work do so because of financial necessity. This is a larger percentage than is found in either the United States, Great Britain, or France (Palmore 1985). But there is also a strong work ethic among elderly Japanese, and younger persons tend to accord older workers considerable respect; in addition, as Erdman Palmore (1985) observes, the elderly generally have job opportunities in Japan, and those aged persons in the highest leadership positions in business, politics, education, and religion usually do not retire until they are very old or their health fails. The proportion of working elderly declines from nearly 80 percent between the ages of 60 and 64 to just under 20 percent at age 80 and above. Nevertheless, there is an important normative distinction between Japan and America when it comes to retirement. As Palmore (1985:51) explains, "In the United States retirement usually means the end of employment; in Japan it usually means reduced work and responsibility, but continued employment."

The Japanese not only are more likely to be employed in old age than in either the United States or Western Europe, but are also more likely to be living with one of their adult children. Although not as large a proportion of Japanese elderly live with their children as is the case in some developing

Asian nations like the Philippines and Singapore (Martin 1988), more elderly live with their children in Japan than in any other developed nation in Western Europe or North America (Watanuki 1986). According to Watanuki (1986:266), "If we only compare industrialized societies, we can say that a high ratio of elderly people living together with their children is peculiar to Japan, and this is the Japanese advantage to be encouraged in order to promote security for the aged." What the aged gain is social support and what their adult children gain is a residence usually in their parents' home—in a nation where housing is expensive and space for homes is scarce. They also gain assistance with household tasks and an enhanced opportunity for young wives to be employed outside the home, because child care facilities are not extensive in Japan. In addition, maintaining a residence with one's aged parents is consistent with the traditional care and respect given to the elderly in Asian societies. According to S. Philip Morgan and Kiyosi Hirosima (1983), living with one's parents is not an anachronism, but is an adaptive strategy for many in Japanese society. Morgan and Hirosima state:

> Extended residence is an accepted tradition in Japanese society supported by strong intergenerational ties, by an emphasis on duty to parents, and by less emotional interdependence between spouses than in Western settings. Also, the Japanese economic system more heavily rewards senior employees so that interfirm moves, which entail geographical mobility, are less frequent. Finally, the extremely expensive housing in Japan, inadequate child care facilities, and less extrafamilial support for the aged make extended residence more attractive in Japan. In short, extended residence seems to fit better with modern Japanese society than with similarly modern nations of the West such as the United States.[3]

Attitudes toward co-residence may be changing somewhat. Watanuki (1986) notes that there can be strain from co-living with aged parents, especially for daughters-in-law who are expected to care for their aged parents-in-law. Linda Martin (1988) also observes a growing preference among better educated elderly to live apart from their children. In 1950, some 87.3 percent of all elderly Japanese lived with their children, but the percentage had declined to 64.6 percent by 1985 (Watanuki 1986). However, despite this decline, the practice of extended residence is not likely to disappear in Japan (Morgan and Hirosima 1983); the proportion of aged Japanese living with their adult children is likely to remain at about 50 percent, which is much higher than in Western nations (Martin 1988). In the United States, for example, in 1987 only 13 percent of the aged lived with a family member other than their spouse; however, this figure includes persons who live with their children and those who live with siblings or other relatives.

3. S. Philip Morgan and Kiyosi Hirosima, "The Persistence of Extended Family Residence in Japan: Anachronism or Alternative Strategy?" *American Sociological Review* 48 (1983): 280.

Another feature of aging in Japan that differs from Western societies is the respect accorded to old people. Palmore (1985) suggests that the high proportion of elderly living with their children is indicative of a continuing high level of respect and affection for the aged by their families. Palmore also notes features of the Japanese language (the honorific form) that are used in speaking to elders to show the proper degree of respect or deference. In addition, aged family members have special places to sit (a seat of honor) at family gatherings and meals, and they are served first at mealtime with the choicest portion of food. The aged also, according to custom, pass through doors before younger persons and bathe first in family baths. Japan also has a special holiday for the aged, Respect for Elders Day, which involves public ceremonies and family activities honoring old people. And Japan has a National Law for the Welfare of the Elders, passed in 1963, guaranteeing a "wholesome and peaceful life" for the aged as a matter of government policy. Although the status of the aged may have declined somewhat in modern Japan, as compared with pre–World War II conditions, Palmore finds that the status of the elderly is returning to relatively higher levels and has traditionally remained higher than in Western countries.

Palmore concludes that the disengagement theory of aging does not apply in Japan, where the elderly are not pushed out of the social mainstream when they are old, nor do the aged themselves wish to withdraw completely from participation in social and economic matters. Palmore also finds that industrialization has not resulted in low status for the aged, as modernization theory would claim. Rather, Palmore finds that the activity theory of aging applies best to the Japanese situation in that the older Japanese tend to maintain high levels of activity if their health permits and the more active Japanese elders tend to be the most satisfied with their lives.

Japan, as discussed in Chapter 2, has the highest life expectancy in the world. According to 1985 figures, the average Japanese lives 77.1 years; the Swedes follow, with the second highest longevity in the world, at 76.6 years. Americans, in contrast, had a life expectancy in 1985 of 74.6 years. Palmore observes that elderly Japanese are relatively happy and healthy; they have free medical care beginning at age 70; and the status and respect accorded to them by their family and the general public are among the highest in the world at present. Japanese elderly, more than those in other industrialized nations, also tend to be more socially integrated into their families. Japan thus appears to be one of the best countries in the world in which to experience old age. But this does not mean that Japan is a paradise for aging. The approach of the Japanese government to aging is to stress self-reliance. Aged Japanese do not receive lavish or extensive old-age pensions from the government, but are required to rely strongly on pensions from employers and savings in one of the most expensive countries in the world. This situation helps explain why the Japanese have one of the highest rates of savings in the world. It also helps explain why a majority of older Japanese continue to work in old age.

As Palmore (1985:55) points out, "In Japan most men continue to work at least until age seventy despite 'retirement' at age fifty-five." Many older Japanese no doubt work in order to remain active in late life and because of the strong work ethic in the country, but for many older Japanese, it is necessary for them to work in order to supplement their old-age benefits.

CHINA

Unlike the other countries discussed in this chapter, the People's Republic of China is a Communist society with one-party rule. The Communists came to power in China in 1949 following a civil war with Nationalist forces. The country remained isolated from non-Communist nations until 1972, when government, cultural, and business contacts were reestablished with the United States and other Western countries in order to further economic development. Although showing tendencies toward allowing greater individual freedom and expression among its population in the 1980s, the Chinese government ruthlessly crushed a student-led prodemocracy movement in 1989 and currently ranks as one of the less tolerant Communist states.

China is of particular interest to gerontologists because of its large and rapidly aging population. With over 1 billion people, representing 22 percent of the world's entire population in the 1980s, China has more people in general and more older people in particular than any other country on the globe. In addition, China is going to overtake Japan in the early twenty-first century as the world's fastest-aging society. What this means is that by the middle of the twenty-first century, China will have a higher proportion of older people in relation to its total population than any other country. According to U.S. Census Bureau (1987) projections, some 40 percent of China's population will be over age 65 by 2025. In terms of absolute numbers, China's elderly population is expected to increase from 53 million in 1985 to over 178 million in 2025. Clearly, China is facing a major demographic and social evolution with respect to aging.

The greatest increase in China's older population is due to declines in fertility and increases in life expectancy that are characteristic of aging societies everywhere. What makes China different is that the large size of its population is in the process of producing greater numbers of older people at a faster pace than elsewhere. According to Jersey Liang and his associates (Liang, Tu, and Chen 1986), China's birthrate fell 50 percent between 1950 and 1982, whereas life expectancy rose from 42.2 years for males and 45.6 years for females during 1953–1964 to 61.6 years for males and 63.2 years for females in 1964–1982. By 1985, overall life expectancy in China was 65.8 years.

Liang and associates point out that about 80 percent of all workers in urban areas are employed in the public sector, which consists of government and Communist party employees and persons working in education, science, industry, and cultural enterprises. Age 60 is the average retirement age for men, and age 55 is the average retirement age for women. However, mandatory retirement is often not required for persons with special skills and positions of political leadership. In order to qualify for a pension, which pays from 60–100 percent of the individual's preretirement salary, the person needs to have been employed in the public sector for at least ten years. The amount of the pension is based upon years of service and credit for revolutionary work. Workers in the public sector have the best retirement situation in China in that they receive the largest pensions and free medical care. Other urban workers in light industry and handicrafts receive pensions that are not as generous as those given state workers, and they do not receive health insurance benefits. They must work twenty years to receive a pension that is 45–50 percent of their last wages. Workers in the few private businesses in China do not receive any public pension at all. Old-age pensions, in fact, are not widespread in China. Less than 25 percent of all persons of retirement age receive a pension, and pensions are especially rare for rural dwellers. Nor does reaching old age bring any special entitlement to health insurance; health insurance benefits when one is elderly are dependent on earlier coverage.

The majority of Chinese elderly depend on their family for support in old age. The government requires that families be responsible for their aged parents under a marriage law; thus, most old people live with their children and depend on them for financial support as well (Liang, Tu, and Chen 1986; Martin 1988; Olson 1988). The bulk of China's population is provided for this way, especially in rural areas where 80 percent of all Chinese live. Under Chinese law, farm workers are to be provided "five guarantees" by their collective farm, which include food, clothing, medical care, housing, and burial expenses. "However," Liang and associates (1986:1359) point out, "it soon became apparent, such guarantees were to apply only to old people who had no pensions or grown sons to support them." Thus, aged persons, without pensions or family support from a son, are provided welfare from either their neighborhood committee in cities or production brigade on collective farms. Many elderly men also find postretirement jobs to provide them with income.

Historically, China, like Japan and other Asian societies, has been characterized as according the elderly relatively high status. Confucian teachings stressing parental authority, the extended family, ancestor worship, and veneration of the aged were influential in China for much of its recorded history (Sher 1984). However, in reality, only upper socioeconomic groups had the economic resources to support large extended households, practice ceremonies associated with Confucian ancestor worship, and consolidate power in the senior family heads (Yin and Lai 1983). Under Communist rule, the status of aged landholders, members of upper and middle socioeconomic groups, and rich peasants was significantly downgraded. But this was primarily a form of social class rather than age discrimination, as the Communists under Mao Tse-tung sought to destroy the influence of China's elderly capitalists. Peter Yin and Kwok Lai describe the circumstances for the aged bourgeoisie:

> Hence, compared to what their situation might have been in traditional China, this bourgeoisie subcohort of elderly adults lost the most social and parental status, and power. In traditional China they would have been venerated by the young, but under the Maoist state, they were despised. Within the family, the same situation prevailed: In traditional China they would have had a large multigenerational household, control of property, and near absolute obedience from the younger generation; under Maoism, they had small families, no property, and little control over their children. Although the literature has noted the decline of older people in Maoist China, it applies almost exclusively to this subcohort of the elderly adults.[4]

Thus, criticism directed against the elderly was motivated by reasons of ties to capitalism rather than age itself. Other aged persons, namely, workers and less affluent peasants, maintained a higher degree of status in China, whereas the greatest status and power in society accrued to the Communists in general and to its political leadership in particular. As Yin and Lai (1983) explain, although the new government deliberately diminished the status of the aged, respect for parents was still emphasized, and obedience to parents was to continue unless it conflicted with the demands of the state. Moreover, youth did not come to power in China under Mao; the most powerful persons in both the central and regional governments were elderly and remain so in the post-Mao period. China's government, with very few exceptions, is controlled by very old men.

The position of the aged in Chinese society has slowly returned to the point that old people generally now have higher status and respect than in the immediate aftermath of the Communist takeover (Yin and Lai 1983; Sher 1984). Whether such status will continue, however, remains an open question, because modernization, such as that taking place in China in the late twentieth century, often lessens the social value of the aged (Cowgill 1986). Whether this will happen is not clear, because the leadership of the Chinese Communist government is elderly; many educated older people, trained in capitalist business methods prior to 1949, have technical and managerial skills needed for modernization; and veneration for the aged is a Chinese cultural tradition, just as it is in Japan, where modernization did not result in diminished status for the aged. Furthermore, with nearly 40 percent of its population over the age of 65 in 2050, China cannot afford to diminish the

---

4. Peter Yin and Kwok Hung Lai, "A Reconceptualization of Age Stratification in China," *Journal of Gerontology* 38 (1983): 611.

respect and position of such a large segment of society. Aging is going to be a dominant factor in Chinese life in the twenty-first century, regardless of its politics.

SUMMARY

This chapter has examined the social policies pertaining to the support of the elderly in the United States, Canada, Great Britain, Germany, France, Japan, and China. Each country is unique in its provision of income and medical care to the aged. Yet there are some common features: (1) the percentages of elderly are increasing rather than declining or remaining stable; (2) the cost of supporting increased numbers and percentages of the aged in the future remains a social policy problem, and no clearly superior method has yet been discovered to increase revenues significantly; (3) national governments are generally supportive of assisting the elderly in maintaining a positive standard of living; and (4) there is likely to be a worldwide crisis in the twenty-first century about national spending for the elderly as their numbers increase and those of younger persons decrease.

Moreover, among Western welfare states, the link between welfare benefits and poverty has tended to be severed, for the United States and the Western countries discussed in this chapter have clearly expanded their support for the aged to include all social classes. Thus, the right of citizenship, rather than social class position, has evolved as the basis for extending state-sponsored benefits to all old people. In non-Western societies, as seen in Japan and China, traditional aspects of Asian society emphasizing family responsibility for elderly parents still prevail to a large extent. A major difference between the West and Asia is that the family remains more of a pillar in Asia for support of the elderly. Family support seems particularly pronounced in China, the only Communist country and the poorest nation discussed in this chapter. The vast majority of old people in China have no pension and must depend on their family. The Soviet Union, however, the other great Communist state, does not share the Asian (Confucian) tradition of family support for the elderly, and the Soviet government provides a state pension to its citizens. About a third of the 58 million Soviet pensioners in 1985 received a pension of about $95 per month, but the official poverty line was $85 monthly, which indicates that many Soviet elderly have only a minimum level of subsistence.

The aged worldwide share problems of declining health and decreased income, but—as the development of social security for the aged in the countries discussed in this chapter indicates—the clear trend is toward the continued allocation of state resources to support the elderly. There are almost as many different ways to accomplish this as there are countries, yet national governments have committed themselves to this end at various periods during the twentieth century. Consequently, increased national resources for the elderly appear to be the norm in modern twenty-first century societies—provided the means can be found to pay for them without sacrificing the future of the young.

Death and Dying

Death comes to everyone, and all human societies have developed social arrangements for containing its impact upon the living. Yet attempts to define death as something so indeterminate that it can be denied or easily avoided have not been successful strategies in coping with both the meaning and process of dying, either on an individual or societal level. Death is an inevitable biological and social experience of all people and represents the final stage of the aging process.

Beginning in 1965 with Barney Glaser and Anselm Strauss's seminal work *Awareness of Dying*, social scientists have become increasingly interested in studying the process of death and dying in contemporary society. The study of attitudes toward death has made that topic one of the most recent sources of significant theoretical and applied insight into human behavior. Initially, most of the research concerning death dealt with the problem of death as a solitary and perhaps cruel experience in modern hospitals, where the dying patient was often found to be socially and psychologically isolated. Hospital staff and the dying patient's family appeared inhibited in their attempts to interact with the patient in an open and socially meaningful manner. The process of dying was itself hidden as much as possible to minimize the effect of death on all concerned, especially the living. Now it seems that our attitudes toward death may be changing, not only in the academic disciplines, but in American society generally. Although it remains to be confirmed that we are actually in a period of "death revolution," which some writers suggest will see the elimination of the fear of death in advanced industrialized societies, the contemporary approach toward death is to deal with it as a natural part of the human condition. It is hoped that this approach will help us to understand our own lives and ease our fears about the inevitability of mortality in a more open, honest, and satisfying manner.

DEATH AND THE INDIVIDUAL

The basic problem that humans have in dealing with death is fear. Some researchers have maintained that modern Western nations are not "death-denying" societies because everyone is not afraid of death, such as aged persons who fear dependency and disability more than death itself (Kellehear 1984). However, in a review of the literature on attitudes toward death, Elizabeth Kübler-Ross (1969), one of the most noted scholars on death and dying, points out that death has been and remains a fearful and frightening event to most human beings and that fear of death is universal throughout the human species. Many studies in psychology and psychiatry have documented the fact that this strong, deep-rooted fear motivates many people to seek secure environments and to avoid activities and situations that could result in premature death (Kammerman 1988; Weisman 1985). Sigmund Freud, for example, believed that fear of death was a primary motivation for social cohesion as people sought security and strength from group membership. Even though some people may not overtly express a fear of death and dying, Herman Feifel and Allan Branscomb (1973) have suggested that nearly everyone fears death. In a survey, Feifel and Branscomb noted that over 70 percent of their respondents verbally denied they were afraid of death. However, at a second level of testing, which involved reactions to images of death, the respondents began to demonstrate ambivalent attitudes. At a third level of testing, involving word and color-word associations, nearly 95 percent of the respondents revealed a subconscious fear of death. Even people who characterized themselves as extremely religious indicated "a demonstrable fear of death" on the subconscious level.

Fear of Death and Dying

Although many fears have been identified in connection with death, the primary fear is fear of the unknown—the dread of not knowing what happens as you die and when you are dead. Barney Glaser and Anselm Strauss (1968) say that when death occurs slowly, the dying patient is forced to cope with death by overcoming the fear of loss of self and the fear of dying as physical, and perhaps mental, disintegration. Avery Weisman (1985) indicates that a fear of dying evokes ideas about decay, destruction, and obliteration. No one can share his or her experiences of death with the living; yet reports are available from people who have nearly died of a heart attack or from an accident of some kind. Although such reports do give clues about the experience of life's final moments, the reader should be cautioned about accepting the validity of such accounts because they obviously cannot be verified.

A study by Russell Noyes, Jr. (1972) of the process of dying found that many people who report being close to death have similar experiences. Using descriptions of dying experiences, both autobiographical and clinical, Noyes developed a model of the death experience consisting of three stages: resistance, review, and transcendence.

The initial stage of *resistance* to death begins when a person struggles for survival, realizing that death may be imminent. This resistance is characterized by marked anxiety but not disabling panic. If even the slightest possibility of survival remains, the person often feels an enormous surge of energy that may enable him or her to survive by alert mental activity and feats of strength. But, conversely, this upsurge of energy is countered by a powerful desire to surrender, and the person is caught between the impulse to fight and the impulse to surrender. If the person is dying gradually, Noyes claims that as energy wanes, life seems to be dependent on an inner struggle to maintain it. He (Noyes 1972:177) states: "it is as though their will to live sustains them and as though without it they might simply let themselves go and, in a sense, will their deaths."

The second stage of *review* appears after all hope of survival has apparently disappeared and the person surrenders to his or her fate. Death is faced calmly, perhaps with a sense of tranquility. At this particular point, Noyes says that the person begins to review past life experiences from a detached perspective, as if the ego had become an entity capable of observing itself act out the past. The present author has interviewed people who reported similar experiences after being close to death as a result of automobile and industrial accidents. These people believed that they, in fact, left their hospital beds and "hovered" about the room, able to view themselves and others as a detached consciousness. Parapsychologists term this experience an "out-of-the-body" phenomenon, which may be a negation of death on the part of the dying person. Here the subject views his or her body as near death, but exists outside it, thus becoming a detached witness. Some people, according to Noyes, report viewing scattered scenes or all the important events in their lives in this "detached" state. He suggests that the certainty of loss of one's future may necessitate a return to the past to make one's existence real in a final grip on life. The phenomenon of the ego splitting from the body may also lessen personal anxiety by reducing death to solely bodily annihilation.

The final phase is *transcendence*. Here the person's perspective becomes more distant, and one experiences oneself as outside of time or beyond the past and future. This altered sense of time represents complete immersion in the present moment. Another characteristic feeling is a sense of loss of control, as if one is held by a superior power. At this point, the person experiences feelings of oneness or unity with other human beings and the universe. Death is near.

Although providing some interesting insights, Noyes's analysis of the death process cannot be considered conclusive by any means. His descriptions were rendered by people generally in good health who were suddenly threatened with death. We do not know if these experiences are typical or how accurately most people identify their dying moments. Then, too, the mystical state of consciousness reported during transcendence may not be shared by all dying people, but just those who have a tendency toward such modes of perception. Not all people near death report such experiences (Kastenbaum 1981). "If they did," states Jack Kammerman (1988:105), "you would expect all people coming close to death to have them, which they don't." Other variables, such as age, sex, personality, and culture, may also be very important in influencing near-death experiences. Still, the similarities among those cases reported by Noyes and other researchers (Moody 1976; Ring 1980) suggest important guidelines for future research into the experience of dying.

Research by Raymond Moody, reported in his book *Life After Life* (1976), suggests that the out-of-the-body phenomenon and the review of one's past life are especially common elements of the dying process. Moody, a physician, interviewed several people who were supposedly near death at some time in their lives, and he described the typical experience of death as follows:

> A man is dying and, as he reaches the point of greatest physical distress, he hears himself pronounced dead by his doctor. He begins to hear an uncomfortable noise, a loud ringing or buzzing, and at the same time feels himself moving very rapidly through a long tunnel. After this, he suddenly finds himself outside of his own physical body, but still in the immediate physical environment, and he sees his own body from a distance, as though he is a spectator. He watches the resuscitation attempt from this unusual vantage point and is in a state of emotional upheaval.
>
> After a while, he collects himself and becomes more accustomed to his odd condition. He notices that he still has a "body," but one of a very different nature and with very different powers from the physical body he has left behind. Soon other things begin to happen. Others come to meet and help him. He glimpses the spirits of relatives and friends who have already died, and a loving, warm spirit of a kind he has never encountered before—a being of light—appears before him. This being asks him a question, nonverbally, to make him evaluate his life and helps him along by showing him a panoramic, instantaneous playback of the major events of his life.[1]

Moody goes on to explain that the dying man is caught up in intense feelings of joy and peace, but somehow he realizes that it is not time for him to die. Reluctantly, he returns to his physical body and lives. Kenneth Ring (1980) followed up Moody's research in a study of 102 people to determine if they had near-death experiences. Half did not, and the other half experienced some five stages consisting of (1) the affective component (sensing peace and

1. Raymond A. Moody, *Life After Life* (New York: Bantam, 1976), 121–122.

well-being), (2) body separation, (3) entering darkness, (4) seeing light, and (5) entering the light. Parallel to stages 2–4 was a decision-making process on whether to return to life; this process included the life review, encounter with a "presence," encounter with deceased loved ones, and the making of the decision. Not everyone passed through all five stages, but the respondents who experienced all or part of this process reported that it was a positive situation. Martha and Rainer Baum (1980) likewise reported that their review of near-death experiences showed the process of dying to be blissful and devoid of fear. They also noted that the experiences of dying took place in stages, in this case, three stages: resistance, life review, and transcendence.

The stage of resistance raises an important sociological question regarding death. This question concerns the extent to which the "will to live" is responsible for length of life. Although researchers are not aware of what physiological mechanisms may be at work in this process, a body of literature in psychology suggests that perhaps rats, chickens, monkeys, human beings, and even cockroaches become unusually susceptible to death when they discover that they have no control over what is happening to them and that further action is futile (Seligman 1974). The experience of American prisoners of war during the Korean and Vietnam wars who simply lay down and died, although apparently in good physical health, are examples of this phenomenon.

Research by David Phillips and Kenneth Feldman (1973) found evidence that there are fewer deaths than usual before important ceremonial occasions such as a birthday, a presidential election, and the Jewish Day of Atonement. Using data derived from biographies of famous people, Phillips and Feldman suggest, in accordance with Émile Durkheim's (1961) description of social integration and ceremonies, that people who are strongly integrated into a society feel an obligation to participate in the ceremonies of that society. Thus, people strongly attached to society postpone death in order to be alive during meaningful social ceremonies; people detached from society and uninvolved with its ceremonies may die earlier by just "letting go." Admittedly speculative, this hypothesis does offer interesting possibilities for research concerning the will to live and the social processes that might either reinforce or possibly negate that will.[2]

Current research by Phillips supports this hypothesis. For example, Phillips and E. King (1988) found that mortality rates for Jewish men in

---

2. An interesting example of the possible relationship between a significant social event in a person's life and the will to live is found in the biography of Thomas Jefferson. Jefferson died on July 4th, fifty years to the day after he signed the Declaration of Independence. Jefferson's physician described the scene as follows:

About seven o'clock of the evening of that day, he [Jefferson] awoke, and seeing my staying at his bedside exclaimed, "Oh Doctor, are you still there?" in a voice, however, that was husky and indistinct. He then asked, "Is it the Fourth?" to which I replied, "It soon will be." These were the last words I heard him utter. (Peterson 1970:1008)

California fell sharply below an expected level before the Jewish holiday of Passover and rose by an equal amount above the expected level immediately afterward. Non-Jewish control groups showed no significant fluctuation in mortality around Passover. In another study, Phillips and Daniel Smith (1990) found the same pattern among elderly Chinese women in California for the Harvest Moon Festival. Mortality dipped 35 percent before the Harvest Moon Festival and rose 34 percent in the week thereafter. Chinese men and young Chinese women did not show the same pattern in mortality, nor did a control group of Jewish men. However, the Harvest Moon Festival in Chinese culture is a ceremonial custom in which the central role is assumed by the senior woman of the household, who is responsible for the preparing of special foods. Research such as this suggests that people may be able to prolong living in some cases in order to reach particularly important social events.

The other major fear of the unknown is fear of what happens after death. Beliefs about existence after death are common in most cultures, and one of the primary functions of religion is to reduce anxiety by providing answers concerning life after death. However, research about effects of religion in allaying fear of death has been inconclusive (Dumont and Foss 1972). Kübler-Ross (1969) found in her research with terminally ill patients that religious patients seemed to differ little from those who were not religious. Very few patients could be identified as being truly religious or as confirmed atheists. Most held beliefs somewhere between the two extremes, and their philosophical perspectives were usually not strong enough to relieve them of the fear of dying. Kübler-Ross observed that people with less education, little sophistication, and few professional obligations or social ties had the least difficulty facing death. Those persons experiencing the greatest difficulty were characterized as ambitious, attempting to strive for control of their environment and for accumulation of material goods. Although they had many social ties, they exhibited few meaningful personal relationships and usually faced death alone.

But fear of the unknown is not the only fear related to the experience of dying. At least five other significant fears have been identified: (1) fear about not being able to pursue or to complete certain goals, (2) fear of what will happen to dependents, (3) fear of the loss of self-mastery or control over one's destiny, (4) fear of punishment for sins, and (5) fear of isolation and separation from loved ones and treasured objects. All of these fears, either singly or in combination, can produce a considerable degree of anxiety in an individual concerned about death.

Strategies for Dealing with Death: Childhood, Adolescence, Adulthood

Because fear of death tends to be universal—defined by existentialist philosophers as the human being's "most profound awareness"—numerous strategies have been employed by individuals and society for coping with death anxieties. In very early *childhood*, there is generally no conception of what death means, and the discovery of the phenomenon of death is not usually accompanied by great emotion (Anthony 1968, 1972). Often the child's discovery of death occurs as a simple incident in day-to-day living when the child explores his or her environment and perhaps finds a dead object such as a bird or insect. Sylvia Anthony (1968) tells us that usually there is a definite interval between a child's first questions about death and the arousal of emotion connected with the idea of dying. Death is commonly associated with the child's understanding of his or her world and may be reviewed as going to sleep, going on a trip, or going up in the sky.

Anthony suggests that anxieties regarding death do not appear until around the ages of 3–5, when the child realizes the possibility of loss of someone upon whom the child depends or the loss of one's own self. D.G. Prugh and associates (1953), for example, found that among hospitalized children, types of death anxiety varied according to age; children under the age of 6 were thought to be highly anxious about separation from other people. Thus, death seems to disturb the very young child mostly in regard to the thought of separation, loneliness, or abandonment.

Many young children, however, do not develop death anxieties. They are usually able to control their fears about death perhaps because they do not perceive death as the end of life. The dead may be viewed as being simply another category of the living who are less than alive or who live somewhere else, such as in heaven. As a defense against death anxiety, many children are taught that there is an afterlife. Often the perception of young children regarding death may involve a close relationship between death and birth; someone dies and then returns as a baby. Many games that children play also include a death theme in which death is not defined as a permanent or finite state. Children who are "killed" while playing "soldier" or "cowboys and Indians" are expected to come back to life at an appropriate time. This view of death is reflected in children's literature, where death is seen as an event that can be undone; the dead hero can be returned to life by magic or the intervention of good fairies and spirits.

Although there is general agreement in the research literature concerning three- to five-year-olds' fears of death as separation, there has been serious disagreement about the characteristics of death anxieties in the six- to ten-year-old age-group. Much of the initial research consisted of data collected from observations of terminally ill children that found that this age-group lacked the intellectual ability to develop an extensive concept of death (Debuskey 1970). These children apparently experienced little anxiety about dying unless adults intervened to point out to the child the seriousness of the illness. Other research suggested that although six- to ten-year-olds could not fully conceptualize death, nonetheless they were aware that something very serious was wrong with them (Easson 1970). John Spinetta (1974) has strongly criticized this research, however, on the grounds that its conclusions rested largely on observations of parents and hospital staff rather than on direct observation of the children; also, when the studies were based upon observations of the child, they lacked objective measures, with little or no use of control groups for comparison.

Other studies strongly suggest that six-to ten-year-olds are aware of what death means. E. H. Waechter (1971) asked a set of four matched groups of children who were fatally ill, children with chronic but not fatal illnesses, children with temporary illnesses, and normal, nonhospitalized children to construct stories about themselves using a set of pictures. Waechter found a greater number of overtly expressed death themes among the fatally ill children. She concluded that this age-group is not only subjectively aware of dying, but also able objectively to express that awareness.

Spinetta, Rigler, and Karon (1974) tested Waechter's conclusion in an experiment involving a group of twenty-five children fatally ill with leukemia and a control group of twenty-five chronically ill children with nonfatal diseases. The six- to ten-year-olds were matched not only by age-group, but also by sex, race, grade in school, and amount of medication. The children were asked to tell a story about a sick friend by placing in a model of a hospital room dolls representing a sick child and significant adults (nurse, doctor, mother, father) in their *usual* places. Later the children were asked to repeat the story by putting the dolls in places they would *like* them to be. Because the dying children placed the adult dolls at such a significantly greater distance from the doll of the sick child, Spinetta and associates inferred that the placement of the dolls by the dying children was reflective of a growing sense of psychological separation from both the people and the circumstances of the hospital environment. In interviews with parents and hospital staff, they found additionally that adults reported a decrease in the frequency, intensity, and quality of interaction with the dying child. Although the parents wished for the child's recovery and attempted to provide great affection, they also wished to withdraw from the child to protect themselves emotionally when the child died. The hospital staff likewise reported a reluctance to become emotionally involved for similar reasons.

Accordingly, Spinetta and associates ask some important questions: Does the dying child reflect the unresponsive feelings of adults, or does the child try to prepare for death by separating from parents? Does the dying child prefer to be left alone for reasons of his or her own choosing or because he or she senses embarrassment on the part of adults? Spinetta does not provide answers to these questions, but he does suggest that whatever the reason, the fatally ill child is aware of death and perhaps dies psychologically isolated from other people.

Spinetta concludes:

It seems clear . . . that the fatally ill 6- to 10-year-old child is concerned about his illness and that even though this illness may not always take the form of overt expressions about his impending death, the more subtle fears and anxieties are nonetheless real, painful, and very much related to the seriousness of the illness that the child is experiencing.[3]

Once children near *adolescence*, around the age of 10 or so, they develop adult concepts of death that recognize that death is not only inevitable, but also final. Yet adolescents generally fear death less than other age-groups because death is not an immediate threat and they are reasonably sure of a full life. Actually, the outward aspects of death often appear very funny to them. They construct jokes and rhymes about death and enjoy laughing at movie and television scenes containing exaggerated expressions of bloody mayhem. Anthony (1968) calls the adolescent's mockery of death "a half-way house" to the defenses against death anxiety available to the adult.

Human beings like to think that somehow the individual personality is not meant to die and that something personal about themselves is able to survive death. However, the strategies that exist for use by the *adult* in the desire for eternal survival are limited to those of (1) sexual reproduction, (2) belief in an afterlife, or (3) belief in reincarnation. Sexual reproduction allows adults at least to imprint themselves genetically upon succeeding generations. Belief in an afterlife is derived from either religion or a personal philosophy of existence. Some people embrace religion and try to live the kind of life that "qualifies" for life after death in heaven. Other people have their own perhaps nonreligious belief in a life or existence of some type after death, perhaps as a spirit or energy form in the cosmos, or the adult may believe in reincarnation. Several accounts have been written by people who are convinced they were born, lived, and died at a time in the past and have returned to the present to live another life. Otherwise, the adult must cope with the idea of death as the total end of experience and an eternity of nothingness.

Strategies for Dealing with Death: The Dying Patient

Despite the particular strategy an individual selects to contain the fear of death, the time arrives for most people (except for infants, comatose patients, or those persons dying sudden and unexpected deaths) to confront the process of dying in old age. Two of the most noted studies describing this process are those of Kübler-Ross (1969) and Glaser and Strauss (1965, 1968). Kübler-Ross identified five stages of coping with dying: (1) denial and isolation, (2) anger, (3) bargaining, (4) depression, and (5) acceptance. Not everyone may go through each of these stages, nor do so in the order prescribed by Kübler-Ross, but the sequence she suggests was typical of most patients in

---

3. John J. Spinetta, "The Dying Child's Awareness of Death: A Review," *Psychological Bulletin* 81 (1974): 259.

her study. The first stage of *denial and isolation* consists of the patient's shock and dismay at the disclosure of impending death. Often the initial awareness of death is accompanied by resentment against other people who are not dying or against fate itself. Sometimes patients in the stage of denial will "shop around" for another physician to disprove a previous diagnosis of terminality. Most patients, according to Kübler-Ross, demonstrate at least partial denial of their deaths at some point in their efforts to cope with the dying process.

Glaser and Strauss also found attempts at denial in their study of terminal patients. Some of these attempts included refusal to seek further information from physicians, refusal to discuss their illness and death with anyone, favorable comparisons of themselves with other dying patients, emphasis upon the future, a state of being highly active, and the attempt to juggle time. This last strategy consisted of setting a particular point in time as a survival goal and, after reaching that time, selecting another future time, and so on.

Throughout all of the stages outlined by Kübler-Ross, dying patients expressed hope that death could somehow be averted. Usually this hope was based on the possible discovery of a new drug or sometimes upon the skill of physicians. Stewart Alsop (1973) a journalist dying of cancer, said that such hope allowed the dying person to die more easily. Although the patient may be told he or she *may* die or *probably* will die, Alsop thought that the patient should not be told he or she *will* die.

Kübler-Ross observed that very few patients are able to maintain a "make-believe" world in which they are healthy up until the final moments of living. When denial of one's death can no longer realistically be maintained in the face of medical evidence, the second stage of anger appears. Often this anger is displaced on family, friends, the hospital staff, or God. Kübler-Ross said this can be a very difficult time for those who must interact with the dying patient. The next stage, *bargaining*, usually does not last very long. This stage represents an attempt to postpone death by good behavior or good deeds. Perhaps in return for some special service, dying patients hope they will be granted an extension of life. The fourth stage, *depression*, occurs usually prior to the acceptance of death. Here the patient knows definitely that absolutely nothing can be done to change his or her fate. The great majority of patients, according to Kübler-Ross and Glaser and Strauss, come to terms with their depression sufficiently to go on to the final stage of *acceptance*.

If the patient has had enough time and perhaps assistance in working through the other stages of reaction to dying, Kübler-Ross found that the patient usually reaches the stage of acceptance. During this stage, the patient is no longer angry or depressed, but recognizes the inevitability of death. This is not a happy period, but one characterized by Kübler-Ross as "almost devoid of feelings." Pain and struggle may be over, and all that usually remains is the wait for death. Glaser and Strauss, however, tell us that acceptance may be either active or passive. Passive acceptance consists of calm resignation as described by Kübler-Ross, but active acceptance involves preparing for death by becoming philosophical about life and death, settling personal and financial affairs, becoming very religious, or elimnating the distressing prospect of dying a painful and lingering death by committing suicide. Some patients accept the fact of their dying but decide to fight it by intensive living, by seeking out marginal or "quack" doctors for miracle cures, or by volunteering to participate in medical research and experiments that might produce a cure.

Alsop (1973) provided a particularly insightful account of the acceptance of death in his book *Stay of Execution*. Although he did not welcome the prospect of dying, it was difficult to accept a life of pain and weakness with a dependency upon medication and blood transfusions. To be without the possibility of ever returning to a normal life and to feel very, very sick made the thought of dying far less terrible to him. Alsop (1973:23) finally reached the point where he believed that just as a sleepy man needs to sleep, a dying man needs to die, and that a time comes when it is both wrong and useless to resist.

DEATH AND SOCIETY

Like individuals, societies develop attitudes toward death that are reflected in the establishment of normative practices designed to contain death's presence. To assess the American perspective regarding death, it is useful to compare its evolution from social thought of Western Europe during the Middle Ages to the present. According to Philippe Ariès (1974), the French social historian, death in Western society in the twelfth century could be characterized as "tamed death" because it seemed to lack the anxieties common to the twentieth century. People in the Middle Ages did not desire to die, or at least they were in no hurry to do so; but when they realized that death was near, the art and literature of the period suggest that people usually died simply, as if death were a familiar aspect of living. Death was supposedly viewed as the collective destiny of the species, and the simplistic, perhaps naive, acceptance of death was acceptance of the order of nature.

Except for sudden or unexpected death, the deaths that occurred during the Middle Ages usually involved a familiar ritual. First, the dying person was supposed to lie down in bed, if at all possible, in order to die. Then, the actual process of dying consisted of a ceremony organized by the dying person, who was expected to follow a prescribed sequence of behaviors intended to conclude life. The dying person was supposed to express sorrow about the end of life and to recollect beloved persons, events, and things. He or she was expected to pardon for any disapproved acts the usually numerous companions who gathered around the deathbed; this was followed by a final prayer in which the dying person requested forgiveness of sins. After a priest administered absolution, all that remained was the wait for death. Dying was a public and familiar act, and the dying person's room was a social setting to be entered freely by relatives, friends, and neighbors. For example, as Ariès points out, no portrayal of the deathbed scene between the twelfth and eighteenth centuries failed to include the appearance of children. Usually there was no great show of emotion at the deathbed, because behavior was guided by the dying person in the formally prescribed death ritual.

In modern society, people no longer experience death in this simple ceremonial manner. Instead, the modern version of dying has been characterized by fear, anxiety, and social isolation. What happened? What caused our attitudes toward death to change? Ariès claims that from the Middle Ages on, death in Western society was subtly modified into a pervasive dread. One source of this change, as noted by Ariès, is found in Christianity. Inspired by the book of Matthew, the Christian death scene during the Middle Ages emphasized the idea of judgment; that is, the weighing of souls by Christ the Judge according to the deeds, both good and bad, committed during the person's lifetime. The eternal destination of heaven and hell for the dying person was at issue and, notwithstanding its cosmic essence, judgment was peculiar to each individual. Thus, the security of death as a collective rite was joined by the anxiety of interrogation and personal trial.

Medieval Christianity was certainly not wholly responsible for the changing attitudes toward death, but it was influential. Another important factor in attitudes toward death in the Middle Ages, according to Ariès (1981) was a love of life among the more affluent social classes. At this time, Ariès (1981:138) states, "Death was not only an end to being but a separation from having: One must leave behind houses and orchards and gardens." During the eighteenth century, romanticism, with its emphasis on love of nature and the expression of strong emotion, also viewed death as a painful rupture from the beauty of nature and the joy of living things. Acute anxiety over death was a norm sanctioned by a society strongly aware of the pain of separation from persons and objects that were loved and valued. Another important attitude that first emerged full-blown in the nineteenth century, the Age of Rationalism, was the notion of guilt about personal failure to accomplish certain goals. Ariès (1974:105) summarizes this latter attitude as a "passion for being, an anxiety at not sufficiently being."

The twentieth century marked the efforts of society to control death by making it as unobtrusive a social process as possible. Emphasis was placed on the "acceptable" death, which was a death that could be tolerated by the survivors. This idea had its origin in the belief of the Middle Ages that there was a close relationship between death and an individual's personal biography. It was thought that each person's life flashed before his or her eyes at the moment of death; the dying person's attitude at that time would thus provide his or her biography with its conclusion and final meaning. Death was believed to be the occasion when human beings were most able to know themselves. Consequently, to die well or to experience a good death became very important. The twentieth century intepretation of this attitude, however, was concerned not with the benefit of the individual but with society. The antithesis to an "acceptable" death was the graceless, fearful, and embarrassing death that caused strong emotions and revulsion among other people and a disruption of social life. Therefore, modern society sought to control death and to make it as acceptable as possible by hiding it.

Societal control of the impact of death was significantly assisted by two contemporary phenomena: (1) the occurrence of dying generally among people furthest removed from the mainstream of social life and; (2) the displacement of the traditional site of dying from the home to the hospital. Approximately two-thirds of all deaths in industrialized societies are the result of old age. Deaths associated with the aging process occur largely among people who have retired from work and who no longer have parental responsibilities. These deaths rarely interrupt the smooth-functioning society.

Hospitals have become the place to die because the care provided there is usually not possible in the home. Today in American society, only a minority of people die at home, and the number is decreasing rapidly. About 70 percent of all deaths occur in hospitals and nursing homes (Kammerman 1988). Fewer than one-third of the deaths in American society take place at home, at work, or in public places. The removal of most deaths from the home has caused the traditional death ritual to disappear. Death in the hospital is controlled not by the dying person or his or her family, but by the physician and the hospital staff, who define not only the circumstances of death but the exact moment of dying.[4] Access by family and friends to the dying patient can also be controlled by the hospital, so that death occurs under the jurisdiction of relative strangers to the dying person. Such a controlled death is disruptive to neither the general functioning of the hospital nor the society at large.

The Social Organization of Dying

Two major studies on death in sociology, those of David Sudnow (1967) and Glaser and Strauss (1965), provide illustrations of the death environment in American society. Sudnow (1967) studied the organization of dying by using participant observation in two hospitals: a large urban West coast

---

4. The medical and legal definition of death is no longer the traditional criterion of heart stoppage because of the possible restoration of heart action, even when there is no longer the remotest possibility of the patient's recovering consciousness and brain functions. The basis for defining death is that of a "flat" or isoelectric electroencephalogram denoting "brain death," which is taken after signs of respiratory and circulatory failure.

charity institution and a private, general hospital in the Midwest. Most of Sudnow's observations took place in the charity hospital, which he described as a setting for the concentration of death. Three-fourths of the patients were over age 60, and there was an average of three deaths daily. Most of the deaths occurred on the medicine and surgery wards. The personnel on these wards encountered death so frequently that it was considered routine. The routinization of dying was made easier, both at the charity and the private hospitals, because almost all of the deaths were preceded by a coma. Comatose patients were regarded as being essentially dead, and they could be disattended as a social object.[5] Of the some two hundred deaths he witnessed, Sudnow noted that not a single death was of the "Hollywood" variety, where the dying person's last sentence was interrupted by a final breath.

Those people having the most contact with death in the hospitals were generally lower echelon employees. Once a patient died, except for the autopsy, the physician lost interest in the body. The higher one's position in the status hierarchy of the hospital as a nurse or a physician, the less likely was one to witness dead bodies or physically handle corpses. The handling of corpses was considered "dirty work" in the value system of the hospital, and whenever possible ward personnel would leave a body to be processed by the next work shift.

Sudnow saw the hospital as an environment of occurrences, with deaths being an occurrence mainly definable in reference to its similarity to other deaths experienced by the personnel. Although any given death could give pause for retrospective comment by staff members, the mention of deaths was usually routine except for those involving unusual events, such as obtrusive settings or styles of dying, accidents, diagnostic or treatment errors, or the high social status of a patient. The age of the dead person could also cause comment, especially the deaths of children. General philosophical consideration by the staff on death and dying did not naturally occur.

Although the staff sought to minimize and routinize death as much as possible for themselves, the organization of dying was constructed in such a way as to hide the fact of dying from patients and visitors. Most hospitals, for example, locate the morgue in a relatively inaccessible part of the hospital basement. Sudnow (1967:51) quotes a text in hospital administration: "The hospital morgue is best located on the ground floor and placed in an area inaccessible to the general public. It is important that the unit have a suitable exit leading onto a private loading platform which is concealed from hospital

5. As suggested by Erving Goffman, Sudnow (1967:74–75) has made a distinction between "clinical death" (signs of death based upon physical examinatin), "biological death" (cessation of cellular activity), and "social death" (the point at which a person is treated like a corpse although still alive clinically or biologically). "Social death" was not simply the asocial treatment of a dying patient by the hospital staff, but was the beginning of social activities commonly associated with death: planning the autopsy, grieving, preparing the obituary notice, contacting insurance companies, disposing of personal effects, arranging for the funeral, etc.

patients and the public." Often the patient whose death was imminently expected was moved to a private room to avoid troubling other patients, and bodies were not removed from these rooms during visiting hours to avoid upsetting visitors.

There was, however, a difference between the charity and private hospitals in regard to the presence of family and friends at the dying patient's bedside. At the private hospital, relatives were considered entitled to be present at the bedside at the moment of death. The dying person did not preside over the gathering, as in the traditional death ritual; nonetheless, the experience of death was not solitary, as it was in the charity hospital. Dying patients were shielded from relatives at the charity hospital in order to minimize disruption of hospital routine and processing of the body. The justification for this action was to protect the relatives from the "unpleasantness of seeing someone die." If death was regarded as imminent, family members were urged by the staff to go home and await further news or to wait in waiting rooms or in the corridors, not in the patient's room. The result was that relatives were usually not present at the time of death and were summoned only after the staff had completed its processing duties.

Awareness Contexts

Glaser and Strauss developed a typology of awareness contexts based upon both participant observation and personal interviews in six hospitals in the San Francisco Bay area. These awareness contexts—closed awareness, suspected awareness, mutual pretense awareness, and open awareness— were all derived from observing the social settings and the control of information about dying in the hospital. Glaser and Strauss found that the physicians were reluctant to disclose impending death to the patient, and nurses were not expected to do so without the consent of the responsible physician. Thus, patients were generally required to take action to get information about the extent of their illness and were often prevented by the staff from asking questions about dying. Awareness contexts were not relevant if the patient was comatose, an infant, someone whose knowledge of death was not important to the staff, or in emergency situations. Awareness contexts pertained when the patient was conscious and the staff managed knowledge of the patient's dying.

Closed awareness is a social condition where the staff knows the patient is dying but the patient is unaware of the fact. It is based on the following structural conditions: (1) inability of the patient to recognize the signs of dying; (2) reluctance of the staff to discuss dying with the patient; (3) reluctance of family members to discuss the patient's condition with the patient; (4) organization of the hospital itself, which is designed to conceal information; and (5) lack of anyone to help the patient find out the facts, including

other patients. When any of the above conditions was lacking, other awareness contexts were possible. *Suspected awareness* is a situation in which the
patient is suspicious but does not know that an illness is terminal. The patient
is then forced to draw information from whatever sources are available to
confirm his or her suspicions. *Mutual pretense awareness* is a somewhat
more comfortable situation; the patient is aware of a terminal condition and
refuses to talk about it, and the staff is under no obligation to discuss dying.
This arrangement usually worked to contain emotions unless either party to
the interaction broke down while trying to maintain the pretense. *Open
awareness* is a condition in which everyone knows and openly acknowledges
the terminal situation. The patient is held responsible for his or her behavior
and is expected by the staff to face death with dignity, to sustain responsible
ties to family and friends, and to cooperate with the staff. This last condition
was most acceptable to the staff. Although there are no formal norms for the
"ideal" death, Glaser and Strauss make the important point that people just
can't help judging other people.

The Glaser and Strauss study differs somewhat from Sudnow's research because most of the patients observed by Glaser and Strauss were not
comatose, paid for their own hospital care, and were of a higher social status.
Unlike patients in the Sudnow study, they were in a better position to
negotiate the dying process. Nevertheless, in both studies the staff saw death
as inconvenient and managed interaction with the dying patient so as to
minimize disruption.

Desensitizing Death: Coroners and Physicians

The implications of the Sudnow and the Glaser and Strauss studies
contribute to an understanding of the social psychology of those people
whose occupations and professions require routine exposure to death. The
findings of other attitudinal studies should also be noted. For example, Kathy
Charmaz (1975) reported that county coroner's deputies employed self-
protective strategies to avoid the emotion of the death scene and to maintain
the routine character of their work (ascertaining the cause of death, establishing the identity of the deceased, protecting the property of the deceased, and
locating the relatives of the deceased to whom the announcement of death
could be made). In making the announcement to relatives, most deputies
expressly avoided using the word *dead* and substituted the words *fatally
injured* or *passed away*, if they made any direct reference to death at all.
Sometimes they just gave progressively meaningful cues in the conversation
so that the relatives would realize what had happened and would themselves
say the word *dead*. The deputies were also prompt to turn the situation
around by asking about funeral and burial arrangements, so that the responsibility for the occasion was thus symbolically shifted to the relatives.

According to Charmaz, one of the most striking features of the attitudes shown by the deputies was the extent to which they reflected typical cultural taboos. The deputies demonstrated an avoidance of death, were uncomfortable during the expression of grief by survivors, and showed an absence of personal philosophy either about death in general or about their own deaths in particular. Instead, they subjectively interpreted death as being a by-product of their work rather than the focus of it. This approach was exemplified by the comment of one deputy (Charmaz 1975:304), who stated: "That's not a body lying there. It's an *investigation*. You have to look at it as an investigation, not as a person lying there." The deputies supported an occupational ideology that prevented them from becoming involved in the situation on the grounds that they would then be unable to perform their work properly. Robert Clark and Emily LaBeff (1982) found in a study of physicians, nurses, law enforcement officers, and clergy that death telling was an aspect of their jobs that they strongly disliked. Typically, they would try to prepare the next of kin for the worst before delivering the news. In an earlier study of over two hundred physicians on the staff of Michael Reese Hospital in Chicago, Donald Oken (1961) found that 90 percent of the doctors stated a preference for not telling cancer patients that their condition was terminal. In discussing their diagnosis with the patient, the use of euphemisms was the general rule. Patients would be told they had a "lesion," a "mass," or perhaps a "tumor," but terms like "cancer" and "malignancy" were avoided.

Despite this strong reluctance to level with a cancer patient, there was essentially unanimous agreement among the physicians that some family member must be told. Not only were legal and ethical considerations important in disclosing the diagnosis to some relevant person but, Oken believed, the physician had a strong need to share the burden of knowledge that someone was going to die. The primary reason cited by the doctors for not wanting to tell the patients they had terminal cancer was "clinical experience." "Clinical experience" consisted of the physicians' opinion that most people did not want to know, that they know already, or that they should not be told so that they should not give up or become depressed. However, Oken found that the real determinant for avoiding the disclosure of a terminal diagnosis was an emotion-laden, a priori judgment related to a fear of how the patient would react to the information (become angry, commit suicide) and the physician's underlying feelings of pessimism and futility about cancer.

Oken further explained that the physicians interviewed generally agreed that patients feared cancer because its diagnosis was equated with suffering and certain death. What was impressive was that the physicians themselves felt very much the same way, and these feelings were in conflict with their strong desire to prevent suffering and save lives. Oken stated:

> Situations of this kind, associated with intense charges of unpleasant emotions, call forth a variety of psychological defenses which reduce the intensity of

feelings to manageable proportions. Among such defenses are those which involve the avoidance, negation, or denial of the existence of some unpleasant fact, and acting as if it were not real.[6]

Oken's research took place in the 1960s, when physician-patient communication about death tended to be highly indirect (Glaser and Strauss 1965). The general trend today among physicians is to be more straightforward in notifying patients and next of kin about illness. They may prepare the recipients for the news somewhat in advance, but it is not likely they will keep this information from the patient. Nevertheless, differences in styles of death telling remain among professionals, and it appears that physicians tend to be rather elaborate when they announce deaths. Police officers, for example, tend to be more direct than physicians in telling about death; physicians, on the other hand, take a more technical approach by relying on a large repertoire of explanations and giving what is essentially a detailed, orderly, blow-by-blow description of the situation (Clark and LaBeff 1982).

Robert Coombs and Pauline Powers (1975) have characterized medical school and the teaching hospital as the locale in which medical students and physicians learn to cope with death in an objective manner (while at the same time denying its subjective implications). Coombs and Powers identified five developmental stages in this process: (1) idealizing the doctor's role, (2) desensitizing death symbols, (3) objectifying and combating death, (4) questioning the medical model, and (5) dealing with personal feelings. In the initial stage, medical students tend to demonstrate the same emotional attitudes toward death that are common among laypersons; for example, they found the "coolness" of the qualified physician's approach to death to be "offensive." Nevertheless, they generally realized that they themselves needed to control their emotions about death if they were to become good physicians. In the second stage, they began to become desensitized to the symbols of death as a result of their experience dissecting cadavers, attending autopsies, and working in the pathology laboratory. In addition, they began to acquire the knowledge and medical terminology that allowed them to adopt an intellectual perspective toward disease.

The third stage of objectifying and combating death came when the medical students started working in the hospital and were exposed to dead and dying patients. They realized more fully at this time the necessity of detaching themselves from the trauma associated with death in order to protect themselves from their own personal feelings and be able to work effectively as a doctor. One way medical students socialize themselves to deal with the emotional side of death, as found in another study by Frederic Hafferty (1988), is the telling of cadaver stories and jokes. Another important

6. Donald Oken, "What to Tell Cancer Patients: A Study of Medical Attitudes," *Journal of the American Medical Association* 175 (1961): 1127.

desensitizing technique found by Coombs and Powers (1975), which was modeled by the clinical faculty, was the student's denial of the subjective features of death. Coombs and Powers explained it this way:

> In other words, the clinician learns to view dying patients not as people with feelings, but as medical entities, specimens, or objects of scientific interest. By adopting a scientific frame of mind, utilized so effectively in their previous work with dead bodies, clinicians can effectively avoid the uncomfortable inner feelings which occur when they are exposed to dying patients.[7]

Some (but apparently not all) of the medical students and physicians in the Coombs and Powers study experienced a fourth stage of socialization to death that questioned the medical model. As they perceived it, the medical (scientific) model of treatment tended to dehumanize patients and to define doctors as little more than technicians. From this perspective, it became unrealistic to think that all patients could be cured; thus, in some cases it might be inappropriate to prolong life unnecessarily. Some physicians apparently did not experience this fourth stage; their ego was easily inflated when they were cast in the role of a healer who had powers over death. "When his self-esteem was involved," stated Coombs and Powers (1975:262–263), "it is imperative that he prevent death from occurring, for death makes him feel vulnerable. But if he can keep the 'corpse' alive for a few more days or weeks, his mastery over death is demonstrated." This so-called God complex, regarded by many physicians as incompatible with good medical practice, was nonetheless an observable phenomenon.

What socialization had generally accomplished up to the time of the fifth stage of dealing with their own personal feelings about death was that the doctors had been conditioned to repress their personal anxieties and fears. However, Coombs and Powers (1975:263–264) found: "Our interviews with physicians revealed rather dramatically how much repressed emotionality exists among medical practitioners." When pressed to discuss their own feelings about death and dying, both on a professional and a personal level, the most common strategy employed by the physicians to cope with their own fears was that of avoidance. In a comment reminiscent of the Sudnow (1967) and Glaser and Strauss (1965) studies, Coombs and Powers stated:

> Typically every effort is made in the hospital to shield oneself from mourning relatives. In the emergency room quiet crying is tolerated, but if any kind of emotional outburst occurs, relatives are usually hustled off to the chapel as fast as possible. "We isolate them so that their grief is not so obvious," a physician said. "It isn't done cruelly, but frankly, it is done more to protect the emergency room staff than to help the family."[8]

---

7. Robert H. Coombs and Pauline S. Powers, "Socialization for Death: The Physician's Role," *Urban Life* 4 (1975): 258.

8. Ibid., 265.

What is suggested by these studies is a tendency of people who confront death regularly to develop a self-protective psychology that consists of a behavioral and cognitive pattern of avoidance and negation of the death experience through the process of objectification. Dead and dying people come to be defined as "cases" or "investigations" rather than as people. Meanwhile, personal fears and anxieties about the subjective meaning of death are suppressed. The objectification of death is justified on the grounds that the professional be able to carry on—"do a good job." Yet despite an outward appearance of control over emotions, the process does not always function smoothly. Some physicians and others who deal with death experience a considerable amount of subjective stress because of it (Clark and LaBeff 1982; Coombs and Powers 1975; Oken 1961).

CHANGING ATTITUDES TOWARD DEATH

Death in the wider context of American society has not been socially disruptive because, as Robert Blauner (1966) explained, the impact of death has been controlled through bureaucratization. Hospitals care for the terminally ill and manage the crisis of dying; mortuaries attend to the problem of disposal of the dead and the transition ritual of the funeral. The handling of death by these specialists and the isolation of the dying experience in hospitals and nursing homes have minimized the average person's exposure to death. Blauner described the modern hospital as a "mass reduction" system because it tends to reduce the individuality of its dying patients.

Yet, as Blauner noted, this system cannot be fully achieved because of the tension between death and bureaucracy. Bureaucracies are committed to routine and unemotional administrative procedures. Death, on the other hand, is laden with considerable emotionality, not only the deep-rooted fear of one's own dying, but also the grief and bereavement of survivors, which can elicit some of the strongest emotions of human existence. Several studies have found grief, mourning, and bereavement for a deceased person to be long-lasting; it can cause decreased appetite, weight loss, difficulty in concentration, sleep disturbances, and depression (Carr 1985; Lund et al. 1986; Lund 1987). No matter how much effort and control is exerted by a society to contain and routinize death and dying through bureaucratic procedures, such procedures are not in themselves satisfying alternatives for handling a strongly emotional and personal event.

However, an exception is found in Victor Marshall's (1975) study of a retirement community on the eastern seaboard of the United States. Marshall observed that the residents organized themselves as a community of dying to legitimatize death as an appropriate (although not necessarily positive) event because they had "lived their lives." The residents were able to socialize each other to their impending deaths through frequent conversations about it and the presence of role models with which to anticipate their own dying. All in all, when a death occurred, the residents managed a "low-key" approach to the way in which that death was observed. Marshall agreed with Arlie Hochschild (1973) that individuals are better able to face their deaths if they can observe, in a kind of role-modeling process, that the deaths of others take place within a taken-for-granted framework.

Attitudes toward death in American society had reached a point of change in the 1970s. The fundamental cause of the change was the recognition of the failure of efforts to hide and deny the process of dying, which had resulted in death's becoming a depersonalizing and lonely experience. The humanistic approach appears to be slowly but steadily returning. Also, as Diana Crane (1975) observed, there is an increasing desire to exert autonomy in areas where formerly the individual had allowed others to make decisions. Consequently, many individuals desire to control not only their own life but also their own death and the factors contributing to it. Furthermore, Crane noted that the development of certain life-sustaining machines and techniques, such as dialysis for kidney disease and organ transplantation, have stimulated questions about the use of medical technology and the quality of the lives that are thus prolonged.

There is considerable evidence to support the contention that attitudes toward death in American society are changing. A tremendous amount of material on death has been produced and presented in the mass media, particularly in the form of books. Colleges, universities, and schools of medicine, nursing, and public health are adding courses on the social and psychological aspects of death. Twenty years ago, practically none of these courses existed; in fact, medical schools offered courses dealing only with clinical facets of death. There has also been recognition in the last few years that large general hospitals have not been very good places to die. To cope with this problem, numerous clinics and seminars have been established to train in-service hospital personnel to handle dying patients more humanely. One particular approach is to encourage physicians and nurses to deal with the reality of their own deaths and their own personal philosophies about life and death. If health practitioners are unable to change the medical outcome of a disease, yet have faced the possibility of their own deaths, it is believed that they can perhaps be supportive of the dying patient in that patient's search for meaning during the remaining portion of his or her life.

Crane (1975:10) has summarized changing attitudes toward death as providing the context for the emergence of a loosely coordinated, norm-oriented social movement with two major goals: (1) improvement in the quality of interaction between dying people and those who come into contact with them; and (2) enactment of legislation to support the patient's right to refuse treatment. In line with this second goal, there is growing interest in euthanasia, as evidenced by increasing numbers of people who have joined organizations advocating the legality of "mercy killing."

However, the legality of directly ending a life is highly questionable. In the widely publicized Karen Ann Quinlan case of 1975–1976, the parents of a comatose young woman sued the hospital and physicians attending their daughter to require them to cease their life-prolonging measures in a hopeless situation. There was medical evidence that Miss Quinlan had suffered brain damage thought to be due to combined effects of alcohol and sleeping pills (exactly what happened was never fully determined) and was not likely ever to regain consciousness. The hospital staff refused to cease treatment and deliberately allow their patient to die. Eventually, the parents won the right to have their daughter removed from the hospital to a nursing home, where the parents had the choice of whether or not to continue extraordinary life-prolonging measures. In the late 1980s, in other cases, an elderly physician was charged with manslaughter for assisting his terminally ill wife, who wanted to die, in taking an overdose of drugs, as was a father who disconnected his young brain-dead son from his life support system while holding hospital staff members at gunpoint. Both men were acquitted, but these cases illustrate the moral and legal dilemmas associated with mercy killings.

At the core of this dilemma is the position of the physician, who has a special ethical duty to preserve life. So long as the patient is legally competent to make a decision to die, it is arguable that the patient has the right to do so. But what happens when the patient is not legally competent because he or she is comatose or insensible due to pain or drugs? There is often no answer to this question, other than the decision of a physician to terminate treatment made on a case-by-case basis. Some states have legislation based upon the right of a patient to refuse treatment. If the patient is not competent, an agent, such as the next of kin, could be appointed to make the decision on the patient's behalf to authorize cessation of treatment. The physician would therefore be protected from having to make a moral (and nonmedical) judgment about what is best for the patient, and the responsibility would rest instead on the family or some court-appointed agent who would be regarded as representing the patient's interest.

Jan Hendrick van den Berg (1978), a Dutch psychiatrist, argues, however, that physicians themselves lose sight of the patient's interest when they resort to technical procedures—new surgical measures, drugs, and artificial organs—to prolong life when the chance for a genuine recovery is nonexistent and results in endless suffering for the patient and the patient's family. The impact of van den Berg's message is derived from case histories of people suffering terrible physical and mental damage who are kept alive by artificial means simply because the doctor is *able* to do it. The image of the physician that van den Berg projects is that of a technician who has become so absorbed in the power of medical procedures for maintaining life that he or she neglects or ignores the morality of the situation. Although van den Berg's thesis opens up unanswered philosophical questions, including who should have the ultimate responsibility for making these life and death decisions, he argues that the medical profession has abdicated its ethical responsibilities by removing itself from involvement with patients as people. Medicine is portrayed as rather mindlessly pursuing the preservation of all human life, unconditionally and regardless of the consequences. What is needed is a code of medical ethics in which patients and their families are (if possible) given the right to know the existence they will face if modern medical technology is applied in its fullest extent to extend the patient's life. Such people, in van den Berg's view, should not be hostages to medical power. They should have the right to die if that is their desire and they are capable of making an informed decision.

In contrast, supporters of the "hospice" concept insist that the right to die involves a corresponding duty to kill and that euthanasia should not be allowed. Instead, the hospice, a hospital that specializes in the care of the terminally ill, offers an alternative approach (Paradis and Cummings 1986). Tried with some success in Great Britain and the United States, the hospice involves a complete change in the priorities of the physician and nurse. The aim is no longer to cure the patient, but to make the patient more comfortable and his or her dying days more meaningful. The hospice stresses companionship, sense of security, and control of physical symptoms through medical and nursing techniques. The control of pain is very important in order to allow the patient to be as active as possible for as long as possible.

Because modern society has attempted to be more open and intellectual concerning death does not mean that the fear and anxiety of dying can be rationalized away. It simply suggests that the process of dying may become less impersonal and dehumanizing. Perhaps death in the future will return to a modern version of Ariès notion of "tamed death." In the final analysis, however, death will probably remain an experience characterized by various forms of fear.

SUMMARY

This chapter has examined death and dying from the perspective of both the individual and society. The primary problem death presents for the individual is that of coping with the fear of death, particularly fear of the experience itself and of its consequences. Although everyone has difficulty in managing these fears, most people eventually reach a stage of acceptance of death.

At present, death is contained by the larger social system in hospitals, nursing homes, and mortuaries by specialists who ensure that death is not disruptive for society. The result of these practices has been the dehumanization of death in modern society. Evidence is now beginning to mount, however, that attitudes in American society are evolving toward a more humanistic interpretation of the dying experience.

Postscript: The Future of Aging

The future of aging in the world appears to be generally positive. Good health and relatively high standards of living are not only possible but probable for the majority of elderly people in technologicaly developed societies. Although old age remains a period that many, perhaps most, people wish to avoid, it simply isn't possible to do so. Consequently, the optimal strategy for the individual is to approach old age with the idea of enjoying and finding personal satisfaction in the final stage of life. Current social policies are oriented toward providing a basic level of financial support and enhancing the quality of life through social programs in old age. There are no signs that these policies will be changed. Rather, national commitments to the aged are evident in governmental decisions throughout the world.

What is behind this trend is the fact that the world's population of old people, those 65 years of age and over, is increasing to levels never before attained in human history. Although some individuals may not be old at age 65, others are, and the use of age 65 as a general age to regard someone as elderly appears likely to continue. Perhaps at some future time, it may be adjusted upward, but for now, age 65 remains the boundary of old age. The twenty-first century will be the first period of human existence when one out of every five persons is likely to be age 65 or over. By the mid–twenty-first century, the United States, Canada, Australia, Western Europe, Japan, and several Asian countries will have populations of elderly people in excess of 20 percent, and some 40 percent of China's population—a simply incredible proportion—will be elderly if present trends continue.

In advanced industrial societies, old people will be more affluent, better educated, and more involved in politics than ever before. They are likely to be a highly potent social and political force in the world of the near future. Adequate old-age pensions and health care delivery, along with government policies supportive of their needs, will be major features of modern welfare states. The option to continue working will be available to the elderly, and forced retirements are likely to be less common; however, many old people may continue to choose retirement over work. The point is that employment will be generally available for those who want it, and the option to work or retire will be largely the choice of the individual. In fact, incentives for older workers to stay on the job in the form of increased salaries, greater retirement benefits, or shorter work schedules may be common, with the expected decline in numbers and proportions of younger adults in the labor force. Thus, older people are likely to have a greater range of choices about work, retirement, leisure activities, and continued education than ever before. Moreover, the elderly are likely to be relatively healthy throughout much of their old age, perhaps remaining fit until just prior to death. Both preventive care and treatment for illnesses of the aged will increasingly become a major medical specialty in the twenty-first century.

This is not to say that old age will be a time of contentment and satisfaction for all old people. Many will be frail and in poor health; hence, they will simply be unable to find enjoyment in the late stages of their life because of their ailments. The key to happiness in old age is health; without it, even vast sums of money will not be able to compensate for feeling ill and being unable to enjoy one's interests and usual activities of life. Being poor, on the other hand, signifies a life course of social and economic disadvantages culminating in significantly reduced life chances and opportunities for the aged living in poverty. Those who are both poor and sick will clearly be the most disadvantaged of all. Furthermore, there are signs in the 1990s of increased physical and mental abuse of the elderly, often by family members, as ageism and devaluation of the old continues—despite indicators of increased status and well-being for the aged in the future.

The elderly in developing countries will generally lack the quality of life of old people in developed nations, but they nevertheless are sharing in the greater longevity available to people in today's world. Diet, sanitation, health care, and lifestyle are prolonging lives throughout the world. High birthrates and relatively lower death rates in developing countries will result in large populations in general and greater proportions of old people in particular. The result is that—at the midpoint of the twenty-first century—some 69 percent of all aged persons on the globe will live in the less-developed states and regions of the world. Moreover, poor countries are likely to find it difficult to provide adequate health, social, and financial services for this large population.

As for the theories formulated to explain the social aspects of aging, no single theory provides a comprehensive explanation to date. However, disengagement theory works well in explaining those situations where older people, having been moved out of their jobs and replaced by younger workers, are themselves opting for the retirement role. Some aged persons may not wish to become disengaged, and the option to remain employed is likely to be more available than in the past, but there comes a time when disengagement may be preferred by the aged individual. For many people, some form of disengagement is inevitable in old age, and disengagement theory helps us to understand this process. The theory is most applicable to those situations in which the aged are disengaged (pushed out) from the mainstream of society and, at the same time, disengage themselves (pull away) from society to pursue their own late-life interests.

Activity theory, another major theoretical approach in social gerontology, is actually a theory of successful aging. Activity theory is based upon the premise that middle-age norms of activity constitute the standards by which older people are judged; thus, the more active an elderly person, the happier and more satisfied that person will be with his or her life. Activity theory would lead us to believe that disengagement is not desired or inevitable for the aged. Rather, being involved in chosen activities and remaining an active part of one's social environment best depict what is important for old people. Of course, not every elderly person can remain active indefinitely, and activity theory does not really explain what happens when this occurs. Nevertheless, activity theory helps us recognize the value of activity in the lives of the elderly.

Another important perspective on aging is continuity theory, which posits that a person's personality in old age is generally consistent with his or her personality when younger. That is, elderly people typically retain the same overall personality they had earlier in their adult life; they are simply older. Although disengagement theory explains tendencies toward disengagement in old age and activity theory shows us the merits of being active when elderly, continuity theory indicates that personality is little changed, if at all, by the aging process. Each of these theories explains a selected aspect of aging. Two other approaches, age stratification theory and modernization theory, apply a broader interpretation to the aging experience. Age stratification theory, a relatively complex theoretical concept of aging, provides a method for analyzing age cohorts as they pass through the life course. People are seen as generations filling the same or similar roles of the cohorts in front of them who have passed on to another stage, yet are different from other generations because of different historical events and experiences. Modernization theory, in turn, explains how old people typically occupy valued statuses and roles in developing societies, but become devalued as the process of industrialization and modernization favors the skills and energies of the young. Yet Japan is an exception to this trend because of its cultural emphasis upon honoring the aged and a family's ancestors. And, as modern societies mature and come to terms with large numbers of elderly in their midst, modernization theory maintains that elderly people regain higher status.

These theoretical perspectives represent important contributions to understanding social factors influencing aging. Other, more general, theoretical approaches in sociology—such as conflict theory (which can explain how the elderly function as a particular interest group in competition with other interest groups for social resources) and symbolic interaction theory (which can contribute knowledge concerning the development of self-concepts and small-group interaction in old age)—have been underutilized to date. But each has considerable potential for theory construction in social gerontology. In sum, significant theoretical concepts have been made, but more remains to be done.

As the world moves into the twenty-first century, the various nations on the globe will become increasingly concerned with old-age policy. Efforts to hold down the cost of health care and pensions for the elderly are not likely to be successful as the aged population expands. Unfortunately, a superior method has not yet been discovered to increase revenues significantly for government support of the aged. But the governments of the world will all more or less be required to expand and improve health and social services for old people. Therefore, although the elderly are headed toward a more positive life situation in the future, as compared with past generations of old people, their large numbers will require considerably more resources than were required previously. A major political challenge today is to prepare to meet the health, social, and financial needs of the elderly now and in the coming future. Exceptionally large populations of senior citizens will be a reality in the twenty-first century.

References

ABERCROMBIE, NICHOLAS, STEPHEN HILL, and BRYAN S. TURNER. 1984. *Dictionary of Sociology*. Harmondsworth, UK: Penguin.

ABERCROMBIE, NICHOLAS, and ALAN WARDE, with KEITH SOOTHILL, JOHN URRY, and SYLVIA WALBY. 1988. *Contemporary British Society*. Cambridge, UK: Polity Press.

ACHENBAUM, W. ANDREW. 1983. *Shades of Grey: Old Age, American Values, and Federal Policies Since 1920*. Boston: Little, Brown.

———. 1985. "Stitching a Safety Net." *Wilson Quarterly* 9:126–136.

AKERS, RONALD L., and RICHARD HAWKINS, eds. 1975. *Law and Control in Society*. Englewood Cliffs, NJ: Prentice-Hall.

ALSOP, STEWART. 1973. *Stay of Execution*. Philadelphia: Lippincott.

AMANN, ANTON. 1981. *The Status and Prospects of the Aging in Western Europe*. Vienna: European Centre for Social Welfare Training and Research.

ANTHONY, SYLVIA. 1968 "The Child's Idea of Death." In *The World of the Child*, edited by T. Talbot, 315–328. New York: Anchor.

———. 1972. *The Discovery of Death in Childhood and After*. New York: Basic Books.

APPLEWHITE, STEVEN R., ed. 1988. *Hispanic Elderly in Transition: Theory, Research, Policy and Practice*. Westport, CT: Greenwood.

ARDAGH, JOHN. 1987. *France Today*. London: Penguin.

ARIÈS, PHILIPPE. 1974. *Western Attitudes Toward Death*. Translated by P. Ranum. Baltimore: John Hopkins University Press.

———. 1981. *The Hour of Death*. New York: Knopf.

ATCHLEY, ROBERT C. 1976. "Selected Social and Psychological Differences Between Men and Women in Later Life." *Journal of Gerontology* 31:204–211.

———. 1982. "The Process of Retirement: Comparing Men and Women." In *Women's Retirement*, edited by M. Szinovacz, 153–168. Beverly Hills, CA: Sage.

———. 1988. *Social Forces and Aging*. 5th ed. Belmont, CA: Wadsworth.

BAKER, PAUL M. 1985. "The Status of Age: Preliminary Results." *Journal of Gerontology* 40:506–508.

BARASH, DAVID P. 1983. *Aging: An Exploration*. Seattle: University of Washington Press.

BAUM, MARTHA, and RAINER C. BAUM. 1980. *Growing Old*. Englewood Cliffs, NJ: Prentice-Hall.

BECERRA, ROSINA M., and DAVID SHAW. 1984. *The Hispanic Elderly*. Lanham, MD: University Press of America.

BENGSTON, VERN L., MARGARET N. REEDY, and CHAD GORDON. 1985. "Aging and Self-Conceptions: Personality Processes and Social Contexts." In *Handbook of the Psychology of Aging*, edited by J. Birren and K. Schaie, 544–593. 2nd ed. New York: Van Nostrand Reinhold.

BERGER, PETER L., and THOMAS LUCKMANN. 1967. *The Social Construction of Reality*. New York: Anchor.

BINSTOCK, ROBERT H. 1983. "The Aged as Scapegoat." *Gerontologist* 23:136–143.

BLAU, ZENA. 1956. "Changes in Status and Age Identification." *American Sociological Review* 21:198–203.

BLAUNER, ROBERT. 1966. "Death and Social Structure." *Psychiatry* 29:378–394.

BLUMER, HERBERT. 1969. *Symbolic Interaction*. Englewood Cliffs, NJ: Prentice-Hall.

BOWDEN, CHARLES L., and ALVIN G. BURSTEIN. 1974. *Psychosocial Basis of Medical Practice*. Baltimore: Williams & Wilkins.

BRENTS, BARBARA G. 1986. "Policy Intellectuals, Class Struggle and the Construction of Old Age: The Creation of the Social Security Act of 1935." *Social Science and Medicine* 23:1251–1260.

BULTENA, GORDON L., and EDWARD A. POWERS. 1978. "Denial of Aging: Age Identification and Reference Group Orientation." *Journal of Gerontology* 33:748–754.

BUTLER, ROBERT N. 1985. "Geriatric Psychiatry." In Vol. 2, *Comprehensive Textbook of Psychiatry*, edited by H. Kaplan and B. Sadock, 1953–1959. 4th ed. Baltimore: Williams & Wilkins.

CAFFERATA, GAIL L. 1987. "Marital Status, Living Arrangements, and the Use of Health Services by Elderly Persons." *Journal of Gerontology* 42:613–618.

CAIN, LEONARD D. 1987. "Alternative Perspectives on the Phenomena of Human Aging: Age Stratification and Age Status." *Journal of the Applied Behavioral Sciences* 23:277–294.

CARR, ARTHUR C. 1985. "Grief, Mourning, and Bereavement." In Vol. 2, *Comprehensive Textbook of Psychiatry*, edited by H. Kaplan and B. Sadock, 1286–1293. 4th ed. Baltimore: Williams & Wilkins.

CHARMAZ, KATHY C. 1975. "The Coroner's Strategies for Announcing Death." *Urban Life* 4:296–316.

CHILDS, DAVID, and JEFFREY JOHNSON. 1981. *West Germany: Politics and Society*. London: Croom Helm.

CHUDACOFF, HOWARD P. 1989. *Age Consciousness in American Culture*. Princeton, NJ: Princeton University Press.

CLARK, ROBERT E., and EMILY E. LaBEFF. 1982. "Death Telling: Managing the Delivery of Bad News." *Journal of Health and Social Behavior* 23: 366–380.

COCKERHAM, WILLIAM C. 1989. *Medical Sociology*. 4th ed. Englewood Cliffs, NJ: Prentice-Hall.

COCKERHAM, WILLIAM C., GERHARD KUNZ, and GUENTHER LUESCHEN. 1988. "Social Stratification and Health Lifestyles in Two Systems of Health Care Delivery: A Comparison of the United States and West Germany." *Journal of Health and Social Behavior* 29:113–126.

COCKERHAM, WILLIAM C., KIMBERLY SHARP, and JULIE WILCOX. 1983. "Aging and Perceived Health Status." *Journal of Gerontology* 38:349–355.

COHEN, CARL I., JEANNE TERESI, and DOUGLAS HOLMES. 1985. "Social Networks, Stress, and Physical Health: A Longitudinal Study of an Inner-City Population." *Journal of Gerontology* 40:478–486.

COHEN, DONNA, and CARL EISDORFER. 1986. *The Loss of Self*. New York: W. W. Norton.

COMFORT, ALEX. 1976. "Age Prejudice in America." *Social Policy* 7:3–8.

COOLEY, CHARLES H. 1964. *Human Nature and the Social Order*. New York: Schocken.

COOMBS, ROBERT H., and PAULINE S. POWERS. 1975. "Socialization for Death: The Physician's Role." *Urban Life* 4:250–271.

COULTON, CLAUDIA, and ABBIE K. FROST. 1982. "Use of Social and Health Services by the Aged." *Journal of Health and Social Behavior* 23:330–339.

COWGILL, DONALD O. 1986. *Aging Around the World*. Belmont, CA: Wadsworth.

COWGILL, DONALD O., and LOWELL D. HOLMES, eds. 1972. *Aging and Modernization*. New York: Appleton-Century-Crofts.

COWLEY, MALCOLM. 1980. *The View From 80*. New York: Viking Press.

COX, HAROLD G. 1988. *Later Life: The Realities of Aging*. 2nd ed. Englewood Cliffs, NJ: Prentice-Hall.

CRAIG, GORDON A. 1982. *The Germans*. New York: Putnam.

CRANE, DIANA. 1975. *The Sanctity of Social Life: Physicians' Treatment of Critically Ill Patients*. New York: Sage.

CUMMING, ELAINE, and WILLIAM E. HENRY. 1961. *Growing Old: The Process of Disengagement*. New York: Basic Books.

DAHRENDORF, RALF. 1959. Class and Conflict in Industrial Society. Stanford, CA: Stanford University Press.

DAVIS, KINGSLEY, and WILBERT MOORE. 1945. "Some Principles of Stratification." *American Sociological Review* 10:242–249.

DEBUSKEY, M. ed. 1970. *The Chroncially Ill Child and His Family*. Springfield, IL: Thomas.

DENZIN, NORMAN K. 1970a. "The Methodologies of Symbolic Interaction: A Critical Review of Research Techniques." In *Social Psychology Through Symbolic Interaction*, edited by G. Stone and H. Farberman, 447–465. Waltham, MA: Ginn-Bladisdell.

———. 1970b. "Rules of Conduct and the Study of Deviant Behavior." In *Deviance and Respectability*, edited by J. Douglas, 120–159. New York: Basic Books.

DE SWAAN, ABRAM. 1988. *In Care of the State*. New York: Oxford University Press.

DEVINEY, STANLEY, and ANGELA M. O'RAND. 1988. "Gender-Cohort Succession and Retirement Among Older Men and Women, 1951 to 1984." *Sociological Quarterly* 29:525–540.

DOHRENWEND, BRUCE P. 1975. "Sociocultural and Social-Psychological Factors in the Genesis of Mental Disorders." *Journal of Health and Social Behavior* 16:365–392.

DOWD, JAMES J. 1980. *Stratification Among the Aged*. Monterey, CA: Brooks/Cole.

———. 1984. "Beneficence and the Aged." *Journal of Gerontology* 39:102–108.

Dowd, James J., and Vern L. Bengston. 1978. "Aging in Minority Populations: An Examination of the Double Jeopardy Hypothesis." *Journal of Gerontology* 33:427–436.

Drevenstedt, Jean. 1976. "Perceptions of Onsets of Young Adulthood, Middle Age, and Old Age." *Journal of Gerontology* 31:53–57.

Dumont, Richard G., and Dennis C. Foss. 1972. *The American Way of Death.* Cambridge, MA: Schenkman.

Durkheim, Émile. 1956. *The Division of Labor in Society.* New York: Free Press.

———. 1961. *The Elementary Forms of Religious Life.* New York: Collier.

Easson, W. M. 1970. *The Dying Child.* Springfield, IL: Thomas.

Edwards, E. D. 1983. "Native-American Elders: Current Social Issues and Social Policy Implications." In *Aging in Minority Groups,* edited by R. McNeely and J. Cohen, 74–82. Beverly Hills, CA: Sage.

Ekerdt, David J., Lynn Baden, Raymond Bossé, and Elaine Dibbs. 1983. "The Effect of Retirement on Physical Health." *American Journal of Public Health* 73:779–783.

Ekerdt, David J., Raymond Bossé, and Joseph S. LoCastro. 1983. "Claims that Retirement Improves Health." *Journal of Gerontology* 38:231–236.

Ekerdt, David J., Barbara H. Vinick, and Raymond Bossé. 1989. "Orderly Endings: Do Men Know When They Will Retire?" *Journal of Gerontology* 44:528–535.

Erikson, Erik. 1963. *Childhood and Society.* New York: W. W. Norton.

Estes, Carroll L., and Philip R. Lee. 1986. "Health Problems and Policy Issues of Old Age." In *Applications of Social Science to Clinical Medicine and Health Policy,* edited by L. Aiken and D. Mechanic, 335–355. New Brunswick, NJ: Rutgers University Press.

Estes, Carroll L., Steven P. Wallace, and Elizabeth A. Binney. 1989. "Health, Aging, and Medical Sociology." In *Handbook of Medical Sociology,* edited by H. Freeman and S. Levine, 400–418. 4th ed. Englewood Cliffs, NJ: Prentice-Hall.

Evans, Robert G. 1986. "Finding the Levers, Finding the Courage: Lessons from Cost Containment in North America." *Journal of Health Politics, Policy, and Law* 11:585–616.

Fairbank, John King. 1989. *The United States and China.* 5th ed. Cambridge, MA: Harvard University Press.

Farley, Reynolds. 1984. *Blacks and Whites: Narrowing the Gap?* Cambridge, MA: Harvard University Press.

Feifel, Herman, and Allan B. Branscomb. 1973. "Who's Afraid of Death?" *Journal of Abnormal Psychology* 81:282–288.

Fennell, Graham, Chris Phillipson, and Helen Evers. 1988. *The Sociology of Old Age.* Philadelphia: Open University Press.

Fenwick, Rudy, and Charles M. Barresi. 1981. "Health Consequences of Marital-Status Change Among the Elderly: A Comparison of Cross-Sectional and Longitudinal Analyses." *Journal of Health and Social Behavior* 22:106–116.

Ferraro, Kenneth F. 1980. "Self-Ratings of Health Among the Old and Old-Old." *Journal of Health and Social Behavior* 21:377–383.

———. 1988. "Double Jeopardy to Health for Black Older Adults." *Journal of Gerontology* 42:528–533.

———. 1989. "Widowhood and Health." In *Aging, Stress and Health,* edited by S. Markides and C. Cooper, 69–90. New York: John Wiley.

Ferraro, Kenneth F., Elizabeth Mutran, and Charles M. Barresi. 1984. "Widowhood, Health, and Friendship Support in Later Life." *Journal of Health and Social Behavior* 25:245–259.

FILLENBAUM, GERDA G. 1979. "Social Context and Self-Assessments of Health Among the Elderly." *Journal of Health and Social Behavior* 20:45–51.

FILLENBAUM, GERDA G., LINDA K. GEORGE, and ERDMAN B. PALMORE. 1985. "Determinants and Consequences of Retirement Among Men of Different Races and Economic Levels." *Journal of Gerontology* 40:85–94.

FISCHER, DAVID H. 1978. *Growing Old in America*, Expanded Edition. New York: Oxford University Press.

FONER, ANNE. 1974. "Age Stratification and Age Conflict in Political Life." *American Sociological Review* 39:187–196.

———. 1986. *Aging and Old Age: New Perspectives*. Englewood Cliffs, NJ: Prentice-Hall.

FONTANA, ANDREA. 1977. *The Last Frontier: The Social Meaning of Growing Old*. Beverly Hills, CA: Sage.

FRIES, JAMES F. 1980. "Aging, Natural Deaths, and the Compression of Morbidity." *New England Journal of Medicine* 300:130–135.

GALVIN, MICHAEL L., and MARGARET FAN. 1975. "The Utilization of Physician's Services in Los Angeles County, 1973." *Journal of Health and Social Behavior* 16:75–94.

GECAS, V. 1982. "The Self Concept." *Annual Review of Sociology* 8:1–33.

GELFAND, DONALD E. 1982. *Aging: The Ethnic Factor*. Boston: Little, Brown.

GEORGE, LINDA K. 1989. "Stress, Social Support, and Depression over the Life-Course." In *Aging, Stress and Health*, edited by K. Markides and C. Cooper, 241–268. New York: John Wiley.

GEORGE, LINDA K., GERDA G. FILLENBAUM, and ERDMAN PALMORE. 1984. "Sex Differences in the Antecedents and Consequences of Retirement." *Journal of Gerontology* 39:364–371.

GIBSON, ROSE C. 1986. "Blacks in an Aging Society." *Daedalus* 115:349–371.

GIDDENS, ANTHONY. 1989. *Sociology*. London: Polity Press.

GILLEARD, CHRISTOPHER J., and ALI A. GURKAN. 1987. "Socioeconomic Development and the Status of Elderly Men in Turkey: A Test of Modernization Theory." *Journal of Gerontology* 42:353–357.

GLASER, BARNEY G., and ANSELM M. STRAUSS. 1965. *Awareness of Dying*. Chicago: Aldine.

———. 1968. *Time for Dying*. Chicago: Aldine.

———. 1971. *Status Passage*. Chicago: Aldine.

GOFFMAN, ERVING. 1959. *The Presentation of Self in Everyday Life*. New York: Anchor.

———. 1961. *Encounters*. Indianapolis: Bobbs-Merrill.

———. 1963. *Stigma*. Englewood Cliffs, NJ: Prentice-Hall.

———. 1967. *Interaction Ritual*. New York: Anchor.

GOVE, WALTER R., SUZANNE T. ORTEGA, and CAROLYN BRIGGS STYLE. 1989. "The Maturational and Role Perspectives on Aging and Self Through the Adult Years: An Empirical Evaluation." *American Journal of Sociology* 94:1117–1145.

GRAEBNER, WILLIAM. 1980. *A History of Retirement*. New Haven: Yale University Press.

GUBRIUM, JABER F. 1975. *Living and Dying at Murray Manor*. New York: St. Martin's.

GUILLEMARD, ANNE-MARIE. 1986. "State, Society and Old-Age Policy in France: From 1945 to the Current Crisis." *Social Science and Medicine* 23:1319–1326.

HABER, CAROLE. 1978. "Mandatory Retirement in Nineteenth-Century America: The Conceptual Basis for a New Work Cycle." *Journal of Social History* 12: 77–96.

———. 1983. *Beyond Sixty-Five*. Cambridge, UK: Cambridge University Press.

HAFFERTY, FREDERIC W. 1988. "Cadaver Stories and the Emotional Socialization of Medical Students." *Journal of Health and Social Behavior* 29:344–356.

HAUG, MARIE, LINDA LISKA BELGRAVE, and BRIAN GRATTON. 1984. "Mental Health and the Elderly: Factors in Stability and Change." *Journal of Health and Social Behavior* 25:100–115.

HAUG, MARIE R., and STEVEN J. FOLMAR. 1986. "Longevity, Gender, and Life Quality." *Journal of Health and Social Behavior* 27:332–345.

HAVIGHURST, ROBERT A. 1963. "Successful Aging." In *Processes of Aging,* edited by R. Williams, C. Tibbitts, and W. Donahue, 299–320. New York: Atherton.

HAVIGHURST, ROBERT A., and RUTH ALBRECHT. 1953. *Older People.* New York: Longmans, Green.

HENRETTA, JOHN C., and RICHARD T. CAMPBELL. 1976. "Status Attainment and Status Maintenance: A Study of Stratification in Old Age." *American Sociological Review* 41:981–992.

HOCHSCHILD, ARLIE RUSSELL. 1973. *The Unexpected Community.* Englewood Cliffs, NJ: Prentice-Hall.

HUDSON, ROBERT B. 1988. "Social Policy in the United States." In *North American Elders,* edited by E. Rathbone-McCuan and B. Havens, 55–68. New York: Greenwood.

JANIS, IRVING. 1958. *Psychological Stress.* New York: John Wiley.

KAMMERMAN, JACK B. 1988. *Death in the Midst of Life.* Englewood Cliffs, NJ: Prentice-Hall.

KAPLAN, GIORA, VITA BARELL, and AYALA LUSKY. 1988. "Subjective State of Health and Survival in Elderly Adults." *Journal of Gerontology* 43:S114–S120.

KAPLAN, HELEN SINGER. 1974. *The New Sex Therapy.* New York: Quadrangle.

KART, CARY S., EILEEN K. METRESS, and SEAMUS P. METRESS. 1988. *Aging, Health and Society.* Boston: Jones & Bartlett.

KASTENBAUM, ROBERT J. 1971. "Age: Getting There." *Psychology Today* 5:53–54, 82–83.

———. 1981. *Death, Society, and Human Experience.* 2nd ed. St. Louis: Mosby.

KAUFMAN, SHARON R. 1987. *The Ageless Self.* Madison: University of Wisconsin Press.

KELLEHEAR, ALLAN. 1984. "Are We a 'Death-Denying' Society? A Sociological Review." *Social Science and Medicine* 18:713–723.

KENT, D.P. 1971. "The Negro Aged." *Gerontologist* 11:48–51.

KII, TOSHI. 1984. "Asians." In *Handbook on the Aged in the United States,* edited by E. Palmore, 201–217. Westport, CT: Greenwood.

KING, DONALD WEST, NEELA PUSHPARAJ, and KATHLEEN O'TOOLE. 1982. "Morbidity and Mortality in the Aged." *Hospital Practice* 17:97–109.

King's Fund Centre. 1988. *Promoting Health Among Elderly People.* London: King's Fund.

KIRCHNER, CORINNE. 1986. *Data on Blindness and Visual Impairment in the U.S.* New York: American Foundation for the Blind.

KITANO, HARRY H. L. 1985. *Race Relations.* 3rd ed. Englewood Cliffs, NJ: Prentice-Hall.

KLEMMACK, DAVID L., and LUCINDA LEE ROFF. 1984. "Fear of Personal Aging and Subjective Well-Being in Late Life." *Journal of Gerontology* 39:756–758.

KLIGMAN, A. M., G. GROVE, and A. BALIN. 1985. "Aging of Human Skin." In *Handbook of the Biology of Aging,* edited by C. Finch and E. Schneider, 820–841. 2nd ed. New York: Van Nostrand Reinhold.

KORTHASE, K. M., and I. TRENHOLME. 1982. "Perceived Age and Physical Attractiveness." *Perceptual and Motor Skills* 54:1251–1258.

KRAUSE, NEAL. 1986. "Social Support, Stress, and Well-Being Among Older Adults." *Journal of Gerontology* 41:512–517.

———. 1988. "Stressful Life Events and Physician Utilization Among the Elderly." *Journal of Gerontology* 43:553–561.

KRAUSE, NEAL, and THANH VAN TRAN. 1989. "Stress and Religious Involvement Among Older Blacks." *Journal of Gerontology* 44:54–63.

KRONENFELD, JENNIE J. 1978. "Provider Variables and the Utilization of Ambulatory Care Services." *Journal of Health and Social Behavior* 19:133–149.

KÜBLER-ROSS, ELIZABETH. 1969. *On Death and Dying*. New York: Macmillan.

LARSON, REED. 1978. "Thirty Years of Research on the Subjective Well-Being of Older Americans." *Journal of Gerontology* 33:109–125.

LARUE, ASENATH, LEW BANK, LISSY JARVIK, and MONTE HETLAND. 1979. "Health in Old Age: How Do Physicians' Ratings and Self-Ratings Compare?" *Journal of Gerontology* 34:687–691.

LEE, DAVID Z., and KYRIAKOS S. MARKIDES. 1990. "Activity and Mortality Among Aged Persons over an Eight-Year Period." *Journal of Gerontology* 45:S39–S42.

LEVIN, JACK, and WILLIAM C. LEVIN. 1980. *Ageism: Prejudice and Discrimination Against the Elderly*. Belmont, CA: Wadsworth.

LEVKOFF, SUE, PAUL D. CLEARY, and TERRIE WETLE. 1987. "Differences in the Appraisal of Health Between Aged and Middle-Aged Adults." *Journal of Gerontology* 42:114–120.

LEVY, JUDITH A. 1988. "Intersections of Gender and Aging." *Sociological Quarterly* 29:479–486.

LIANG, JERSEY. 1986. "Self-Reported Physical Health Among Aged Adults." *Journal of Gerontology* 41:248–260.

LIANG, JERSEY, EDWARD JOW-CHING TU, and XIANGMING CHEN. 1986. "Population Aging in the People's Republic of China." *Social Science and Medicine* 23:1353–1362.

LICHTER, DANIEL T. 1988. "Racial Differences in Underemployment in American Cities." *American Journal of Sociology* 93:771–792.

LICHTMAN, RICHARD. 1982. *The Production of Desire: The Integration of Psychoanalysis into Marxist Theory*. New York: Free Press.

LINDESMITH, ALFRED R., ANSELM L. STRAUSS, and NORMAN K. DENZIN. 1988. *Social Psychology*. 6th ed. Englewood Cliffs, NJ: Prentice-Hall.

LINN, BERNARD S., and MARGARET W. LINN. 1980. "Objective and Self-Assessed Health in the Old and Very Old." *Social Science and Medicine* 14:311–315.

LOCAYO, CARMELA G. 1984. "Hispanics." In *Handbook on the Aged in the United States*, edited by E. Palmore, 253–267. Westport, CT: Greenwood.

LONGINO, CHARLES F., JR. 1986. *The Oldest Americans: State Profiles for Data Base Planning*. Coral Gables, FL: University of Miami Center for Social Research on Aging.

———. 1988. "A Population Profile of Very Old Men and Women in the United States." *Sociological Quarterly* 29:559–564.

LOPATA, HELENA Z. 1973. "Social Relations of Black and White Widowed Women in a Northern Metropolis." *American Journal of Sociology* 78:1003–1010.

LUND, DALE A. 1987. "Gerontology Update on Bereavement." In *Gerontology Updates*, edited by J. Borup, 27–35. Washington, D.C: U.S. Department of Health and Human Services.

LUND, DALE A., MICHAEL S. CASERTA, and MARGARET F. DIMOND. 1986. "Gender Differences Through Two Years of Bereavement Among the Elderly." *Gerontologist* 26:314–320.

LUND, DALE A., MICHAEL S. CASERTA, MARGARET F. DIMOND, and ROBERT M. GRAY. 1986. "Impact of Bereavement on the Self-Conceptions of Older Surviving Spouses." *Symbolic Interaction* 9:235–244.

LUSKY, RICHARD A. 1986. "Anticipating the Needs of the U.S. Aged in the 21st Century: Dilemmas in Epidemiology, Gerontology, and Public Policy." *Social Science and Medicine* 23:1217–1227.

McAULEY, WILLIAM J., and GREG ARLING. 1984. "Use of In-Home Care by Very Old People." *Journal of Health and Social Behavior* 25:54–64.

McCRAE, R. R., and P. T. COSTA, JR. 1982. *Emerging Lives, Enduring Dispositions: Personality in Adulthood.* Boston: Little, Brown.

McDANIEL, SUSAN A. 1986. *Canada's Aging Population.* Toronto: Butterworths.

McGOLDRICK, ANNE E. 1989. "Stress, Early Retirement and Health." In *Aging, Stress and Health,* edited by K. Markides and C. Cooper, 91–118. New York: John Wiley.

McGOLDRICK, ANNE E., and CARY L. COOPER. 1989. *Early Retirement.* Aldershot, UK: Gower Press.

MacNEIL, RICHARD D., and MICHAEL L. TEAGUE. 1987. *Aging and Leisure.* Englewood Cliffs, NJ: Prentice-Hall.

McTAVISH, DONALD G. 1971. "Perceptions of Old People: A Review of Research, Methodologies, and Findings." *Gerontologist* 11:90–101.

MADDOX, GEORGE L. 1962. "Some Correlates of Differences in Self-Assessment of Health Status Among the Elderly." *Journal of Gerontology* 17:180–185.

MADDOX, GEORGE L., and ELIZABETH B. DOUGLASS. 1973. "Self-Assessment of Health: A Longitudinal Study of Elderly Subjects." *Journal of Health and Social Behavior* 14:87–93.

MANTON, KENNETH G. 1980. "Sex and Race Specific Mortality Differentials in Multiple Cause of Death Data." *Gerontologist* 20:480–493.

MANTON, KENNETH G., and BETH J. SOLDO. 1985. "Dynamics of Health Changes in the Oldest Old: New Perspectives and Evidence." *Milbank Quarterly* 63:206–285.

MARKIDES, KYRIAKOS S., ed. 1989. *Aging and Health.* Beverly Hills, CA: Sage.

MARKIDES, KYRIAKOS, and CARY L. COOPER, eds. 1987. *Retirement in Industrialized Societies: Social, Psychological and Health Factors.* New York: John Wiley.

———. 1989. *Aging, Stress and Health.* New York: John Wiley.

MARKIDES, KYRIAKOS S., and CHARLES H. MINDEL. 1987. *Aging and Ethnicity.* Beverly Hills, CA: Sage.

MARSHALL, T. H. 1964. *Class, Citizenship, and Social Development.* Chicago: University of Chicago Press.

MARSHALL, VICTOR W. 1975. "Socialization for Impending Death in a Retirement Village." *American Journal of Sociology* 80:1124–1144.

MARTIN, LINDA G. 1988. "The Aging of Asia." *Journal of Gerontology* 43:S99–S113.

MASON, EVELYN P. 1954. "Some Correlates of Self-Judgments of the Aged." *Journal of Gerontology* 9:324–337.

MEAD, GEORGE H. 1934. *Mind, Self, and Society.* Chicago: University of Chicago Press.

MEAD, LAWRENCE M. 1985. *The Social Obligations of Citizenship.* New York: Free Press.

MECHANIC, DAVID, and RONALD J. ANGEL. 1987. "Some Factors Associated with the Report and Evaluation of Back Pain." *Journal of Health and Social Behavior* 28:131–139.

MONTEIRO, LOIS. 1973. "Expense Is No Object . . . :Income and Physician Visits Reconsidered." *Journal of Health and Social Behavior* 14:99–115.

MOODY, RAYMOND. 1976. *Life After Life.* New York: Bantam.

MORGAN, S. PHILIP, and KIYOSI HIROSIMA. 1983. "The Persistence of Extended Family Residence in Japan: Anachronism or Alternative Strategy?" *American Sociological Review* 48:269–281.

MORRISON, MALCOLM H. 1986. "Work and Retirement in the Aging Society." *Daedalus* 115:269–294.

MOSSEY, JANA M., and EVELYN SHAPIRO. 1982. "Self-Rated Health: A Predictor of Mortality Among the Elderly." *American Journal of Public Health* 8:800–808.

MUTRAN, ELIZABETH. 1985. "Intergenerational Family Support Among Blacks and Whites: Response to Culture or to Socioeconomic Differences." *Journal of Gerontology* 40:382–389.

MUTRAN, ELIZABETH, and KENNETH F. FERRARO. 1988. "Medical Need and Use of Services Among Older Men and Women." *Journal of Gerontology* 43:S162–S171.

MUTRAN, ELIZABETH, and DONALD C. REITZES. 1981. "Retirement, Identity and Well-Being: Realignment of Role Relationships." *Journal of Gerontology* 37:733–740.

———. 1984. "Intergenerational Support Activities and Well-Being Among the Elderly: A Convergence of Exchange and Symbolic Interaction Perspectives." *American Sociological Review* 49:117–130.

MYLES, JOHN F. 1978. "Institutionalization and Sick Role Identification Among the Elderly." *American Sociological Review* 43:508–521.

———. 1984. *Old Age in the Welfare State.* Boston: Little, Brown.

———. 1988. "Social Policy in Canada." In *North American Elders,* edited by E. Rathbone-McCuan and B. Havens, 37–53. New York: Greenwood.

National Center for Health Statistics. 1986a. "Aging in the Eighties." Preliminary Data from the Supplement on Aging to the National Health Interview Survey, United States, January–June 1984. No. 115. U.S. Department of Health and Human Services.

———. 1986b. "Aging in the Eighties, Impaired Senses for Sound and Light in Persons Age 65 Years and Over." No 125. U.S. Department of Health and Human Services.

———. 1987a. "Use of Nursing Homes by the Elderly." Preliminary Data from the 1985 National Nursing Home Survey. No. 135. U.S. Department of Health and Human Services.

———. 1987b. "Health Statistics on Older Persons, 1986." Series 3, No. 25. Washington, D.C.: U.S. Government Printing Office.

———. 1987c. "Aging in the Eighties, Ability to Perform Work-Related Activities." No. 136. U.S. Department of Health and Human Services.

———. 1989. "Physical Functioning of the Aged, United States, 1984." *Vital and Health Statistics,* Series 10, No. 167. U.S. Department of Health and Human Services.

National Institute of Mental Health. 1987. *Mental Health, United States, 1987.* Washington, D.C.: U.S. Government Printing Office.

NAVARRO, VICENTE. 1986. *Crisis, Health, and Medicine: A Social Critique.* New York: Tavistock.

NEUGARTEN, BERNICE. 1964. *Personality in Middle and Later Life.* New York: Atherton.

———. 1970. "The Old and Young in Modern Societies." *American Behavioral Scientist* 14:13–24.

———. 1971. "Grow Old with Me. The Best Is Yet to Be." *Psychology Today* 5:45–48.

NEUGARTEN, BERNICE L., and DAIL A. NEUGARTEN. 1986. "Age in the Aging Society." *Daedalus* 115:31–50.

NOYES, RUSSELL, JR. 1972. "The Experience of Dying." *Psychiatry* 35:174–184.

OKEN, DONALD. 1961. "What to Tell Cancer Patients: A Study of Medical Attitudes." *Journal of the American Medical Association* 175:1120–1128.

OLSON, PHILIP. 1988. "Modernization in the People's Republic of China: The Politicization of the Elderly." *Sociological Quarterly* 29:241–262.

O'NEILL, J. 1985. "Role Differentiation and the Gender Gap in Wage Rates." In *Women and Work,* edited by L. Larwood, A. Stromberg, and B. Gutek, 50–75. Beverly Hills, CA: Sage.

ORY, MARCIA G., and KATHLEEN BOND. 1989. *Aging and Health Care.* London: Routledge.

OTTEN, MAC W., JR., STEVEN M. TEUTSCH, DAVID F. WILLIAMSON, and JAMES S. MARKS. 1990. "The Effect of Known Risk Factors on the Excess Mortality of Black Adults in the United States." *Journal of the American Medical Association* 263:845–850.

OWEN, J. P., and D. BELZUNG. 1967. "Consequences of Voluntary Early Retirement: A Study of a New Labour Force Phenomenon." *British Journal of Industrial Relations* 5:162–189.

ØYEN, ELSE. 1986. "The Muffling Effect of Social Policy: A Comparison of Social Security Systems and Their Conflict Potential in Australia, the United States, and Norway." *International Sociology* 1:271–281.

PALMORE, ERDMAN. 1968. "The Effects of Aging on Activities and Attitudes." *Gerontologist* 8:259–263.

———. 1969. "Sociological Aspects of Aging." In *Behavior and Adaptation in Later Life,* edited by E. Busse and E. Pfeiffer, 33–69. Boston: Little, Brown.

———. 1971. "Attitudes Toward Aging as Shown by Humor." *Gerontologist* 11:181–186.

———. 1975a. "The Status and Integration of the Aged in Japanese Society." *Journal of Gerontology* 30:199–208.

———. 1975b. *The Honorable Elders.* Durham, NC: Duke University Press.

———. 1981. *Social Patterns in Normal Aging.* Durham, NC: Duke University Press.

———. 1985. *The Honorable Elders Revisited.* Durham, NC: Duke University Press.

PALMORE, ERDMAN B., LINDA K. GEORGE, and GERDA G. FILLENBAUM. 1982. "Predictors of Retirement." *Journal of Gerontology* 37:733–742.

PALMORE, ERDMAN, and KENNETH MANTON. 1974. "Modernization and Status of the Aged: International Comparisons." *Journal of Gerontology* 29:205–210.

PAMPEL, FRED C. 1981. *Social Change and the Aged.* Lexington, MA: Lexington Books.

PAMPEL, FRED C., and SOOKJA PARK. 1986. "Cross-National Patterns and Determinants of Female Retirement." *American Journal of Sociology* 91:932–955.

PAMPEL, FRED C., and JANE A. WEISS. 1983. "Economic Development, Pension Policies, and the Labor Force Participation of Aged Males: A Cross-National, Longitudinal Approach." *American Journal of Sociology* 89:350–372.

PAMPEL, FRED C., and JOHN B. WILLIAMSON. 1985. "Age Structure, Politics, and Cross-National Patterns of Public Pension Expenditures." *American Sociological Review* 50:782–799.

PARADIS, LENORA FINN, and SCOTT B. CUMMINGS. 1986. "The Evolution of Hospice in America Toward Organizational Homogeneity." *Journal of Health and Social Behavior* 27:370–386.

PARKER, S. 1982. *Work and Retirement.* London: Allen & Unwin.

PARSONS, TALCOTT. 1951. *The Social System.* Glencoe, IL: Free Press.

PESCOSOLIDO, BERNICE A., CAROL A. BOYER, and WAI YING TSUI. 1985. "Medical Care in the Welfare State: A Cross-National Study of Public Evaluations." *Journal of Health and Social Behavior* 26:276–297.

PETERSON, MERRILL. 1970. *Thomas Jefferson and the New Nation.* New York: Oxford University Press.

PHILLIPS, DAVID P., and KENNETH A. FELDMAN. 1973. "A Dip in Deaths Before Ceremonial Occasions: Some New Relationships Between Social Integration and Mortality." *American Sociological Review* 38:678–696.

PHILLIPS, DAVID P., and E. W. KING. 1988. "Death Takes a Holiday: Mortality Surrounding Major Social Occasions." *Lancet* 87:728–732.

PHILLIPS, DAVID P., and DANIEL G. SMITH. 1990. "Postponement of Death Until Symbolically Meaningful Occasions." *Journal of the American Medical Association* 263:1947–1951.

PIFER, ALAN, and D. LYDIA BRONTE. 1986. "Introduction: Squaring the Pyramid." *Daedalus* 115:1–12.

PINKNEY, ALPHONSO. 1984. *The Myth of Black Progress.* Cambridge, UK: Cambridge University Press.

PRESTON, CAROLINE E. 1967. "Self-Reporting Among Older Retired and Non-Retired Subjects." *Journal of Gerontology* 22:415–418.

———. 1968. "Subjectively Perceived Agedness and Retirement." *Journal of Gerontology* 23:201–204.

PRESTON, CAROLINE E., and KAREN S. GUDIKEN. 1966. "A Measure of Self-Perception Among Older People." *Journal of Gerontology* 212:63–67.

PRUGH, D. G., E. M. STAUB, H. H. SANDS, R. M. KIRSCHBAUM, and E. A. LENIHAN. 1953. "A Study of the Emotional Responses of Children and Families to Hospitalization and Illness." *American Journal of Orthopsychiatry* 23:70–106.

QUADAGNO, S. JILL. 1982. *Aging in Early Industrialized Society: Work, Family, and Social Policy in Nineteenth Century England.* New York: Academic Press.

———. 1984. "Welfare Capitalism and the Social Security Act of 1935." *American Sociological Review* 49:632–647.

———. 1988a. *The Transformation of Old Age Security: Class and Politics in the American Welfare State.* Chicago: University of Chicago Press.

———. 1988b. "Women's Access to Pensions and the Structure of Eligibility Rules: Systems of Production and Reproduction." *Sociological Quarterly* 29:541–558.

RILEY, MATILDA WHITE. 1971. "Social Gerontology and the Age Stratification of Society." *Gerontologist* 11:79–87.

———. 1987. "On the Significance of Age in Sociology." *American Sociological Review* 52:1–14.

RILEY, MATILDA WHITE, and ANNE FONER. 1968. Vol. 1, *Aging and Society.* New York: Russell Sage Foundation.

RILEY, MATILDA WHITE, ANNE FONER, and JOAN WARING. 1988. "Sociology of Age." In *Handbook of Sociology,* edited by N. Smelser, 243–290. Beverly Hills, CA: Sage.

RILEY, MATILDA WHITE, MARILYN JOHNSON, and ANNE FONER. 1972. Vol. 3, *Aging and Society.* New York: Russell Sage Foundation.

RILEY, MATILDA WHITE, and JOHN W. RILEY, JR. 1986. "Longevity and Social Structure: The Added Years." *Daedalus* 115:51–75.

RING, KENNETH. 1980. *Life at Death: A Scientific Investigation of the Near-Death Experience.* New York: Coward, McCann & Geoghegan.

ROMAN, PAUL, and PHILIP TAIETZ. 1967. "Organizational Structure and Disengagement: The Emeritus Professor." *Gerontologist* 7:147–152.

ROSE, ARNOLD M. 1965. "The Subculture of Aging: A Framework for Research in Social Gerontology." In *Older People and Their Social World,* edited by A. Rose and W. Peterson, 3–16. Philadelphia: Davis.

ROSENFELD, ALBERT. 1985. "Stretching the Span." *Wilson Quarterly* 9:96–107.

ROSENWAIKE, IRA. 1985. "A Demographic Portrait of the Oldest Old." *Milbank Quarterly* 63:187–203.

ROSOW, IRVING. 1967. *Social Integration of the Aged.* New York: Free Press.

————. 1974. *Socialization to Old Age*. Berkeley: University of California Press.

ROSTOW, WALT W. 1978. *The World Economy: History and Prospect*. Austin, TX: University of Texas Press.

RUDMAN, DANIEL, AXEL G. FELLER, HOSKOTE S. NAGRAJ, GREGORY A. GERGENS, PARDEE Y. LALITHA, ALLEN F. GOLDBERG, ROBERT A. SCHLENKER, LESTER COHEN, INGE W. RUDMAN, and DALE E. MATTSON. 1990. "Effects of Human Growth Hormone in Men Over 60 Years Old." *New England Journal of Medicine* 323:1–6.

SCHEUCH, ERWIN K. 1987. "Entwicklung der Bevolkerungsstruktur und unser Gesundheitswesen." *Mensch Medizin Gesellschaft* 12:135–143.

————. 1989. "Theoretical Implications of Comparative Survey Research: Why the Wheel of Cross-Cultural Methodology Keeps on Being Reinvented." *International Sociology* 4:147–167.

SCHWARTZ, ARTHUR, and ROBERT W. KLEEMEIER. 1965. "The Effects of Illness on Some Aspects of Personality." *Journal of Gerontology* 20:85–91.

SELIGMAN, MARTIN E. P. 1974. "Submissive Death: Giving Up on Life." *Psychology Today* 7:80–85.

SELTZER, MILDRED M., and ROBERT C. ATCHLEY. 1971. "The Concept of Old Age: Changing Attitudes and Stereotypes." *Gerontologist* 11:226–230.

SHER, ADA ELIZABETH. 1984. *Aging in Post-Mao China: The Politics of Veneration*. Boulder, CO: Westview.

SMITH, KEN R., and PHYLLIS MOEN. 1988. "Passage Through Midlife: Women's Changing Family Roles and Economic Well-Being." *Sociological Quarterly* 29:503–524.

SPACAPAN, SHIRLYNN, and STUART OSKAMP, eds. 1989. *The Social Psychology of Aging*. Beverly Hills, CA: Sage.

SPINETTA, JOHN J. 1974. "The Dying Child's Awareness of Death: A Review." *Psychological Bulletin* 81:256–260.

SPINETTA, JOHN J., DAVID RIGLER, and MYRON KARON. 1974. "Personal Space as a Measure of a Dying Child's Sense of Isolation." *Journal of Consulting and Clinical Psychology* 42:751–756.

STOLLER, ELEANOR PALO. 1984. "Self-Assessments of Health by the Elderly: The Impact of Informal Assistance." *Journal of Health and Social Behavior* 25: 260–270.

STREHLER, BERNARD L. 1977. *Time, Cells, and Aging*. 2nd ed. New York: Academic Press.

STREIB, GORDON F. 1965. "Are the Aged a Minority Group?" In *Applied Sociology*, edited by A. Gouldner, 311–328. New York: Free Press.

————. 1976. "Social Stratification and Aging." In *Handbook of Aging and the Social Sciences*, edited by R. Binstock and E. Shanas, 160–188. New York: Van Nostrand Reinhold.

————. 1984. "Socioeconomic Strata." In *Handbook on the Aged in the United States*, edited by E. Palmore, 77–92. Westport, CT: Greenwood.

STREIB, GORDON F., and CARROLL J. BOURG. 1984. "Age Stratification Theory, Inequality, and Social Change." *Comparative Social Research* 7:63–77.

STREIB, GORDON F., and CLEMENT J. SCHNEIDER. 1971. *Retirement in American Society*. Ithaca, NY: Cornell University Press.

SUDNOW, DAVID. 1967. *Passing On*. Englewood Cliffs, NJ: Prentice-Hall.

SUZMAN, RICHARD, and MATILDA WHITE RILEY. 1985. "Introducing the Oldest Old." *Milbank Quarterly* 63:177–186.

TAYLOR, ROBERT J., and LINDA M. CHATTERS. 1986. "Patterns of Informal Support to Elderly Black Adults: Family, Friends, and Church Members." *Social Work* 31:432–438.

THOMAS, ELIZABETH C., and KAORU YAMAMOTO. 1975. "Attitudes Toward Age: An Exploration in School-Age Children." *International Journal of Aging and Human Development* 6:29–40.

TORRES-GIL, FERNANDO. 1986. "The Latinization of a Multigenerational Population: Hispanics in an Aging Society." *Daedalus* 115:325–348.

TURNER, BRYAN S. 1987. *Medical Power and Social Knowledge.* London: Sage.

U.S. Census Bureau. 1987. *An Aging World.* Washington, D.C.: U.S. Government Printing Office.

———. 1988. *Aging in the Third World.* Washington, D.C.: U.S. Government Printing Office.

VAN DEN BERG, JAN HENDRICK. 1978. *Medical Power and Medical Ethics.* New York: W. W. Norton.

VERBRUGGE, LOIS M. 1982. "Marital Status and Health." *Journal of Marriage and Family* 41:267–285.

———. 1985. "Gender and Health: An Update on Hypotheses and Evidence." *Journal of Health and Social Behavior* 26:156–182.

VOGEL, EZRA F. 1979. Japan as Number One. Cambridge, MA: Harvard University Press.

WAECHTER, E. H. 1971. "Children's Awareness of Fatal Illness." *American Journal of Nursing* 71:1168–1172.

WALLIMANN, ISIDOR. 1986. "Social Insurance and the Delivery of Social Services in France." *Social Science and Medicine* 23:1305–1317.

WAN, THOMAS T. 1982. "Use of Health Services by the Elderly in Low Income Communities." *Milbank Quarterly* 60:82–107.

WAN, THOMAS T., and SCOTT J. SOIFER. 1974. "Determinants of Physician Utilization: A Causal Analysis." *Journal of Health and Social Behavior* 15:100–108.

WARD, RUSSELL. 1979. *The Aging Experience: An Introduction to Social Gerontology.* Philadelphia: Lippincott.

WARE, JOHN E., JR. 1986. "The Assessment of Health Status." In *Applications of Social Science to Clinical Medicine and Health Policy,* edited by L. Aiken and D. Mechanic, 204–228. New Brunswick, NJ: Rutgers University Press.

WATANUKI, JOJI. 1986. "Is There a 'Japanese-Type Welfare Society'?" *International Sociology* 1:259–269.

WEBER, MAX. 1958. *From Max Weber: Essays in Sociology.* Translated and edited by H. Gerth and C. Mills. New York: Oxford University Press.

WEBSTER, MURRAY, JR., and JAMES E. DRISKELL, JR. 1983. "Beauty as Status." *American Journal of Sociology* 89:140–165.

WEINBERGER, MORRIS, JEFFREY C. DARNELL, B. L. MARTZ, SHARON L. HINES, PEGGY C. NEILL, and WILLIAM M. TIERNEY. 1986. "The Effects of Positive and Negative Life Changes on the Self-Reported Health Status of Elderly Adults." *Journal of Gerontology* 41:114–119.

WEISMAN, AVERY D. 1985. "Thanatology." In Vol. 2, *Comprehensive Textbook of Psychiatry,* edited by H. Kaplan and B. Sadock, 1277–1286. 4th ed. Baltimore: Williams & Wilkins.

WELLS, NICHOLAS, and CHARLES FREER, eds. 1988. *The Ageing Population.* London: Macmillan.

WHITE, LYNN K. 1988. "Gender Differences in Awareness of Aging Among Married Adults Ages 20 to 60." *Sociological Quarterly* 29:487–502.

WILLIAMSON, JOHN B., LINDA EVANS, and LAWRENCE A. POWELL. 1982. *The Politics of Aging: Power and Policy.* Springfield, IL: Thomas.

WILSON, WILLIAM JULIUS. 1987. *The Truly Disadvantaged.* Chicago: University of Chicago Press.

WIRTH, LOUIS. 1945. "The Problem of Minority Groups." In *The Science of Man in the Modern World,* edited by R. Linton, 67–92. New York: Columbia University Press.

Witt, David D., George D. Lowe, Charles W. Peek, and EVANS W. CURRY. 1980. "The Changing Association Between Age and Happiness: Emerging Trend or Methodological Artifact." *Social Forces* 58:1302–1307.

WOLINSKY, FREDERIC D., RODNEY M. COE, DOUGLAS K. MILLER, JOHN M. PRENDERGAST, MYRA J. CREEL, and M. NOEL CHAVEZ. 1983. "Health Services Utilization Among the Noninstitutionalized Elderly." *Journal of Health and Social Behavior* 24:325–337.

WOLINSKY, FREDERIC D., RAY R. MOSELY II, and RODNEY M. COE. 1986. "A Cohort Analysis of the Use of Health Services by Elderly Americans." *Journal of Health and Social Behavior* 27:209–219.

WONG, MORRISON G. 1984. "Economic Survival: The Case of Asian-American Elderly." *Sociological Perspectives* 27:197–218.

YIN, PETER, and KWOK HUNG LAI. 1983. "A Reconceptualization of Age Stratification in China." *Journal of Gerontology* 38:608–613.

Author Index

Abercrombie, N., 170, 193
Achenbaum, W., 153, 157–159, 163, 173–174
Akers, R., 67
Alsop, S., 219–220
Amann, A., 41
Angel, R., 74
Anthony, S., 216, 218
Applewhite, S., 91
Ardagh, J., 200
Ariès, P., 220–221
Arling, G., 104
Atchley, R., 11, 22, 53, 115, 117–118, 123–125, 131, 145, 164

Baker, P., 3, 22
Balin, A., 111
Barash, D., 111, 113–114
Barell, V., 71
Barresi, C., 87
Baum, M., 214
Baum, R., 214
Becerra, R., 91, 143–144
Belgrave, L., 98
Belzung, D., 163

Bengston, V., 56, 139
Berg, van den, J., 231–232
Berger, P., 63, 108
Binney, E., 68
Binstock, R., 118, 134, 171
Blau, Z., 114
Blauner, R., 229
Blumer, H., 50, 63–64, 109
Bossé R., 163
Bourg, C., 59–60
Bowden, C., 11
Boyer, C., 180, 195
Branscomb, A., 211
Brents, B., 177
Bronte, D., 12
Bultena, G., 114
Burstein, A., 11
Butler, R., 98–100

Cafferata, G., 86
Cain, L., 60
Campbell, R., 26
Charmaz, C., 225–225
Carr, A., 229
Caserta, M., 65, 87

Chatters, L., 141
Chen, X., 205–206
Childs, D., 196
Chudacoff, H., 131, 134
Clark, R., 226–227, 229
Cleary, P., 74
Cockerham, W., 71–74, 86–88, 91–92, 196
Coe, R., 75
Cohen, C., 87
Cohen, D., 100
Comfort, A., 131
Cooley, C., 109, 123–124, 128–129
Coombs, R., 227–229
Cooper, C., 163
Cooper, G., 87
Costa, P., 56
Coulton, C., 75
Cowgill, D., 10, 16, 60–62, 119, 129, 133, 135, 207–208
Cowley, M., 112, 116–117, 127–128
Cox, H., 115
Craig, G., 196
Crane, D., 230
Cumming, E., 51
Cummings, S., 232

Dahrendorf, R., 50
Davis, K., 51
Debuskey, M., 216
Denzin, N., 52, 63–64, 109
DeViney, S., 136, 162
Dimond, M., 65, 87
Dohrenwend, B., 98
Douglass, E., 71, 74
Dowd, J., 62
Dowd, L., 139
Drevenstedt, J., 114
Driskell, J., 111–112
Dumont, R., 215
Durkheim, E., 49, 214

Easson, W., 216
Edwards, E., 145
Eisdorfer, C., 100
Ekerdt, D., 163
Erikson, E., 127
Estes, C., 68, 101
Evans, L., 62
Evans, R., 191
Evers, H., 4

Fairbank, J., 118
Fan, M., 75

Farley, R., 140
Feifel, H., 211
Feldman, K., 214–215
Fennell, G., 4
Fenwick, R., 87
Ferraro, K., 71, 74, 87–88, 91, 137, 139
Fillenbaum, G., 71, 163
Fischer, D., 133–134
Folmar, S., 121
Foner, A., 4, 57, 119
Fontana, A., 54–55, 170
Foss, D., 215
Freer, C., 192
Fries, J., 12
Frost, A., 75

Galvin, M., 75
Gecas, V., 106
Gelfand, D., 142
George, L., 87, 136, 163
Gibson, R., 139–141
Gilleard, C., 61
Glaser, B., 158, 210–211, 218–219, 222, 224–225, 227–228
Goffman, E., 109–111, 123–124, 128–129, 131–133
Gordon, C., 56
Gove, W., 125, 127, 170
Graebner, W., 66, 131, 151–153, 173, 177
Gratton, B., 98
Gray, R., 65
Grove, G., 111
Gubrium, J., 72
Gudiken, K., 122
Guillemard, A., 198–199
Gurkan, A., 61

Haber, C., 134, 177
Hafferty, F., 227
Haug, M., 98, 121
Havighurst, R., 53
Hawkins, R., 67
Henretta, J., 26
Henry, W., 51
Hill, S., 170
Hirosima, K., 62, 203
Hochschild, A., 65, 72, 121–122, 230
Holmes, D., 87
Holmes, L., 61
Hudson, R., 187

Janis, I., 86
Johnson, J., 196
Johnson, M., 57

Kammerman, J., 211, 213
Kaplan, G., 71
Kaplan, H., 113
Karon, D., 217
Kastenbaum, R., 11, 213
Kaufman, S., 125–126, 170
Kellehear, A., 211
Kent, D., 138
Kii, T., 147
King, D., 6
King's Fund Centre, 192, 194
Kirchner, C., 86
Kitano, H., 146
Kleemeir, R., 121
Klemmack, D., 132
Kligman, A., 111
Korthase, K., 111
Krause, N., 86–87, 141
Kronenfeld, J., 75
Kübler-Ross, E., 211, 215, 218–220
Kunz, G., 88, 196

LaBeff, E., 226–227, 229
Lai, K., 206–207
Larson, R., 118
LaRue, A., 71
Lee, D., 55
Lee, P., 101
Levkoff, S., 74
Levy, J., 135, 138
Liang, J., 71, 205–206
Lichter, D., 140
Lichtman, R., 67
Lindesmith, A., 52, 109
Linn, B., 71
Linn, M., 71
LoCastro, J., 163
Locayo, C., 143–144
Longino, C., 138
Lopata, H., 137
Luckmann, T., 63, 108
Lueschen, G., 88, 196
Lund, D., 65, 87, 229
Lusky, A., 71, 166

MacNeil, R., 115–116
Maddox, G., 71, 74, 121–122
Manton, K., 62, 91
Markides, K., 55, 87, 90–92, 139,
    142–143
Marshall, T., 176
Marshall, V., 229–230
Martin, L., 39–40, 45, 118, 147, 203,
    206

Mason, E., 119
McAuley, W., 104
McCrae, R., 56
McDaniel, S., 189
McGoldrick, A., 163–164
McTavish, D., 131
Mead, G., 63, 107, 123–124, 128–129
Mead, L., 179, 195
Mechanic, D., 74
Mindel, C., 90–92, 139, 142–143
Moen, P., 136–137
Monteiro, L., 75
Moody, R., 213
Moore, W., 51
Morgan, S., 62, 203
Morrison, M., 151–153, 166
Molsey, R., 75
Mossey, J., 71
Mutran, E., 65, 88, 141, 163
Myles, J., 71–72, 175–177, 179,
    188–192, 195–196

Navarro, V., 67
Neugarten, B., 13, 55–56, 118–120,
    122–123, 132, 170
Neugarten, D., 13
Noyes, R., 212–213

Oken, D., 226–227, 229
Olson, P., 206
Ortega, S., 125, 127, 170
Oskamp, S., 3
Otten, M., 90
O'Neill, J., 137
O'Rand, A., 136, 162
O'Toole, K., 6
Owen, J., 163
Øyen, E., 185

Palmore, E., 54, 62, 117, 121–122, 163,
    165, 202–205
Pampel, F., 62, 137, 139, 148, 150,
    177–178
Paradis, L., 232
Park, S., 137, 148, 150
Parker, S., 163
Parsons, T., 49–50
Pescosolido, B., 180, 195
Peterson, M., 214
Phillips, D., 214–215
Phillipson, C., 4
Pifer, A., 12
Pinkney, A., 140
Powell, L., 62

Powers, E., 114
Powers, P., 227–229
Preston, C., 119, 121–122
Prugh, D., 216
Pushparaj, N., 6

Quadagno, J., 62, 137, 153, 174, 179, 188

Reedy, M., 56
Reitzes, D., 65, 163
Rigler, D., 217
Riley, J., 13
Riley, M., 4, 13, 41, 57–58, 119
Ring, K., 213
Roff, L., 132
Roman, P., 52
Rose, A., 170
Rosow, I., 114–116, 119, 122
Rosenfield, A., 4–5, 7
Rosenwaike, I., 41
Rostow, W., 60
Rudman, D., 5

Seltzer, M., 117
Schneider, C., 53, 56, 163
Scheuch, E., 180, 195
Schwartz, A., 121
Seligman, M., 214
Shapiro, E., 71
Sharp, K., 71, 73
Shaw, D., 91, 143–144
Sher, A., 206
Smith, D., 215
Smith, K., 136–137
Soifer, S., 75
Soothill, K., 193
Spacapan, S., 3
Spinetta, J., 216–218
Stoller, E., 71–72, 74
Strauss, A., 52, 109, 158, 210–211, 218–219, 222, 224–225, 227–228
Strehler, B., 6
Streib, G., 27, 53, 56, 59–60, 163, 170–171
Style, C., 125, 127, 170
Sudnow, D., 222–223, 225, 228

Suzman, R., 41
Swaan, A., 185

Taietz, P., 52
Taylor, R., 141
Teague, M., 116
Teresi, J., 87
Thomas, E., 117–118
Torres-Gil, F., 142–144
Tran, T., 141
Trenholme, I., 111
Tsui, W., 180, 195
Tu, E., 205–206
Turner, B., 67, 170

Urry, J., 193

Verbrugge, L., 18–19, 111, 136
Vinick, B., 163
Vogel, E., 201

Waechter, E., 217
Walby, S., 193
Wallace, S., 68
Wallimann, I., 199–200
Wan, T., 75
Ward, R., 118, 132
Warde, A., 193
Ware, J., 71
Waring, J., 4, 57
Watanuki, J., 202–203
Weber, M., 22
Webster, M., 111–112
Weinberger, M., 87
Weisman, A., 211
Wells, N., 192
Wetle, T., 74
White, L., 111, 114–115, 135–136
Wilcox, J., 71, 73
Williamson, J., 62, 177–178
Wilson, W., 139–140
Wirth, L., 169
Witt, D., 70–71
Wolinsky, F., 71, 75
Wong, M., 146–147

Yamamoto, K., 117-18
Yin, P., 206–207

Subject Index

Activity theory, 48, 53–55, 57, 68–69, 235
Age. *See also* Aging
  median age, 3, 31, 142
    Germany, 3
    Great Britain, 3
    France, 3
    Italy, 3
    United States, 3, 29, 142
  stereotypes, 3, 118, 170
Age Discrimination in Employment Act, 153, 186
Age stratification theory, 48, 57–60, 68–69, 235
Aged
  interest group, 171–174
  minority group, 169–171
  self, 106–129
  society's view, 116–119
  view of themselves, 119–123
Aging
  awareness, 111–115
  biological, 4–9
  demographic patterns
    United States, 16–31, 46
    worldwide, 31–47

  fear, 132
  gender, 17–21, 135–138
  genetic clock theory, 4–6, 14
  life cycle, 10–13, 27
  personality, 56–57, 120–123
  race, 21–22
  sexuality, 113–114, 136
  social policy. *See* Social Policy and aging
  social values, 132–135
  wear and tear theory, 4–6, 14
Ageism, 131–135
Africa, 9, 35, 39, 41
Alabama, 26, 46
Alaska, 29, 46, 145
Aleuts, 22
Alzheimer's disease. *See* Dementia
American Association for Old Age Security, 173
American Association for Labor Legislation, 173
American Association of Homes for the Aged, 173
American Association of Retired Persons, 67, 172–173, 184
American Federation of Labor, 173

American Medical Association, 101
American Nursing Home Association, 173
American Psychiatric Association, 100
American Indians. *See* Native Americans
Andrus, Ethel, 172
Argentina, 142
Area Agencies on Aging, 186
Arizona, 29, 46
Arkansas, 26, 29, 46
Asia, 35, 37, 39, 44–46, 62, 118, 146, 198, 208, 233
Asian Americans, 22, 144–148, 170
  health, 92, 106
  median age, 143
  nursing home residents, 81
Asociacion Nacional Por Personas Mayores, 173
Australia, 33, 41, 198, 233
Austria, 33, 41, 45, 175, 178, 180

Baby Boom generation, 2, 183, 188
Bangladesh, 35, 39
Basic Law (Germany), 196, 198
Belgium, 176
Blacks, 21–22, 25–26, 138–141, 146, 148, 170, 183
  health, 88-91, 106, 139
  life expectancy. *See* Life expectancy, United States
  median age, 143
  median income, 139
  nursing home residents, 81
  retirement, 139–140
Blindness, 81
Bismarck, Otto von, 196

California, 29, 54, 109, 145–146, 173
Cambodia, 146
Canada, 33, 35, 41, 71, 186–187, 198, 200, 208, 233
  old-age pensions, 176, 178
  social policy and aging, 185, 189–191
Canadian Pension Plan, 190
Caribbean, 142
Central African Republic, 39
Central America, 142
China, 7, 33, 35, 37, 39, 44, 46–47, 118, 145–47, 215, 233–234
  life expectancy. *See* Life expectancy, China
  social policy and aging, 185, 205–208

Columbia, 142
Conflict theory, 48, 50, 66–67, 236
Confucianism, 118, 206, 208
Congress, U.S., 101–103, 153, 157, 166, 172–174
Connecticut, 31
Continuity theory, 48, 56-57, 68, 122, 236
Cooley, Charles C., 106, 109, 123–124, 128–129
Czechoslovakia, 39

Death
  awareness contexts, 224–225
  changing attitudes, 229–232
  dealing with death, 218–220
  death and dying, 210–232
  death and the individual, 211–220
  death and society, 220–229
  leading causes, United States, 6–8, 76
Delaware, 29
Dementia, 99–101
Denmark, 33, 175, 184
Diagnostic Related Groups (DRGs), 104, 188
Disengagement theory, 48–53, 57, 68, 235
Durkheim, Emile, 49

Eastern Europe, 33, 39, 41
Ecuador, 7
Education, 26
Eskimos, 22. *See also* Native Alaskans
Ethiopia, 39, 41
Europe, 37, 44
Euthanasia, 230

Florida, 7, 29, 31, 46
France, 3, 37, 41, 49, 186–187, 208
  life expectancy. *See* Life expectancy, France
  old age pensions, 176
  social policy and aging, 185, 198–199
Functionalist theory, 49–50, 68

Gambia, 39, 41
Georgia, 26
Gender, 16–21, 41–44
Gerontology, 3
Gerontology, social, 3–4, 13, 48, 68–69
Germany, 3, 33, 37, 41, 179–181, 186–187, 192, 200, 208

Germany (*cont.*)
  life expectancy. *See* Life expectancy, Germany
  old age pensions, 175, 181, 197
  social policy and aging, 185, 194–198
Goffman, Erving, 106–111, 123–124, 128–129, 131–132
Gray Panthers, 68, 173
Great Britain, 3, 7, 33, 37, 45, 163, 180, 186–187, 190, 200, 208
  life expectancy, *See* Life expectancy, Great Britain
  old-age pensions, 175–176
  social policy and aging, 185, 191–194
Greece, 16, 33, 40–41, 44, 194
Guaranteed Income Supplement (Canada), 190
Guatemala, 35–37

Hawaii, 29, 46, 145–146
Health care delivery, 2
Health, 70–105
  characteristics of the aged, 76–86
  insurance, 2, 101–105, 187, 188, 191, 197
  mental, 93–101
  physical, 75–92
  policy, 101–104, 188
  services utilization, 75–76
Health, status, 71–74
Hispanics, 22, 25–26, 142–144, 146, 148, 170, 183
  health, 90, 106
  median age, 143
  median income, 143
  population growth, 142–143
  retirement, 143–144
Hospice, 232
Hospitalization, 75–76
Hospitals
  admissions, 93–97
  mental, 93–94, 97
  organization for dying, 222–224
Hungary, 37, 39
Hong Kong, 35, 39–40

Income, 23–25, 143
Illinois, 29, 73–74
India, 33, 35, 39, 44, 46
Indonesia, 35
Iowa, 29, 114
Israel, 41, 71
Italy, 3, 33, 176, 180, 194

Jefferson, Thomas, 214
Japan, 16, 33, 35, 37, 39–41, 44–45, 47, 69, 118, 145–147, 171, 198, 208, 233
  life expectancy. *See* Life expectancy, Japan
  old-age pensions, 201–202
  social policy and aging, 185, 200–205
  status of the aged, 62, 204
Johnson, Lyndon, 157

Kentucky, 26
Kenya, 35
Korea, North, 118
Korea, South, 118, 146

Latin America, 198
Life cycle. *See* Aging, life cycle
Life, expectancy, 39–41, 88, 90, 194
  China, 205
  Denmark, 194
  France, 41, 194
  Germany, 194
  Great Britain, 194
  Greece, 194
  Italy, 194
  Japan, 16, 39–41, 47, 204
  Norway, 194
  Sweden, 194
  United States, 1, 13, 16, 18, 21, 39, 41, 46
    blacks, 90
    nonwhites, 88
    whites, 88
Lifestyles, health, 6, 9, 88
Living arrangements, 27–28, 44–45, 203
Looking-glass self, 109, 128
Louisiana, 26, 46

Marital status, 27
Marx, Karl, 50, 66–67
Mead, George H., 63, 106–109, 123–124, 128–129
Medicaid, 101, 104, 188
Medicare, 101–105, 157, 160, 166, 186, 188–189
Medicare Catastrophic Coverage Act, 102, 189
Mental disorder, true prevalence, 97–101
Mental health. *See* Health, mental
Mexico, 35, 142
Michigan, 29, 109

Middle East, 39, 44, 47
Mississippi, 46
Missouri, 29
Mitterrand, Francois, 200
Modernization theory, 48, 60–62,
    68–69, 119, 133, 135

National Association of Retired
    Employees, 173
National Association of State Units on
    Aging, 173
National Caucus on the Black Aged,
    173
National Committee to Preserve Social
    Securtiy and Medicare, 67
National Council of Senior Citizens,
    173
National Council on Aging, 173
National Service Act (Britain), 192
Native Alaskans. *See* Native
    Americans
Native Americans, 22, 144–145, 170
    health, 91–92, 106
    nursing home residents, 81
    retirement, 145
Nepal, 39
Netherlands, 41, 176, 180
Nevada, 29, 46
New York, 29, 74–75, 146
New Mexico, 29
New Jersey, 31
Nebraska, 29, 31
Nevada, 31
North America, 44, 144, 146
North Carolina, 26, 29, 74, 163
Norway, 33, 41, 178, 192, 194
Nursing homes, 77, 81, 102, 104–105

Occupation, 26
Ohio, 29
Old Age Pensions Act (Canada), 190
Old Age Security Act (Canada), 190
Older Americans Act, 186

Pacific Islanders, 22
Pakistan, 7, 39–40
Parsons, Talcott, 49–50
Pensions Act (Britain), 192
Philippines, 35, 45, 146, 203
Physician Payment Reform Act, 103,
    188
Physician visits, 75
Pennsylvania, 29, 31, 75, 109

Poland, 39
Population growth, 1–2, 15
Poverty, 7, 25–26, 87–88, 122, 138–140,
    143, 193, 194, 200
Puerto Rico, 142

Quebec Pension Plan, 190

Race, 21–22, 87–88, 138–149, 170–171
Racial mortality crossover
    phenomenon, 90
Religion, 141, 211, 218, 220
Retirement, 51–53, 62, 87, 102, 115,
    133, 137–138, 140, 150–152, 154,
    158–168, 177, 202
Rhode Island, 29, 75
Rome, 16
Romania, 39
Roosevelt, Franklin D., 174–175

Self, 106–111. *See also* Aged, self
Sierra Leone, 39
Singapore, 35, 39, 45, 203
Social Security, 3, 23-25, 102, 138, 140,
    144, 153, 166–167, 177, 183–184,
    185–188
    beneficiaries, 160, 183
    benefits, 153, 160–161
Social Security Act (U. S.), 153, 157,
    159–160, 166, 173–175, 186, 188
Social Security Act (Britain), 193
Social Security Administration, 10, 103
Social Security Trust Fund, 183
Social policy and aging, 59, 185–209
Socioeconomic status, 22–26, 121–122,
    140–141
Somalia, 39, 41
South America, 142
South Asia, 44, 47
South Carolina, 26, 29
South Dakota, 29
South Korea, 39
Soviet Union, 9, 33, 35, 37, 39, 41
Spain, 41, 142
Sri Lanka, 39
Stigma, 131–132
Stress, 86–87, 162–164
Structural-functionlist theory. *See*
    Functionalist theory
Suicide, 98–99
Sweden, 33, 37, 40–41, 47, 178–180,
    192, 194
Switzerland, 39–41, 176, 178

Symbolic interaction theory, 48, 63–65, 68, 236

Tennessee, 26
Texas, 29, 163
Townsend, Frances E., 173
Townsend Movement, 173–174
Turkey, 33, 61

United States
demographic patterns, 15–31
gender. *See* Gender
geographic distribution, 29–31
health, status of, perceived. *See* Health, status
health, policy for, 101–105. *See also* Health, policy
leading causes of death. *See* Death
life expectancy. *See* Life expectancy, United States
living arrangements. *See* Living arrangements

mental health. *See* Health, mental
old-age pensions, 176–178
race. *See* Race
social policy, 159, 185–189
social security. *See* Social Security
socioeconomic status. *See* Socioeconomic status
welfare state, 175–183, 187, 195–196
Utah, 29

Vietnam, South, 146

Weber, Max, 22
West Virginia, 29
Western Europe, 3, 33, 37, 41, 44–46, 88, 159, 175–177, 179–181, 183–184, 189, 194, 201–203, 233
Wisconsin, 159
Work, 150–158

Yugoslavia, 39